IMAGES
of America

HARVARD

For Kate.

IMAGES
of America

HARVARD

Michael Volmar

ARCADIA
PUBLISHING

ISBN 978-0-7385-1217-6

Published by Arcadia Publishing
Charleston, South Carolina

Printed in the United States of America

Library of Congress Catalog Card Number: Applied For

For all general information, contact Arcadia Publishing at:
Telephone 843-853-2070
Fax 843-853-0044
E-mail sales@arcadiapublishing.com
For customer service and orders:
Toll-free 1-888-313-2665

Visit us on the Internet at www.arcadiapublishing.com.

Contents

ACKNOWLEDGMENTS

Several people and institutions offered essential assistance to this project. Most of the images in this volume are from the library and archive at Fruitlands Museums. In fact, this publication was prepared to enable greater access to this important archival collection of local photographs. Conservation of the William Wright Photo Collection was funded in part through a grant from the Institute of Museum and Library Services and completed by the Northeast Document Conservation Center. A significant number of images of the town were kindly provided courtesy of the Harvard Historical Society. In particular, the author acknowledges the generous help and support provided by Jill Anderson, Roben Campbell, Melanie Clifton-Harvey, and the staff and board of trustees at Fruitlands Museums.

INTRODUCTION

Harvard, Massachusetts, is located about 30 miles west of Boston. The bedrock geology of Harvard was formed through the collisions of continental masses after the breakup of Pangea over 200 million years ago, known as the Acadian orogeny. The view to the west of Harvard looks over former parts of the African and Scottish continental areas left behind and altered after those collisions.

More recently, during the last glacial period, the Wisconsin ice sheet covered this area with perhaps one-mile-thick ice. As the glacial ice receded north, glacial Lake Nashua formed, covering much of the valley west of Harvard. At its maximum extent, glacial Lake Nashua stretched south from Boylston, Massachusetts, and north to Nashua, New Hampshire. At least nine episodes of draining occurred during the existence of glacial Lake Nashua.

Native Americans occupied and colonized the region around 11,000 years ago. During protohistoric and historic times, these people referred to themselves as Nipmuc, or people of the fresh water. They were Algonkian people culturally connected to other groups in southern New England.

In 1653, English settled Lancaster, originally to exploit the sources of bog iron the colonists needed as well as to trade with the Native Americans. As the settlement grew, in 1670 a second division of lands in Lancaster was was laid out in what is now called Still River. By 1732, residents of Still River and lands to the east and north incorporated into the town of Harvard.

In early Harvard, all local matters came before town meeting, which was a joint meeting of the town and the congregation. Corporate control extended to settling neighbors' disputes, reprimanding the religiously or civically errant, and ensuring the tranquility of domestic life. It was a homogenous community of Congregational farmers.

As early as 1740, the enthusiastic impulses of the Great Awakening rippled through Harvard's Congregational Church. Also beginning in the mid-1740s, the French and Indian wars ended a prolonged era of peace and pierced the insularity of parochial Harvard. There were few Tories in Harvard when the Minutemen alarm came on April 19, 1775. After the Revolution, all of her citizens had encountered the outside world through the news and ideas that soldiers brought home. In the 1780s, the experience of nation building had conditioned even rural dwellers like those in Harvard to embrace a world beyond their borders. This exposure manifested itself by the 1790s in a decreased sense of unity and harmony.

During the course of the late 18th and 19th centuries, the town of Harvard and the surrounding area had its fair share of social experiments: Shadrack Ireland and his New Light Baptists, Bronson Alcott's Fruitlands utopia, the Harvard Shaker community, Shakerton and Tahanto single-tax enclaves, Millerites and Adventists of Lancaster, as well as the Paulist Catholic community in Still River.

The Shakers were the most controversial of the new sects. After early, violent resistance to their unorthodox lifestyle (the Shakers eschewed marriage and private ownership, vowing to live and work communistically) and manner of worship (uninhibited expression of the Spirit in dance, song, and visions), the town grudgingly accepted the growing Shaker community.

In the half-century before the Civil War, Harvard experienced the transition from traditional to modern lifeways. Market aspirations, increased mobility, better education, scientific experiment, technological innovation, and expanded print media combined to transform a traditional agrarian way of life into a more scientific approach to farming. However, the land in Harvard was not well suited to these new methods. Harvard's population fell steadily by 10 percent annually from 1850 through 1900. Many people left in search of opportunity in the new economy. Those who stayed behind abandoned farming and turned their rocky, hilly acreage into dairy farms and orchards.

Harvard's most famous utopian experiment was founded by Bronson Alcott in June 1843. Alcott hoped to establish a new Eden, an agrarian, communal society that would be unsullied by the use of money, avoid the exploitation of any other creature's labor or product, and devote itself to the spiritual cultivation of the inner nature. To avoid the evils of money and exploited labor, Alcott and his fellow founder, Charles Lane, planned to have the community draw all its sustenance from the "fruit of the land." The Fruitlands experiment failed at least in part because its participants failed to spend time farming and, perhaps, in part due to the lack of pragmatism directed toward the type of farming they did undertake.

In the early 20th century, people became interested in acquiring Harvard's rural acres. In 1909, Fiske Warren began his first experimental "enclave," leasing his land to those who would agree to his "single tax" contracts. At the outbreak of World War I, the U.S. government purchased large, contiguous tracts of land in Harvard, Lancaster, Ayer, and Shirley to build Camp Devens. At the same time that Warren and the United States were buying land in Harvard, another wealthy outsider was looking to purchase a large estate. Clara Endicott Sears, daughter of Boston Brahmins and a keen student of Americana, sought a "gentlemen's farm," a pastoral retreat from her social life in Boston. Eventually, Sears established and opened four museums to the public on her site: a "restoration" of Bronson Alcott's Fruitlands (1914); the Shaker Museum in honor of, and with donations from, her friend in the Harvard Shaker family (1922); the Indian Museum, inspired by the lithics she uncovered on her property (1928); and the Picture Gallery, displaying primitive portraits of rural, antebellum New Englanders and masterpieces by painters of the Hudson River school (1940). In each of her collections, Sears paid homage to those who had drawn their living or their inspiration from the landscape of New England; through her Colonial heritage and her own working farm, she placed herself among this class of "true Americans."

One

Harvard and Still River

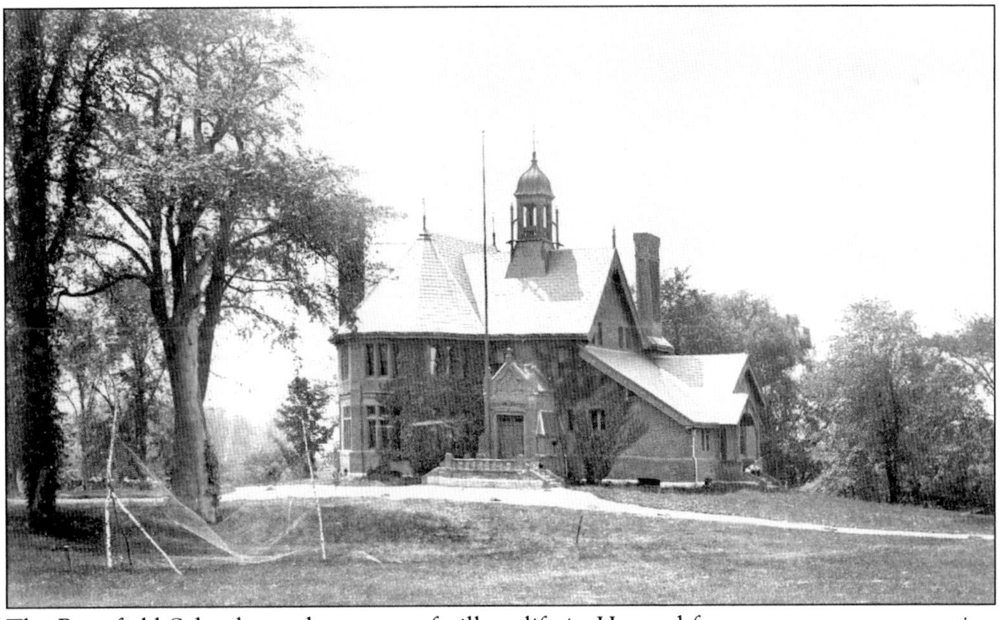

The Bromfield School was the center of village life in Harvard for many years as generation after generation was educated here. Named after Col. Henry Bromfield, a wealthy Bostonian who moved to Harvard in the 18th century, the school was built by his granddaughter in 1874.

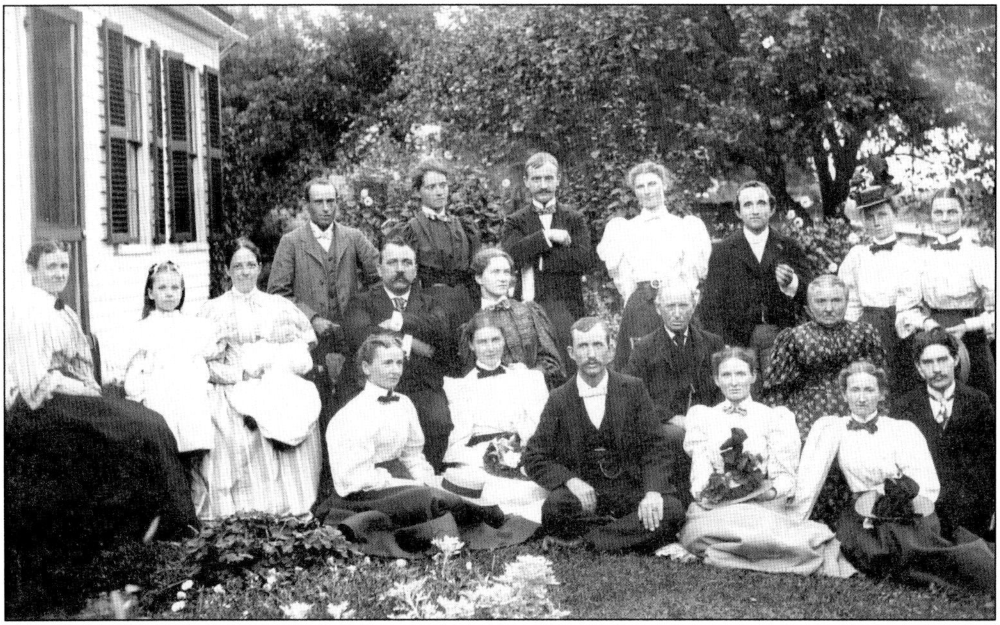

James Madigan is seen with his family and friends in 1897. The Madigans were, and still are, a prominent family in Harvard with several businesses and at least one street named after them.

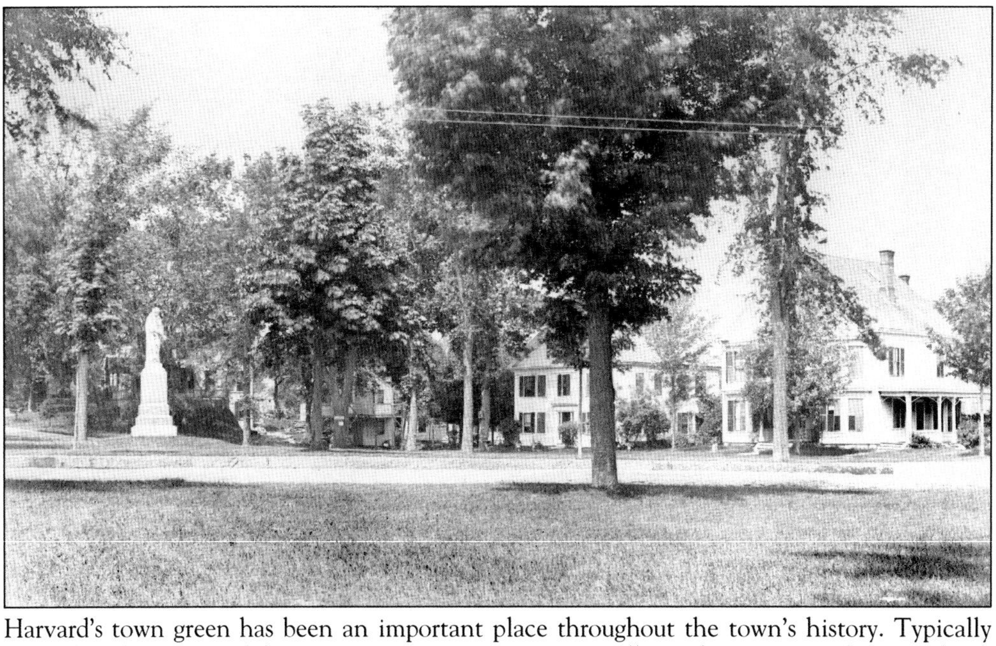

Harvard's town green has been an important place throughout the town's history. Typically located in the center of the town, town greens were originally used as communal grazing land. Later, they became a location for seasonal recreational activities and other gatherings.

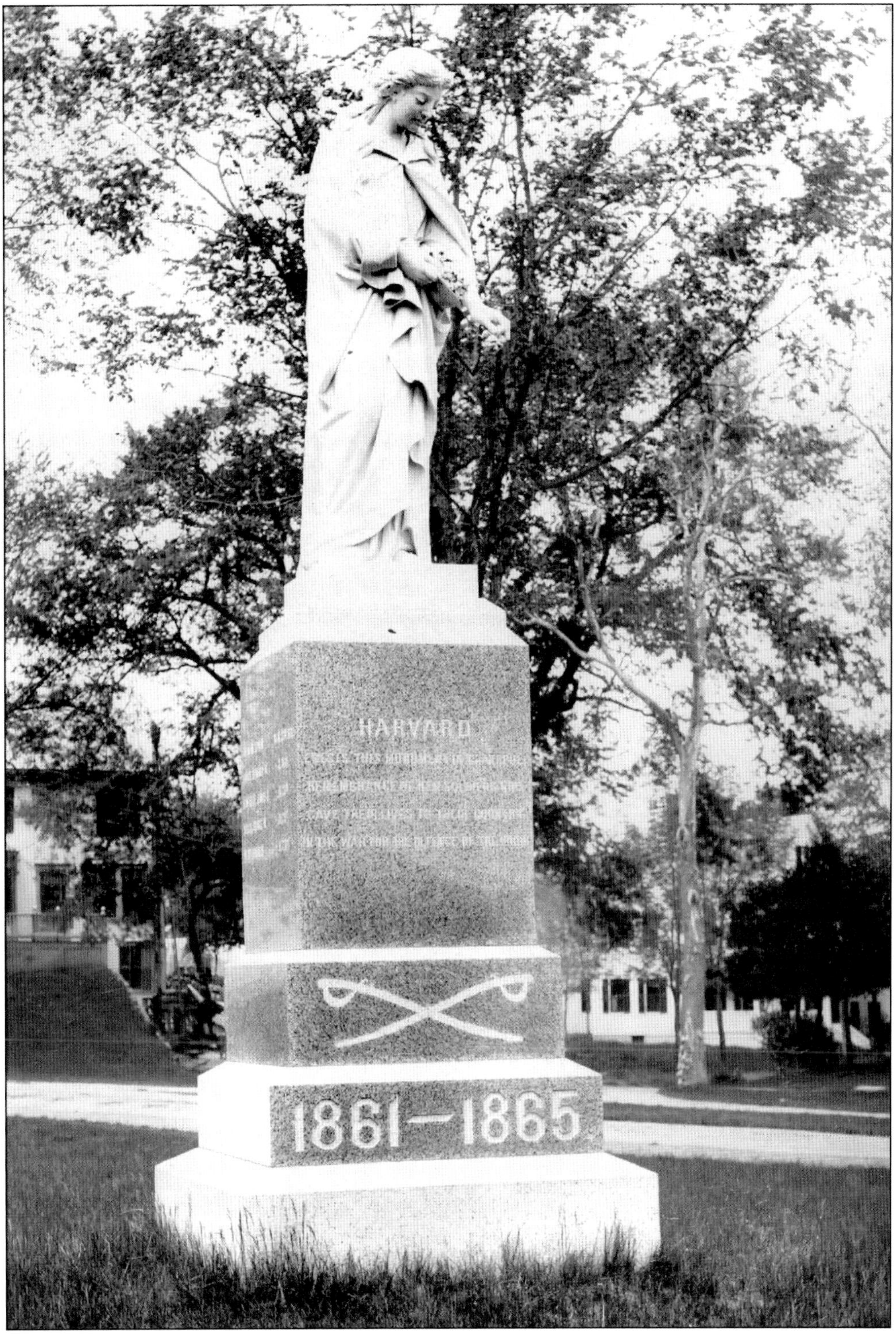

This 1895 photograph shows one of the most prominent features of the town green—a statue commemorating the men from Harvard who served and died during the Civil War.

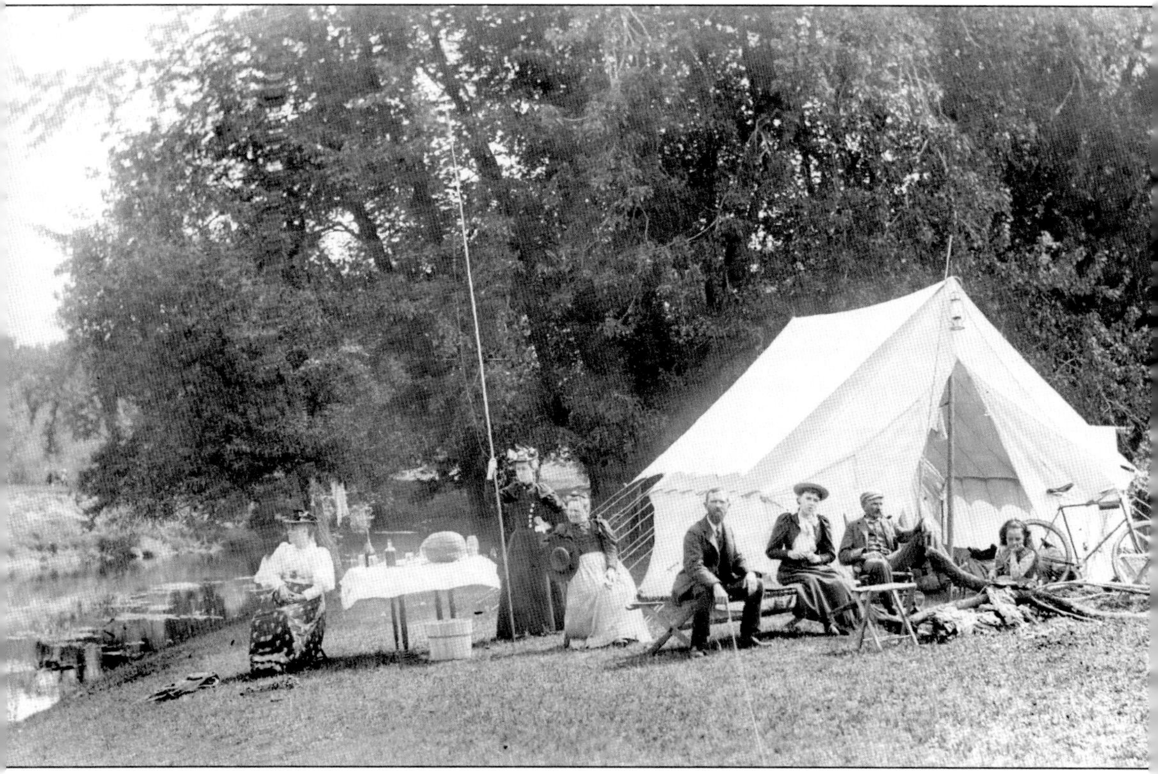

The Wright family holds a picnic along the Nashua River *c.* 1900. The men and women are dressed in Victorian-style clothing, and the image provides an interesting insight into leisure-time activities at the turn of the century. William Wright, shown in the center holding a shutter line, was an amateur photographer who was active from 1880 to 1920. Many of his photographs document the local history of Harvard, Ayer, and other Massachusetts towns.

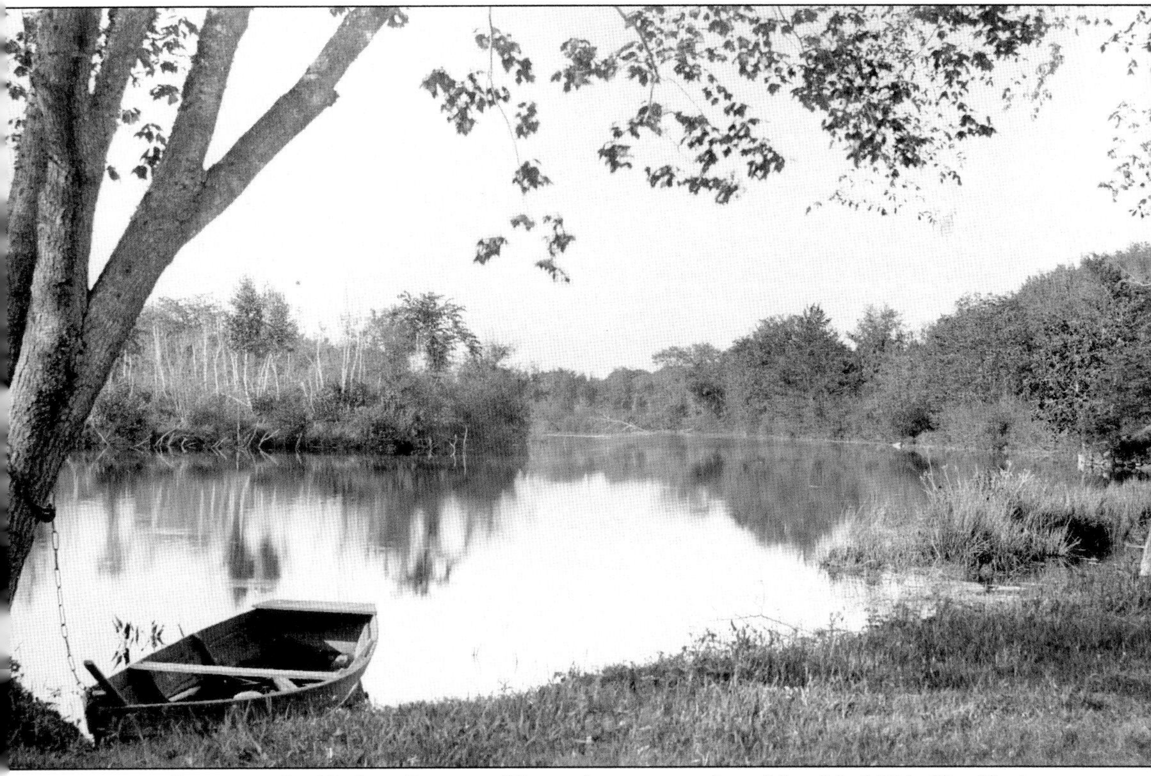

Lovering Farm, on the Nashua River in Harvard, is pictured on May 27, 1894. The Nashua River played an important role in the history of Harvard. When the town incorporated in 1732, the Nashua defined Harvard's western boundary. Some 10,000 years ago, this area was a glacial lake bed. Clay from this glacial lake bottom was also mined to make bricks. The fertile lands along the banks of the river were some of the best agricultural lands in town. Interestingly, patterns of property ownership for these fertile bottom lands differed from the adjacent lands upslope to the east. In general, the choice agricultural bottom land lots were much smaller and changed hands more frequently. Over the years, the river meandered around this flat flood plane, creating a series of oxbows, now the Oxbow Wildlife Refuge. Over the years, the river provided a natural transportation route to Lowell and the Merrimack River to the north. In 1847, the railroad took advantage of the flat land when it built the Worcester Nashua line just to the east of the Nashua River.

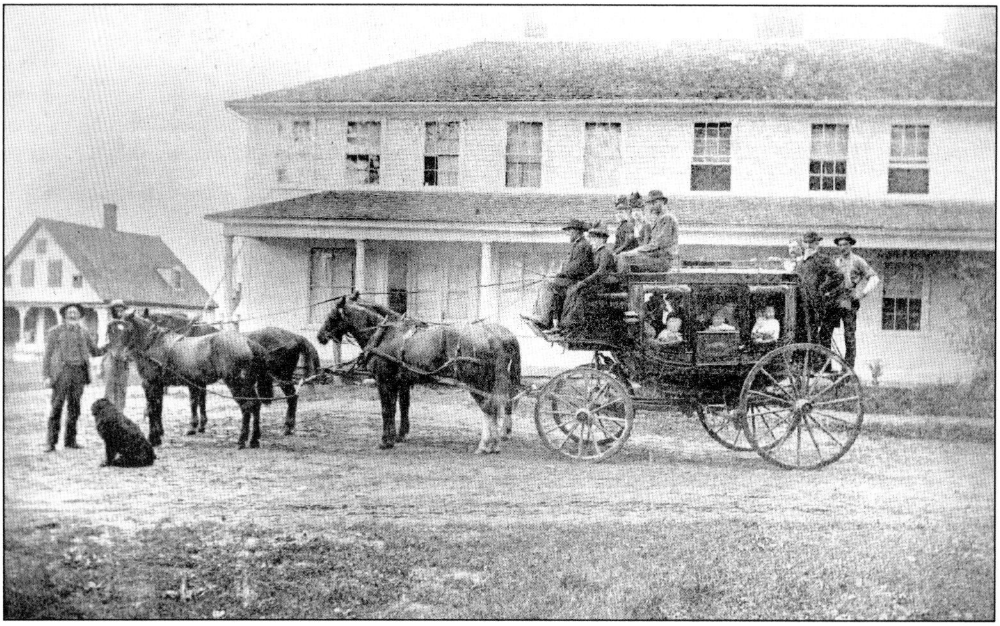

The old stagecoach at Harvard was the primary means of transportation from Harvard to surrounding towns prior to the railroad line's completion in the mid-1840s. In fact, a toll road called the Union Turnpike was built in Harvard in 1805 and remained in use until 1818.

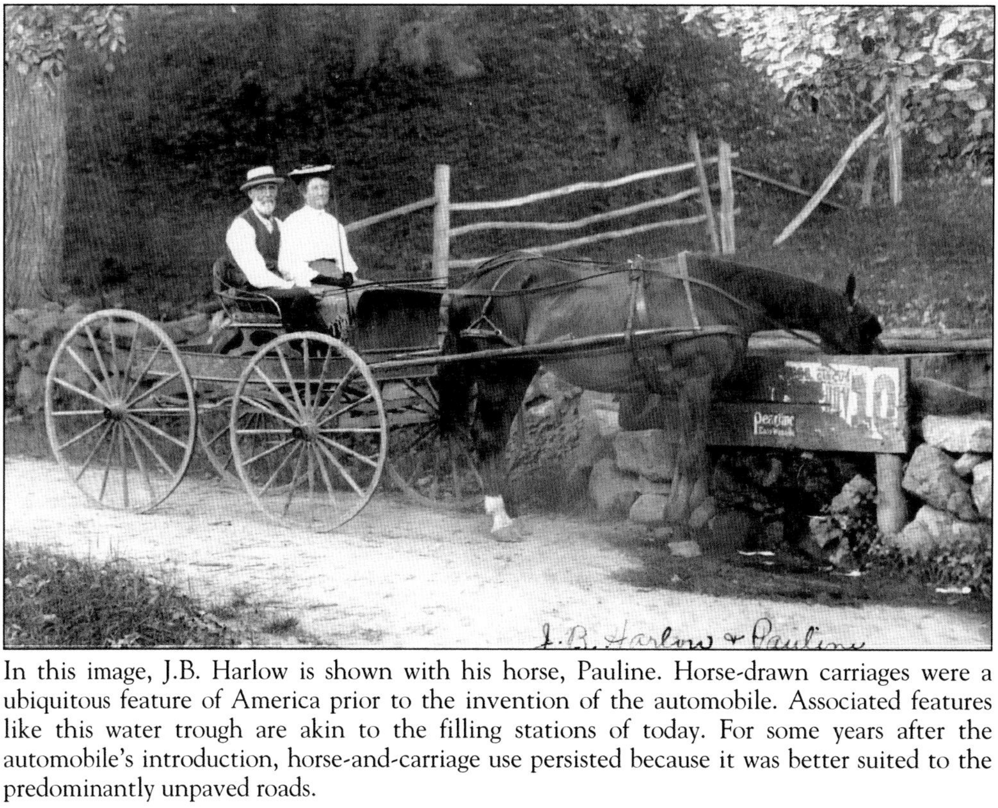

In this image, J.B. Harlow is shown with his horse, Pauline. Horse-drawn carriages were a ubiquitous feature of America prior to the invention of the automobile. Associated features like this water trough are akin to the filling stations of today. For some years after the automobile's introduction, horse-and-carriage use persisted because it was better suited to the predominantly unpaved roads.

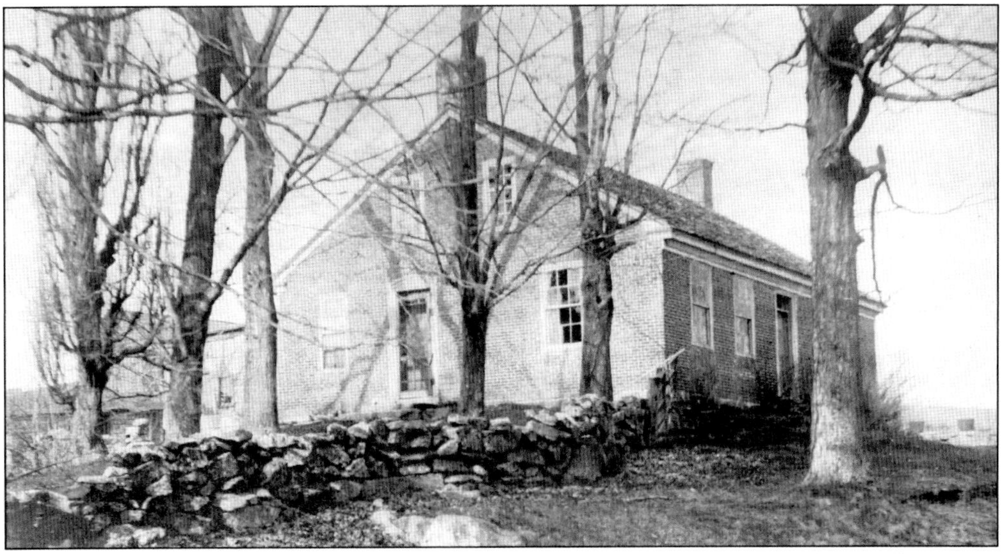

This house was built in 1734 by Thomas Willard. The Willard family moved to Still River in the 17th century. A number of lots were given to the Willards as part of the second division lands of Lancaster—all of which were located along the western slopes of Prospect Hill. When this photograph was taken, the house belonged to Elvira Scorgie, an important town historian in Harvard.

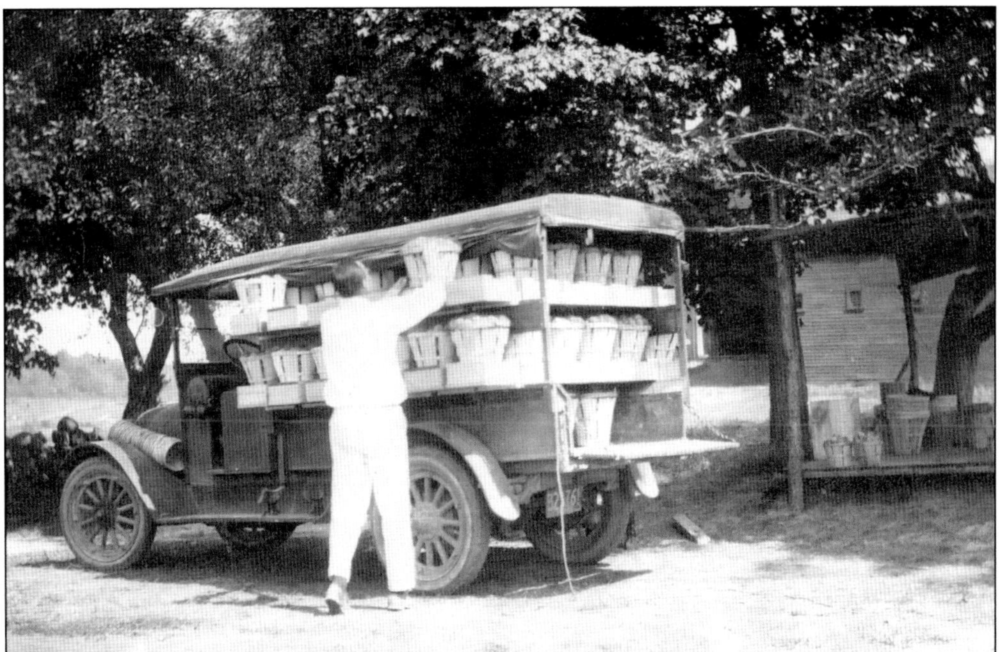

This is a photograph of Phillip H. Babcock loading apples into his truck c. 1920. Apples have always been an important crop for Harvard farmers. Early in the 19th century, they began selling apples in Boston and Lowell. Apples were used by most families for many staple foods, from apple pies to cider.

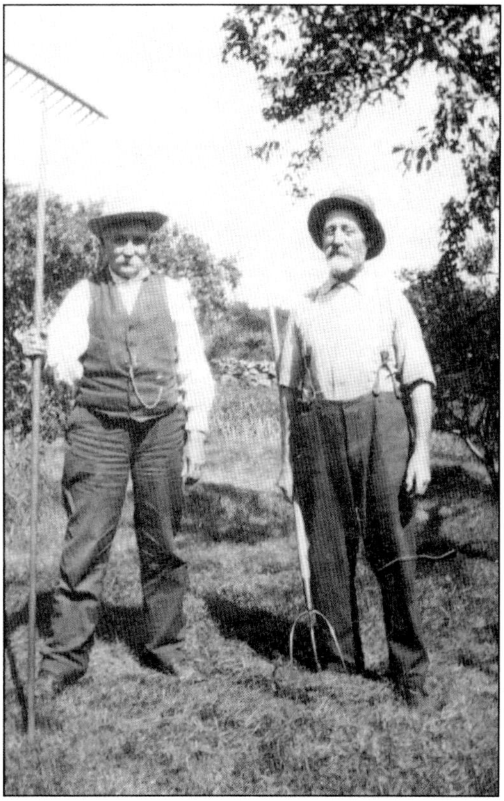

Isaac Baker (left) and John Harlow are pitching hay. Good hay is probably the single most important farm product. Hay needs to be dried before it is stored, to avoid spontaneous combustion or rotting. Once it was cut, people would pile the hay up to dry out before loading it onto wagons to store in the barn.

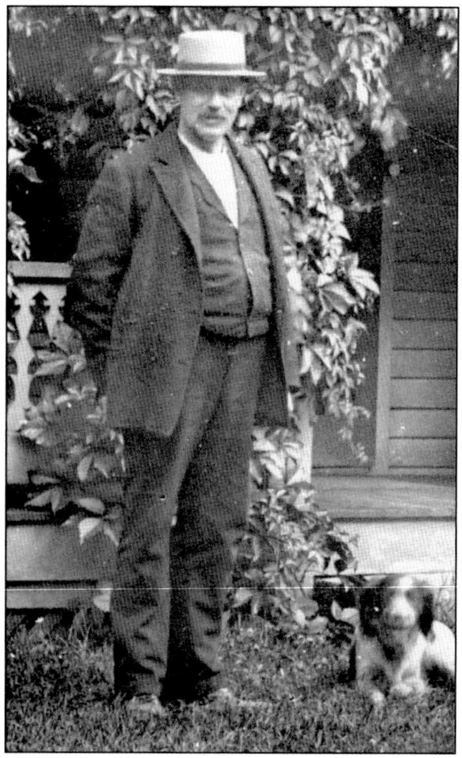

S.P. Morgan and his dog are standing *c.* 1910 in front of a porch that has what might be trumpet vine growing up it. Historic photographs such as this offer us a window into past modes of dress and exterior home decoration.

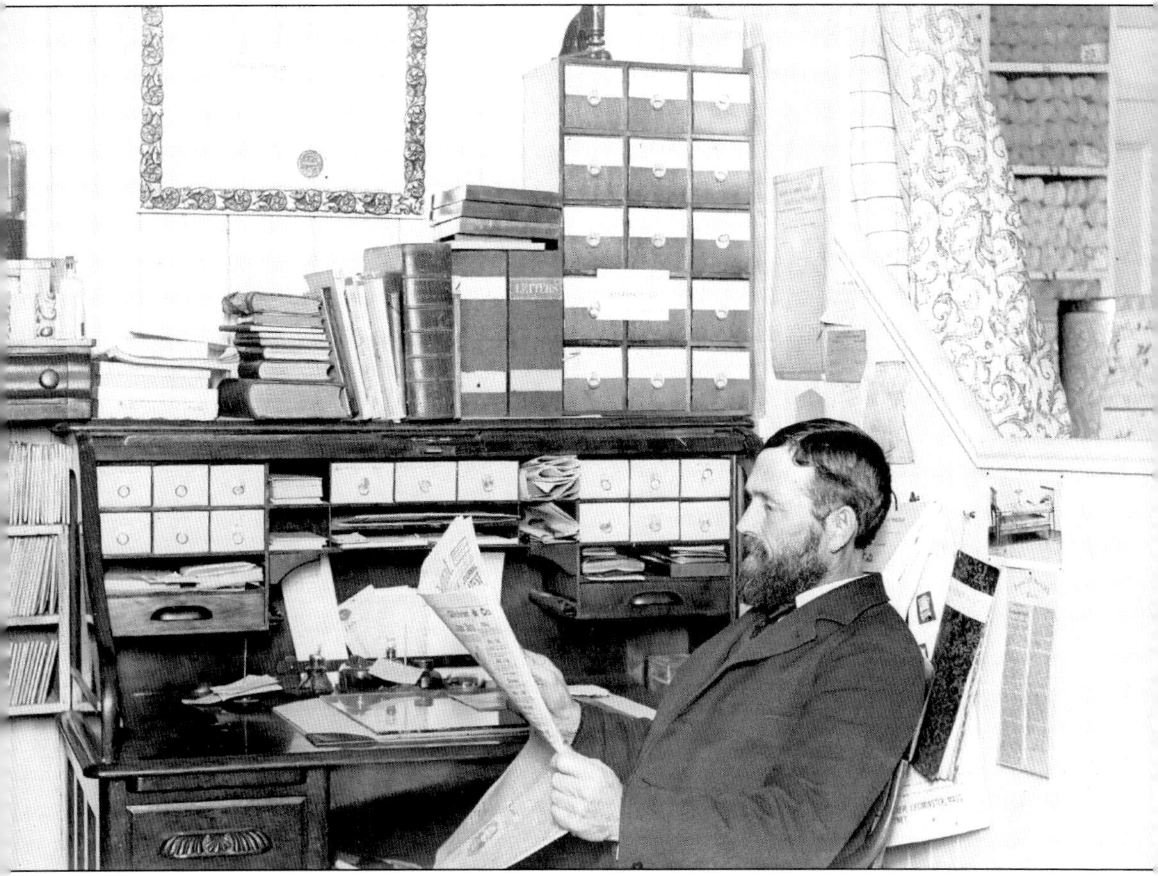

William Wright is pictured here in 1895. Born in 1851, Wright and his father ran a furniture and undertaking business in Ayer, Massachusetts. Around 1880, Wright took up photography, and over the next 40 years, he compiled an impressive collection of photographs of local towns, farms, and other points of interest. He was also a noted authority on local history.

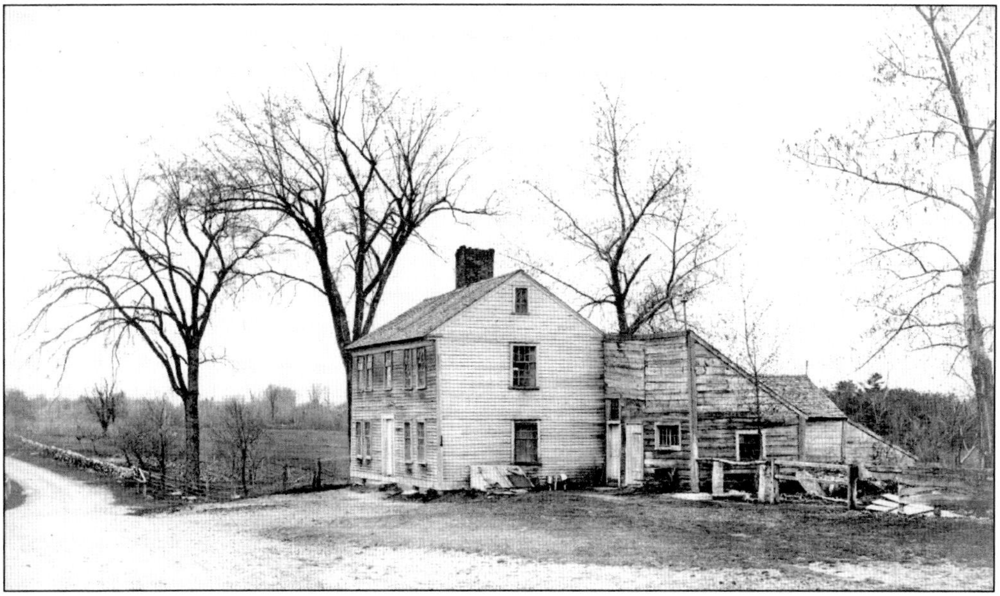

The Abel Stone House, on Ayer Road, is shown on May 5, 1895. This center-chimney Colonial was built *c.* 1720. Contrary to current practice, in the past, people did not always paint their houses. Also, because certain taxes were based on the number and area of windows, some people limited the number of windows they had.

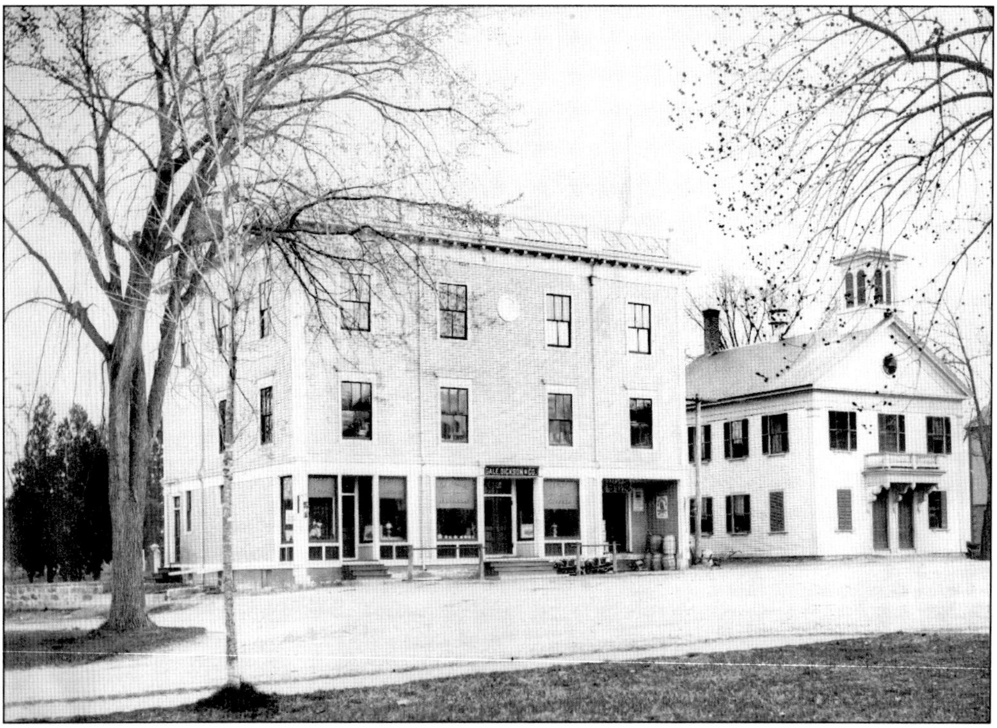

This April 1897 photograph of Harvard center shows the Gale & Dickson General Store to the left and the Congregational church, built in 1821, to the right. It is interesting to note that there are two doorways on the front of the meetinghouse, which is no longer in this location.

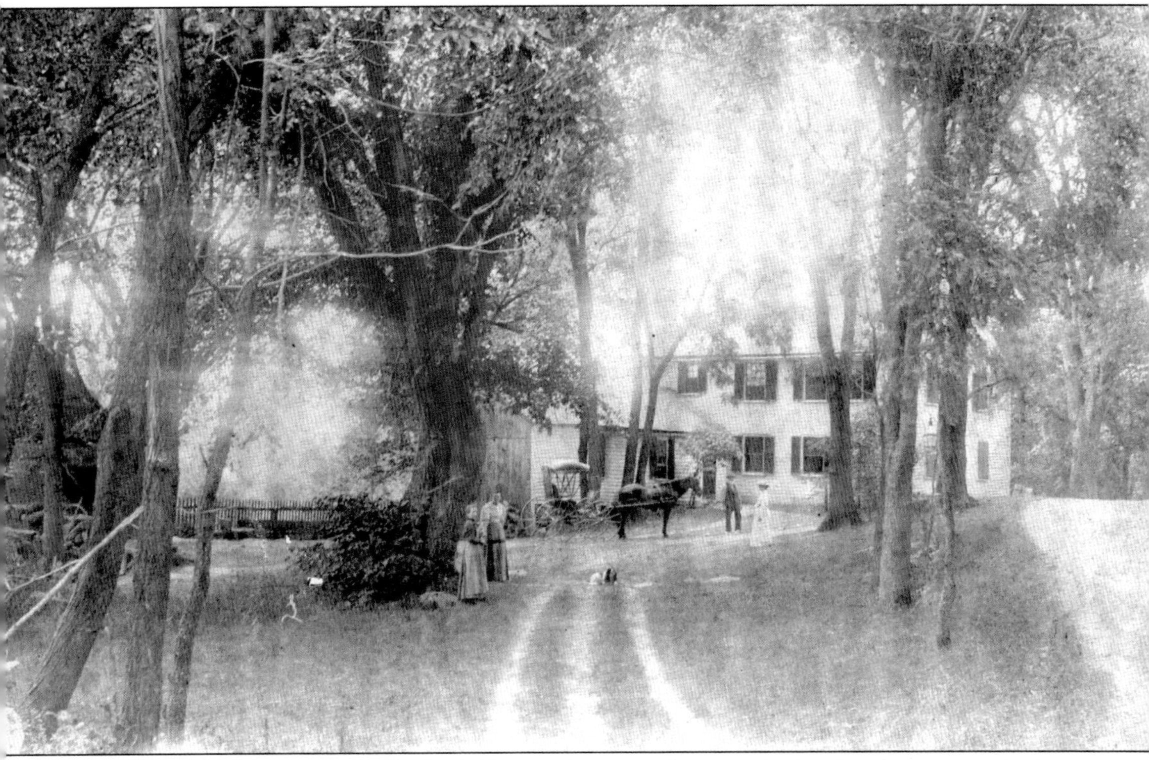

An interesting feature of the Willard House, shown *c.* 1900, includes the driveway with its three tracks; the wagon wheels made the two outer tracks, and the center track was made by the horse's hooves. Closer to the house is the covered buggy the family used for transportation.

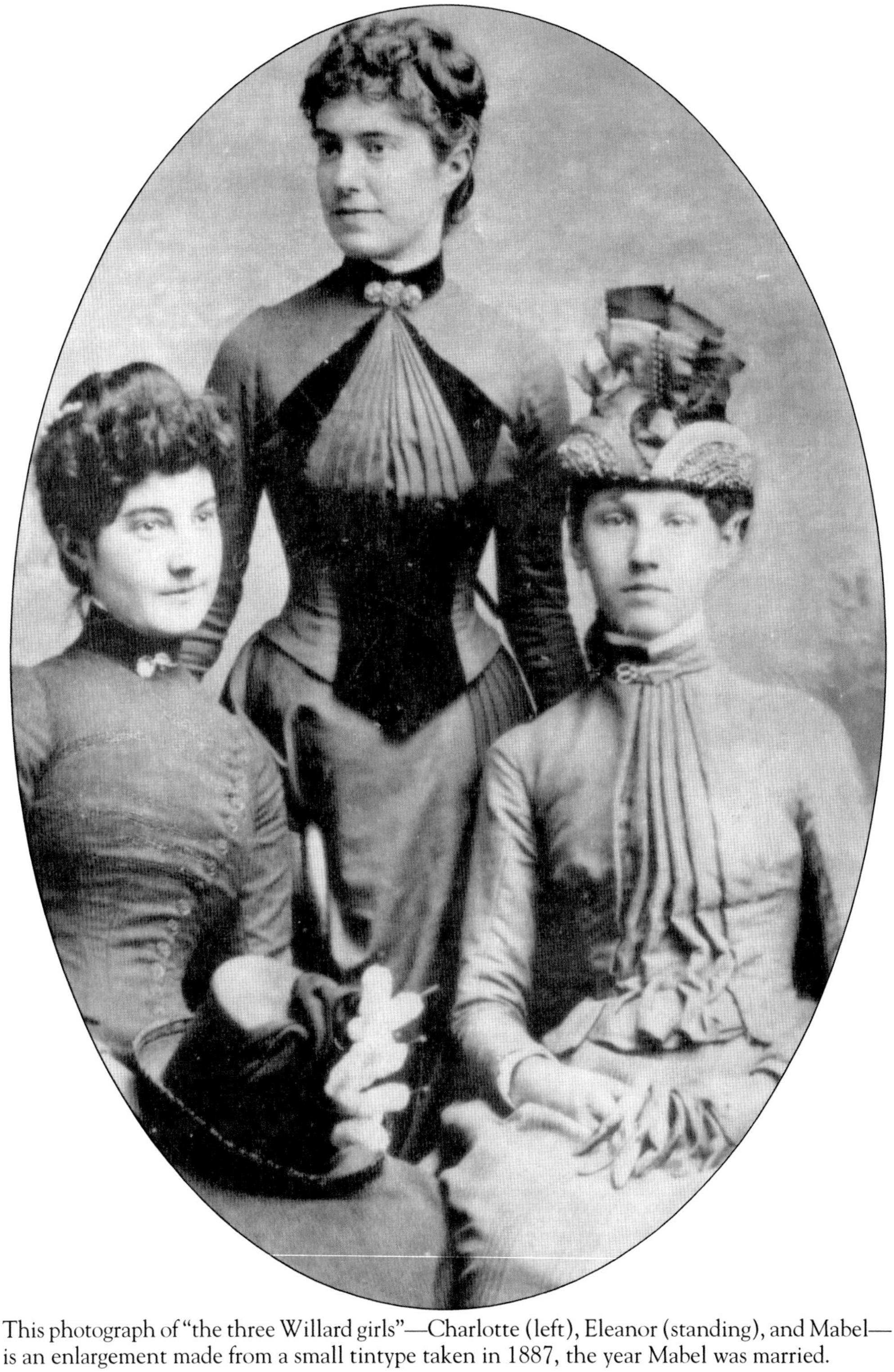

This photograph of "the three Willard girls"—Charlotte (left), Eleanor (standing), and Mabel—is an enlargement made from a small tintype taken in 1887, the year Mabel was married.

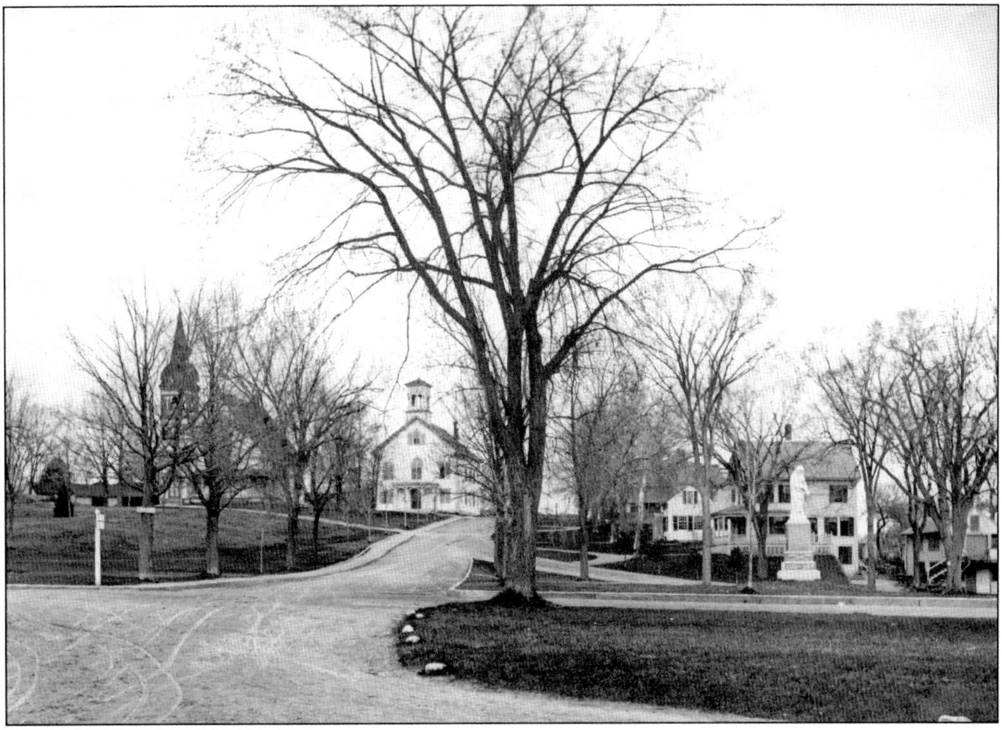

This north-facing picture of the center of Harvard was taken in April 1897. Notice that the streets are not paved and there is no traffic light at the crossroads. Off camera to the left is the Gale & Dickson General Store. In the center of the photograph is the town hall.

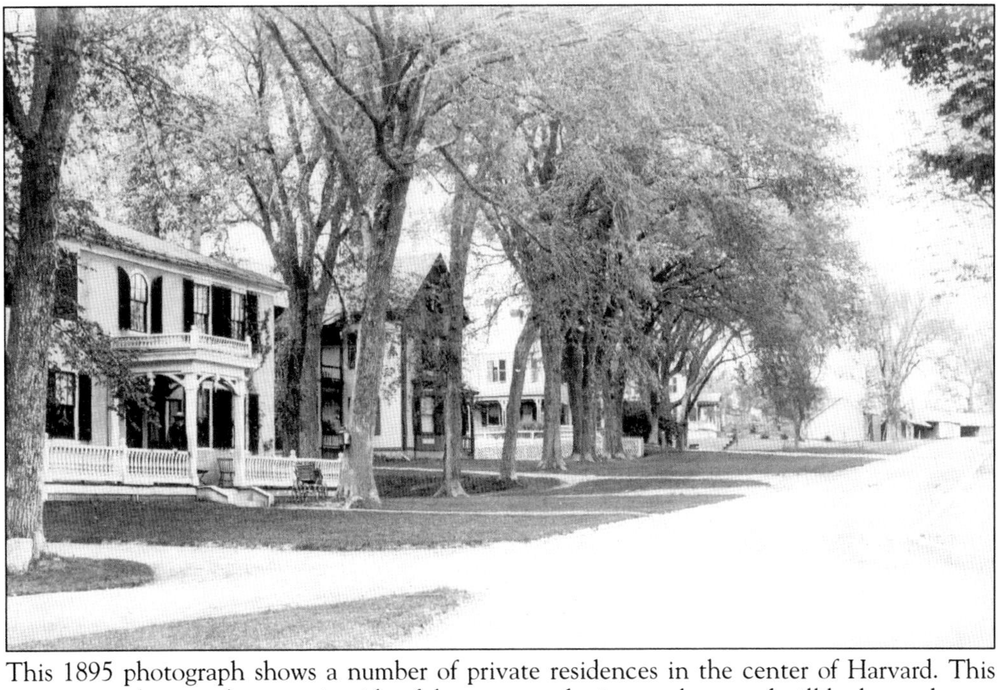

This 1895 photograph shows a number of private residences in the center of Harvard. This image was taken on the opposite side of the green as the image above and still looks north.

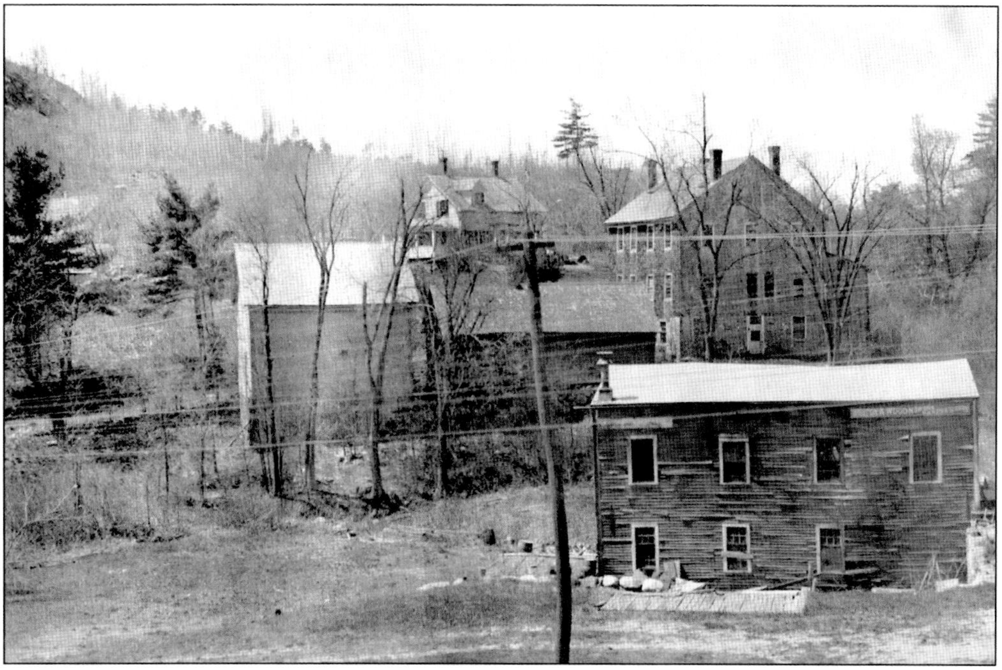

William Wright described the foreground buildings shown as "Old Mills of Harvard, May, 1923." Water power was, and still is, a cheap, efficient, and clean way to power manufacturing plants. Many water-powered mills in Massachusetts were set up to grind grain into flour, cut lumber, and perform other tasks.

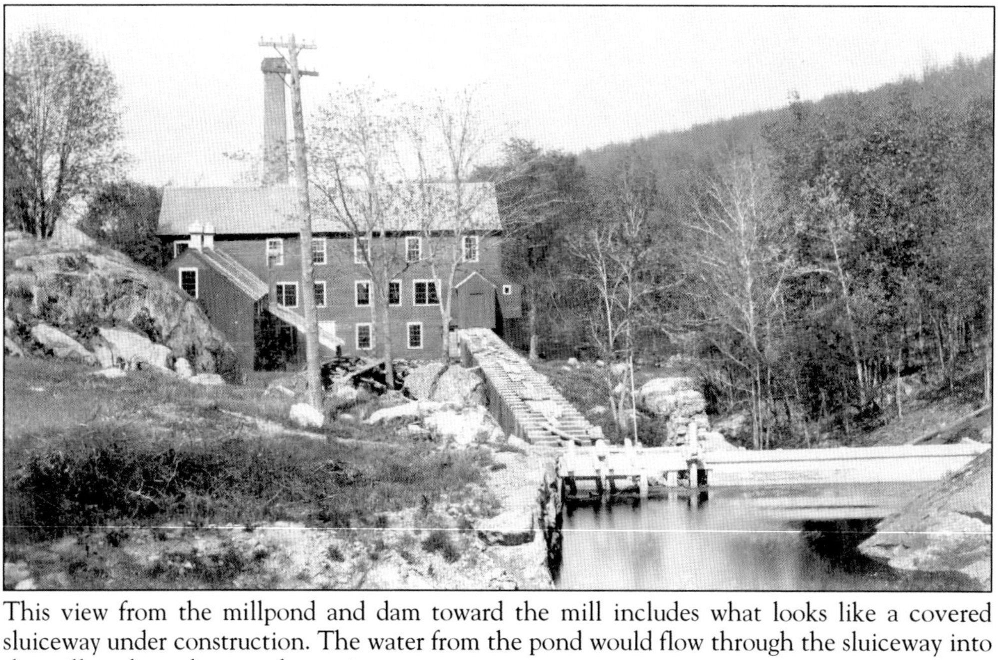

This view from the millpond and dam toward the mill includes what looks like a covered sluiceway under construction. The water from the pond would flow through the sluiceway into the mill works and power the equipment.

Photographed from downstream, a man sits on the slope beside the spillway that leads the water away from the mill. The number and arrangement of chimneys suggests this is a different mill than the one in the previous photograph.

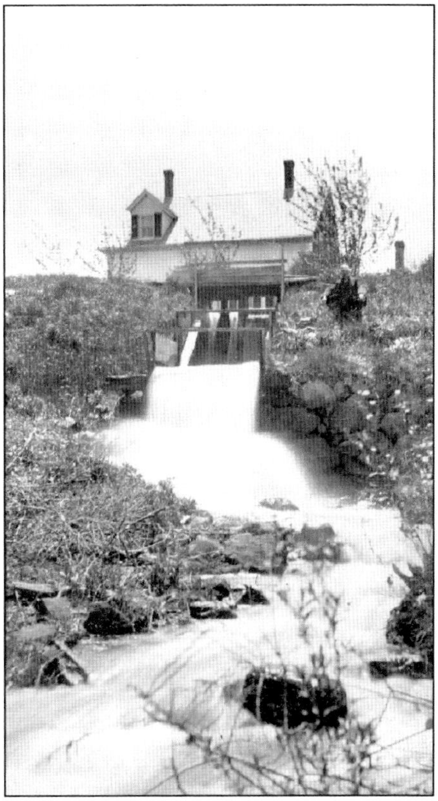

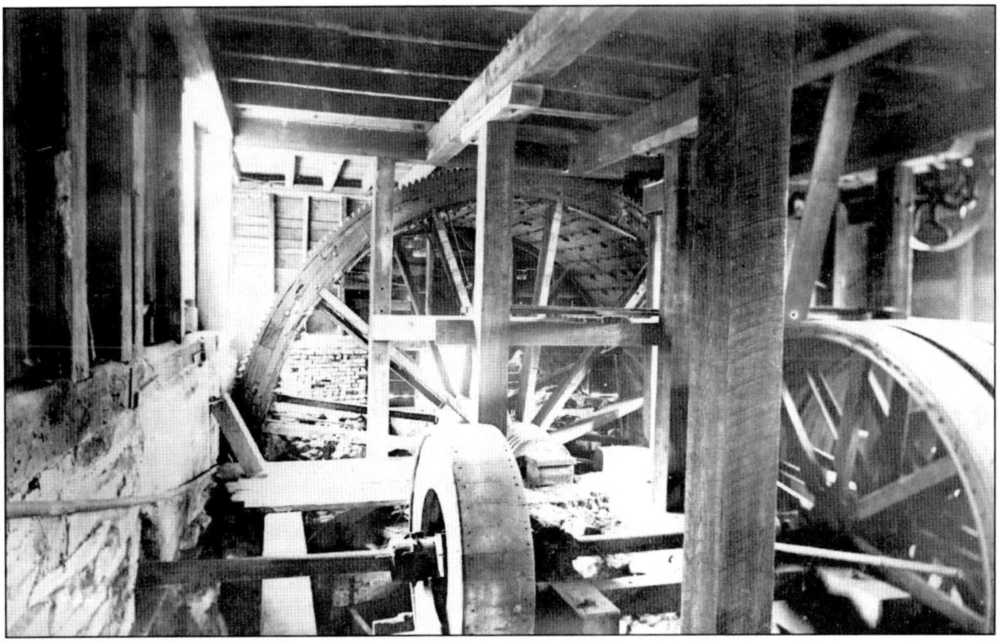

This image provides a glimpse of the complicated arrangement of gears and belts inside a mill that turned flowing water into manufacturing power. For hundreds of years, people in New England relied on waterpower to sustain and grow their communities.

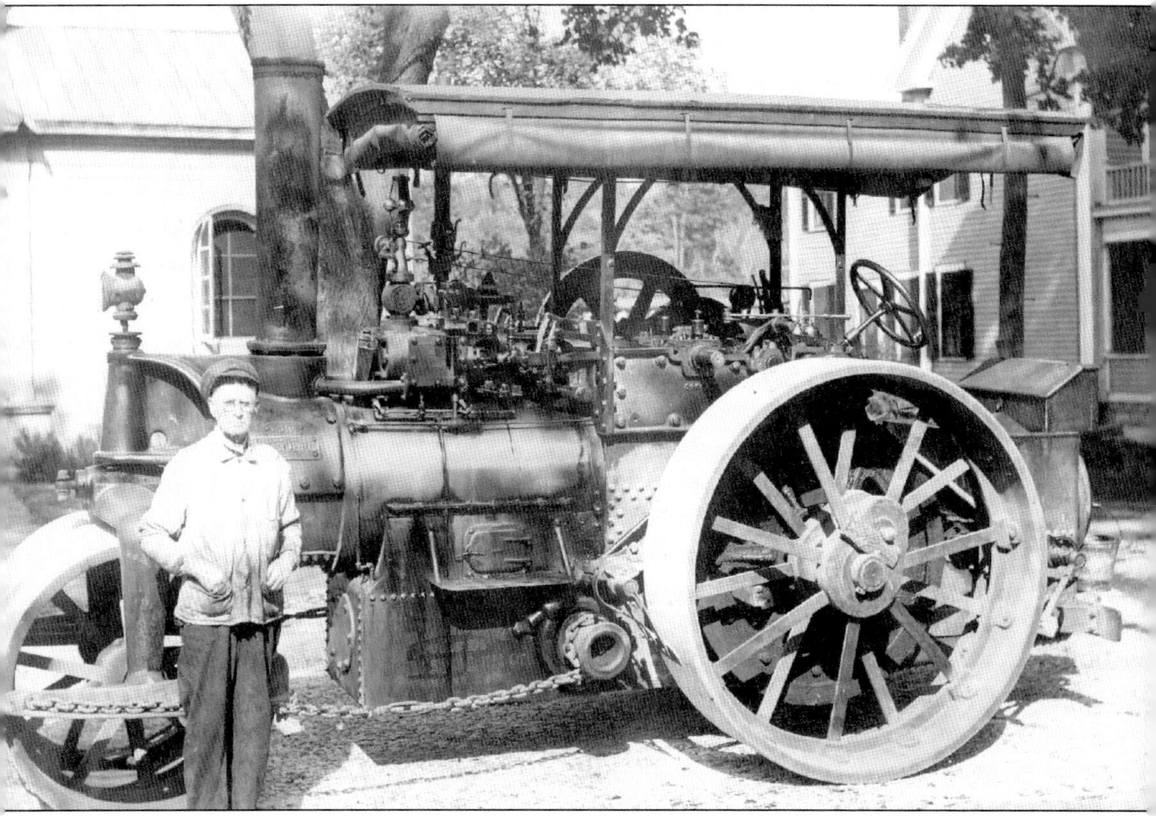

This September 1923 photograph shows the type of steamroller that became prevalent with the development of paved roads. Once completed, these roads facilitated automotive transportation—the second biggest innovation after the railroad.

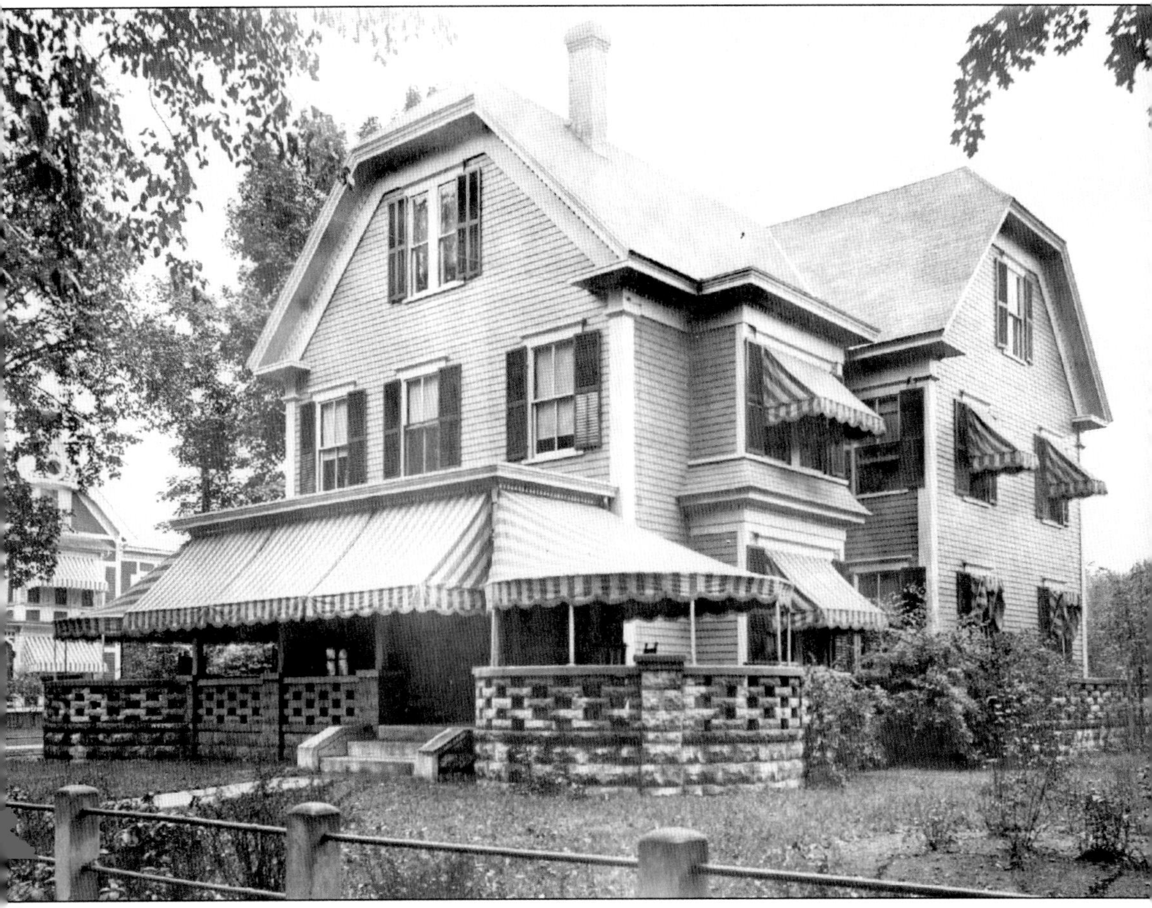
The residence of W.H. Atwood is shown in September 1923.

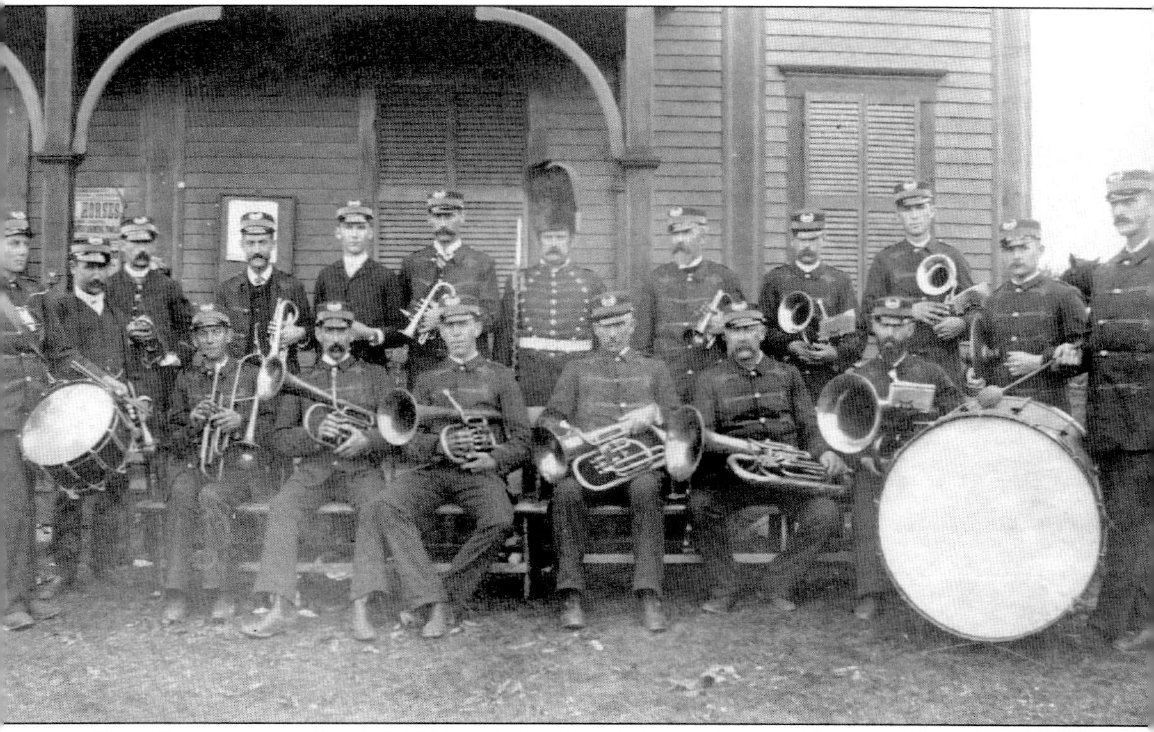

The Harvard cornet band of 1891 includes, from left to right, the following: (front row) Frank Armstrong, Nelson Conleigh, H. Ernest Brown, Warren Willard, Henry Harrod, and John Harlow; (back row) Arthur Armstrong, Clarence Green, F. Cartwright, Arthur Wood, Wilmont Cleaves, Arthur Turner, Warren Fairbanks, William H. Brown, Arthur Bryant, Edgar Cleaves, William Hannah, and George Gale.

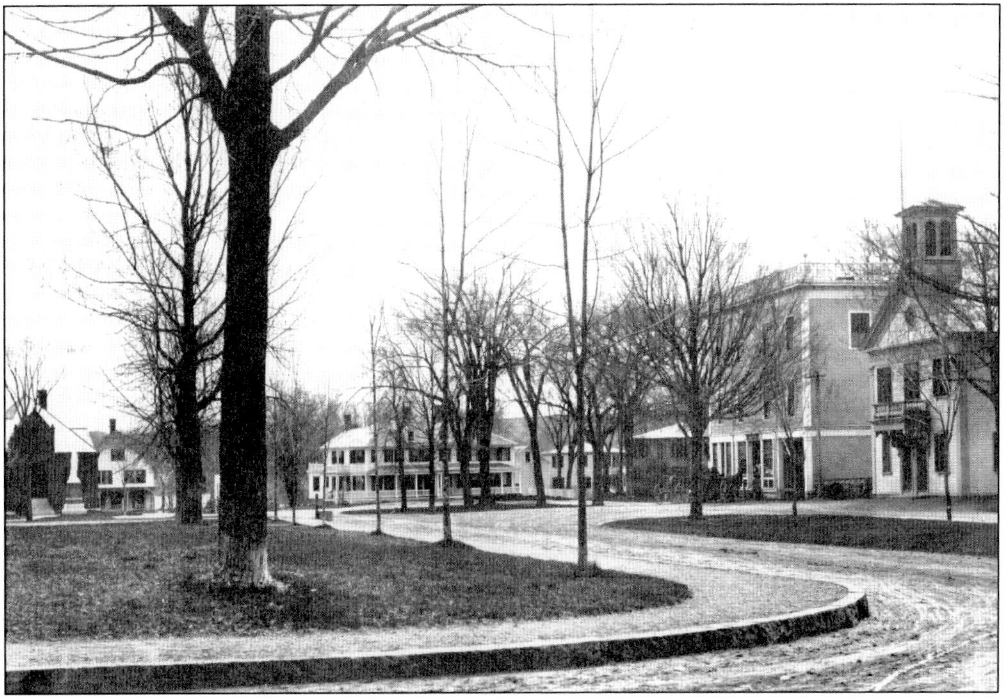

This 1897 image looks east from the center of Harvard. To the right are the church, general store, old town inn, and library.

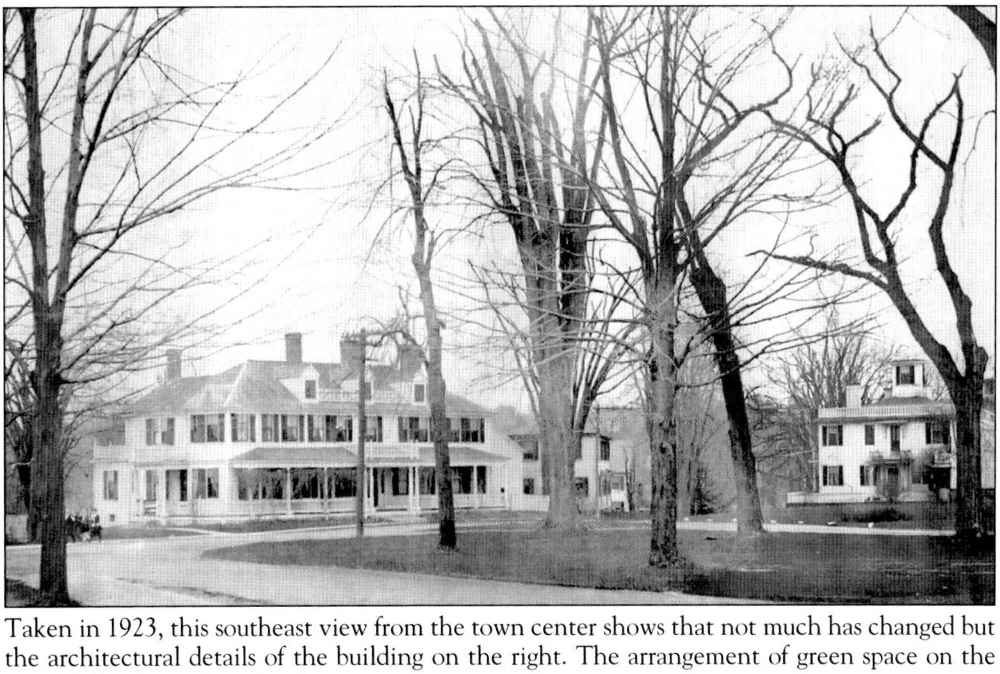

Taken in 1923, this southeast view from the town center shows that not much has changed but the architectural details of the building on the right. The arrangement of green space on the green differs from that of today.

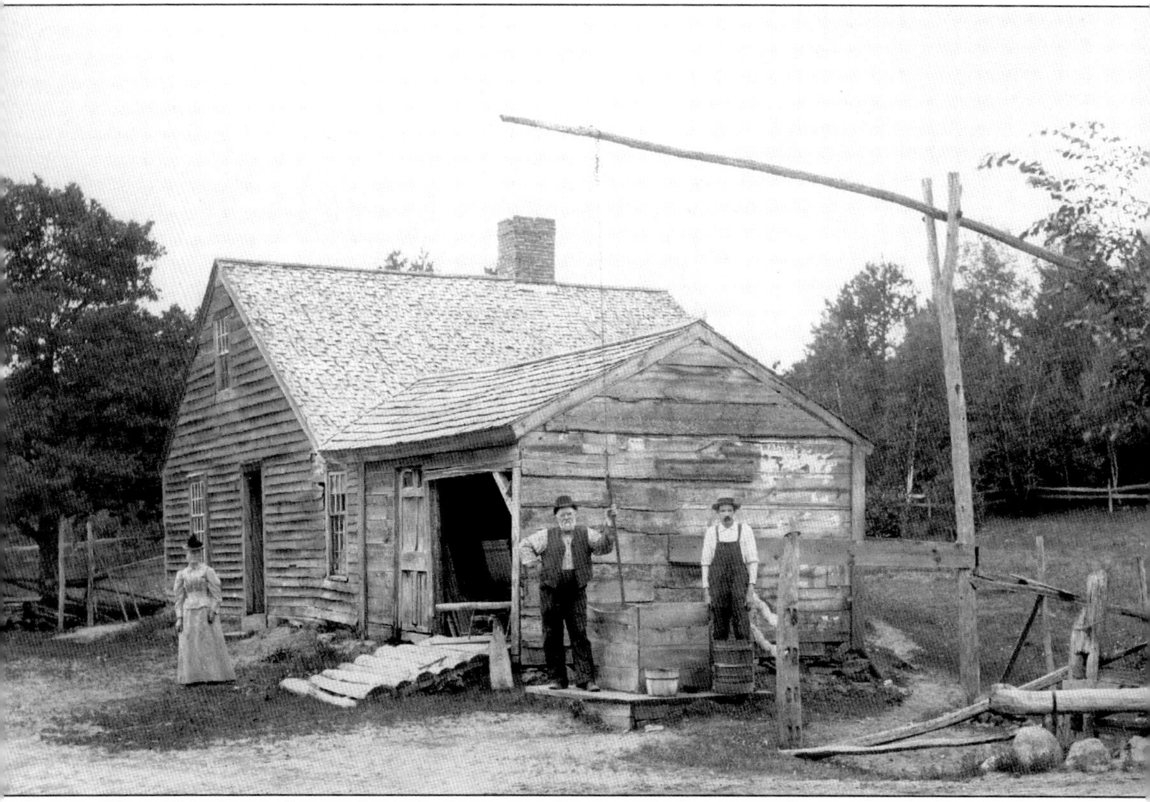

The old Jackson place in Wood's Village is shown in June 1895. The image reveals little except clothing style that differs significantly from much earlier in the 19th century. The two men stand on either side of the house's well.

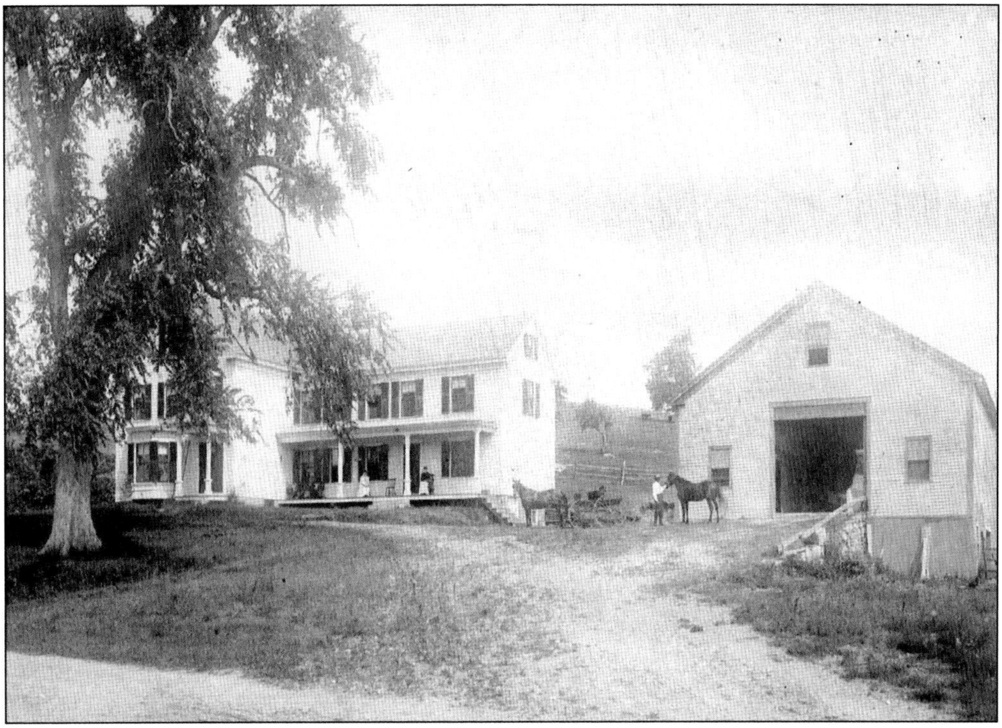

This is the Absolom Gale House, at 42 Still River Road, *c.* 1900. Gale owned the general store in town at this time.

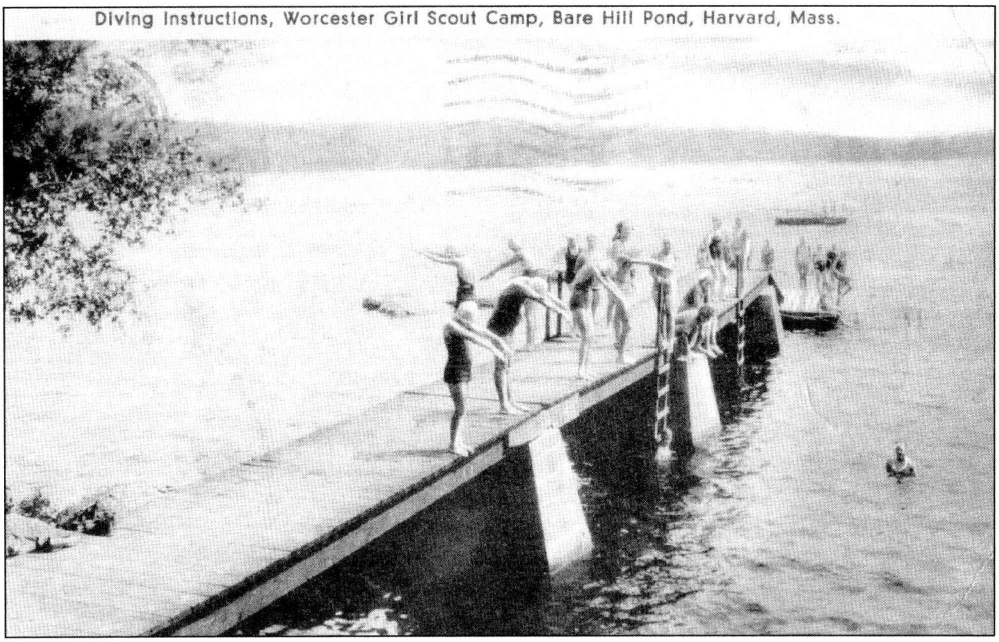

This is a scene at the Girl Scout camp on Bare Hill Pond *c.* 1900. Bare Hill Pond is a man-made pond close to the center of Harvard. While the dock is gone, Camp Green Eyrie still attracts Girl Scout troops throughout the year.

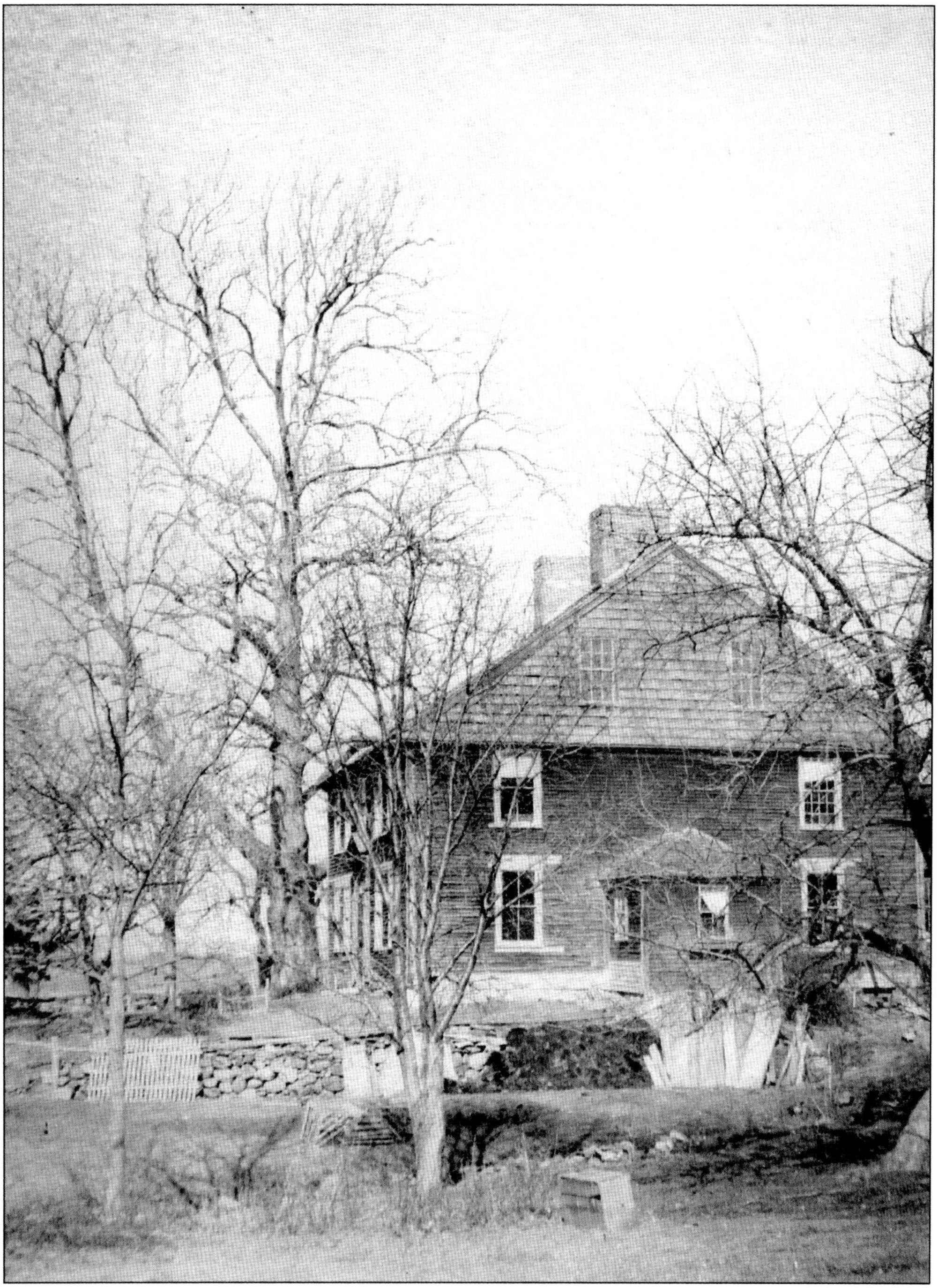

Larger homes like this were more common in the 19th century. Notice the two large chimneys of this two-story home. There is also a difference in the windowpane configuration visible on this end of the house. The upper right has a much smaller and older pane design.

Here are four boys from a Harvard family *c.* 1900. During this period, it was commonplace to dress all young children in dresses.

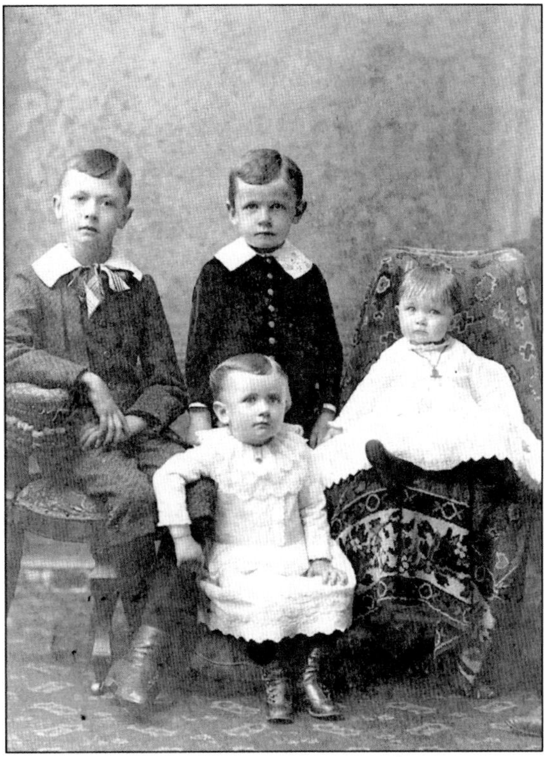

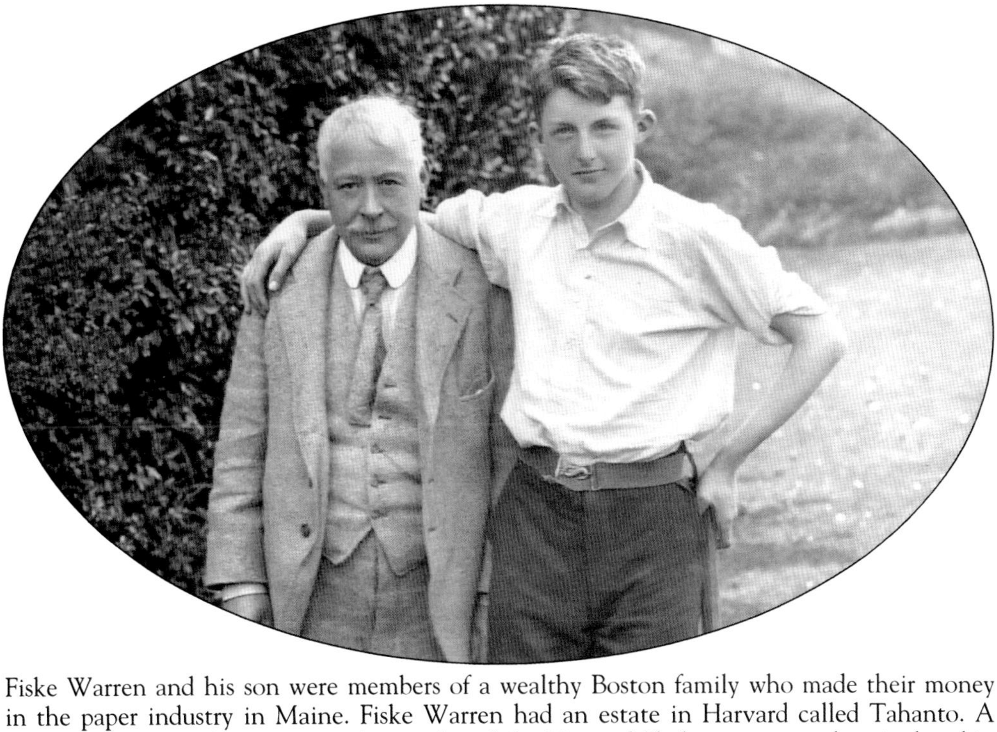

Fiske Warren and his son were members of a wealthy Boston family who made their money in the paper industry in Maine. Fiske Warren had an estate in Harvard called Tahanto. A proponent of a single-tax system, he purchased the Harvard Shaker property when it closed in 1918 and set up a single-tax enclave there and at Tahanto.

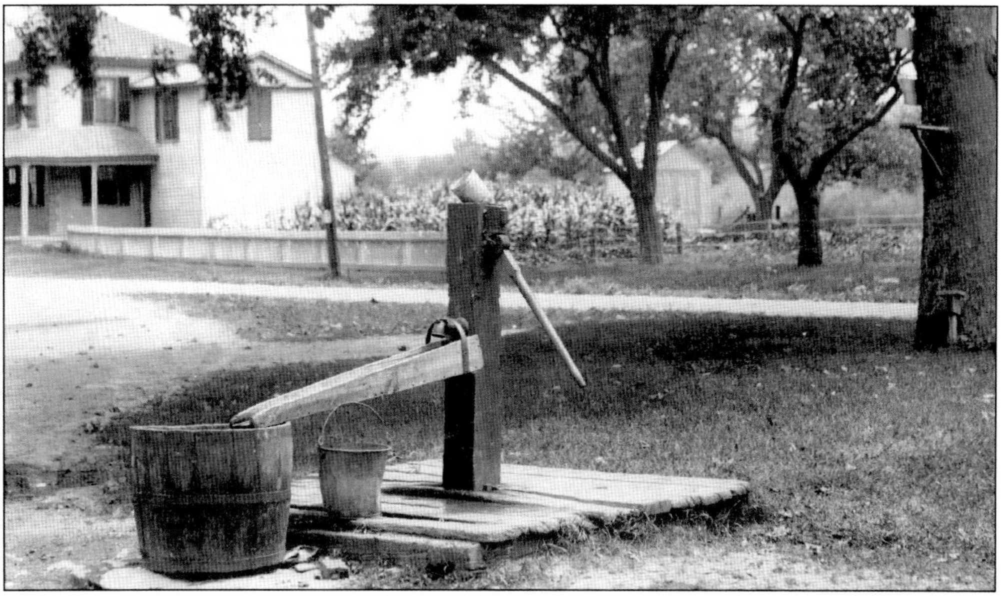

Still River is the western section of Harvard. It was originally the first settlement of people moving north from Lancaster. While Harvard eclipsed Still River in the 18th century, it still retains its own character and identity.

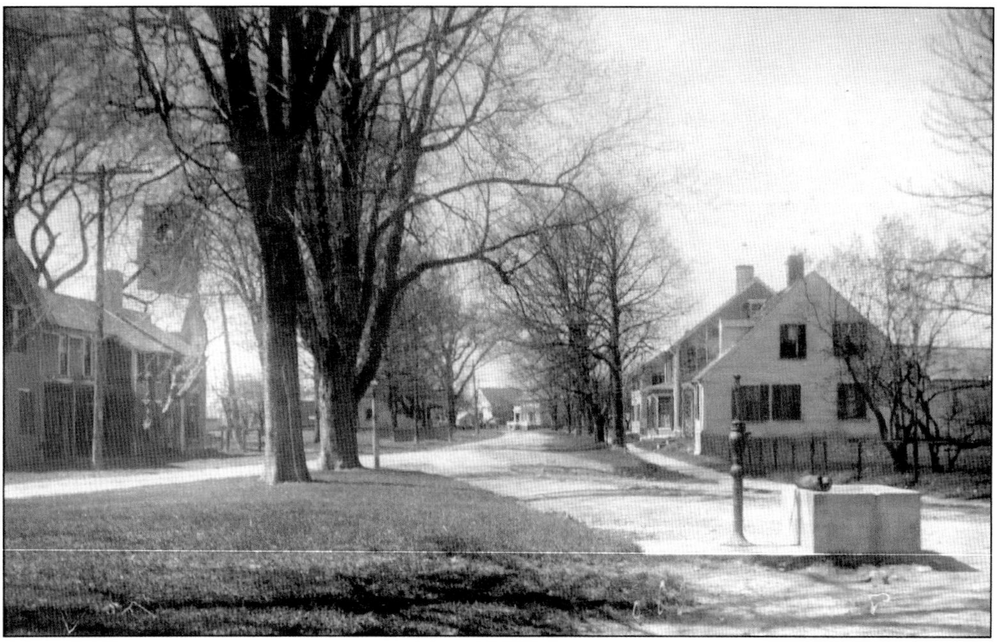

This *c.* 1910 view of Still River center shows the homes of Peter Snow, Levi Howard, Howard Stone, Helen Stone Bigelow, and Donald and Roger Wood.

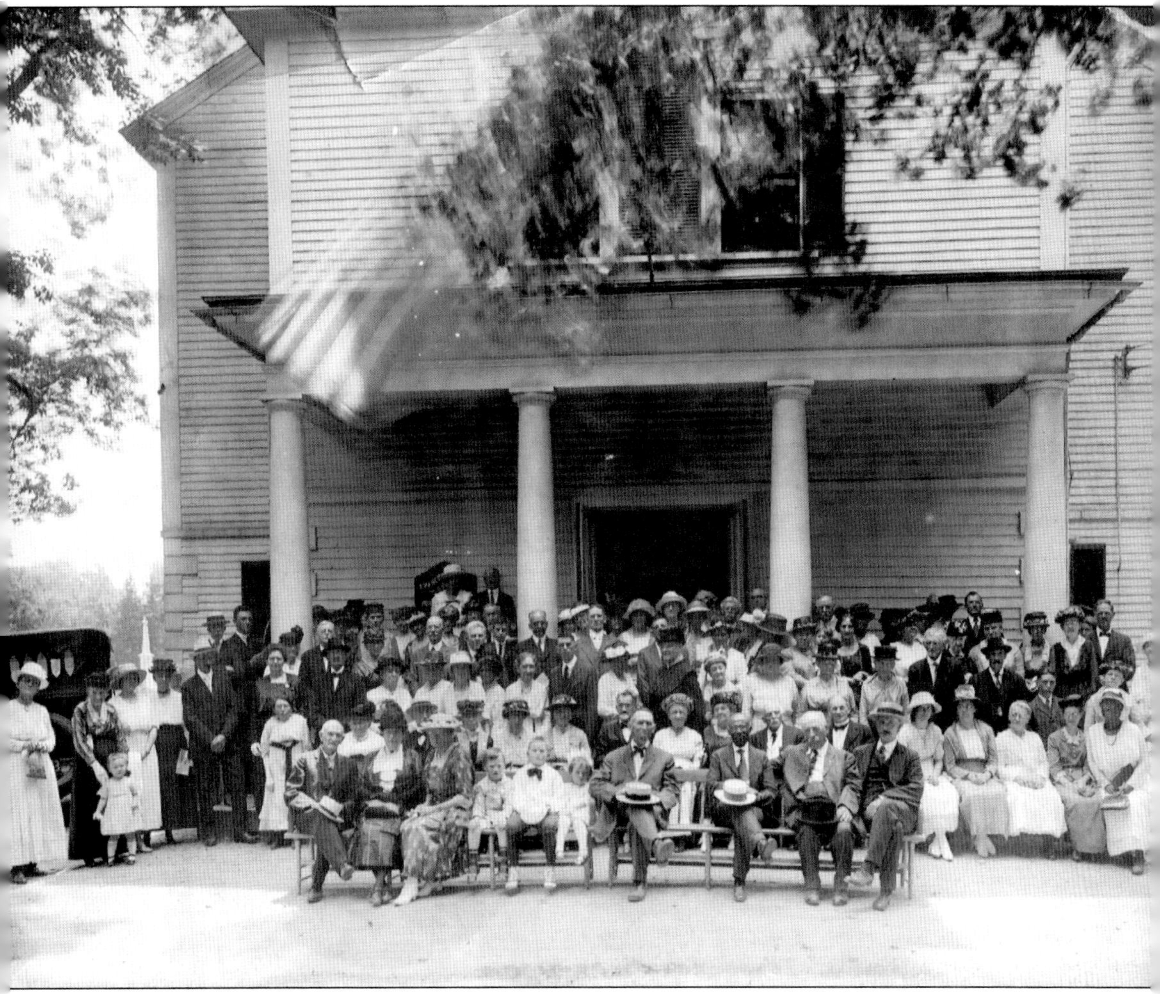

This image marks the celebration of the 100th anniversary of the Harvard Evangelical Church on March 21, 1921.

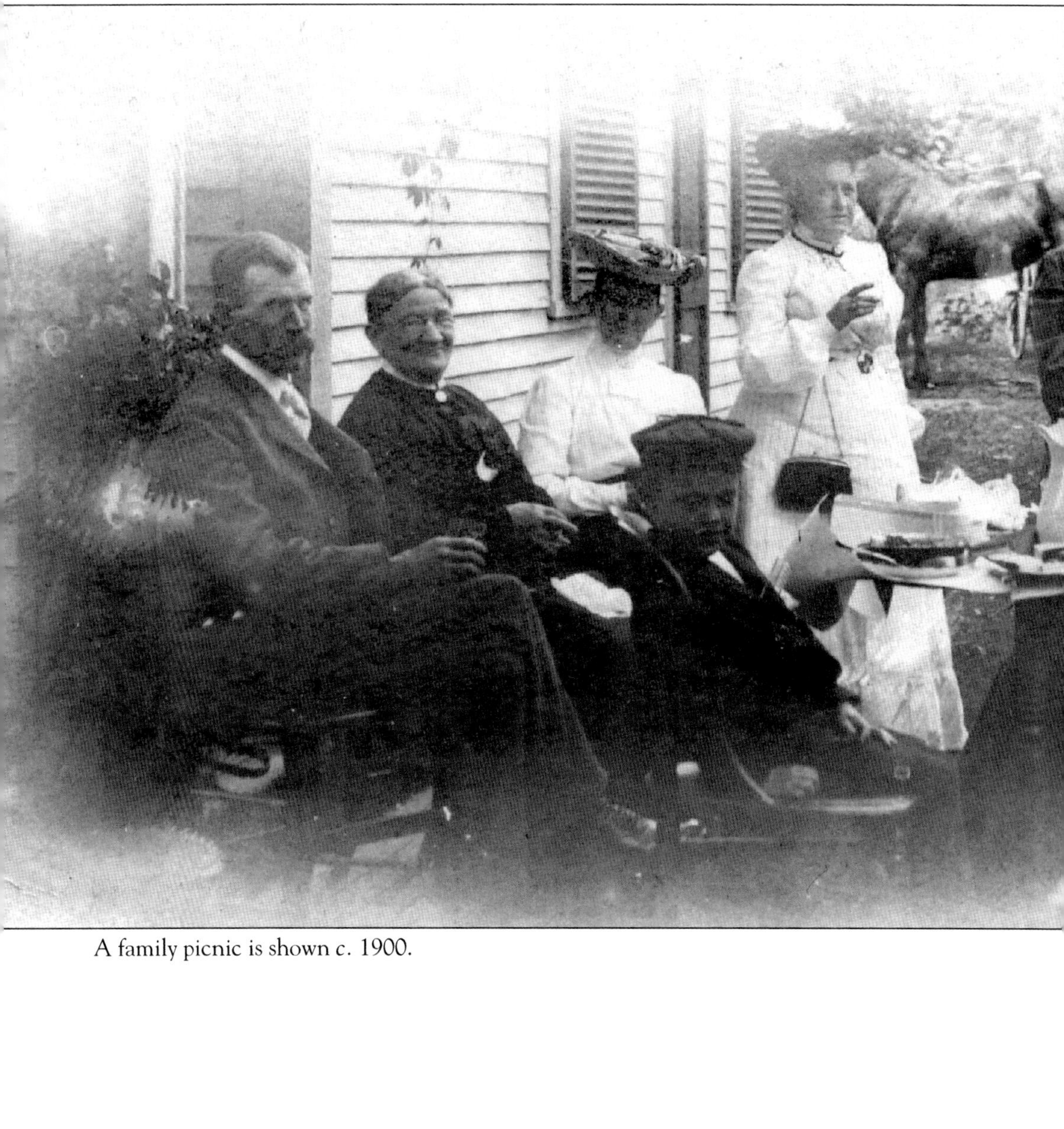

A family picnic is shown *c.* 1900.

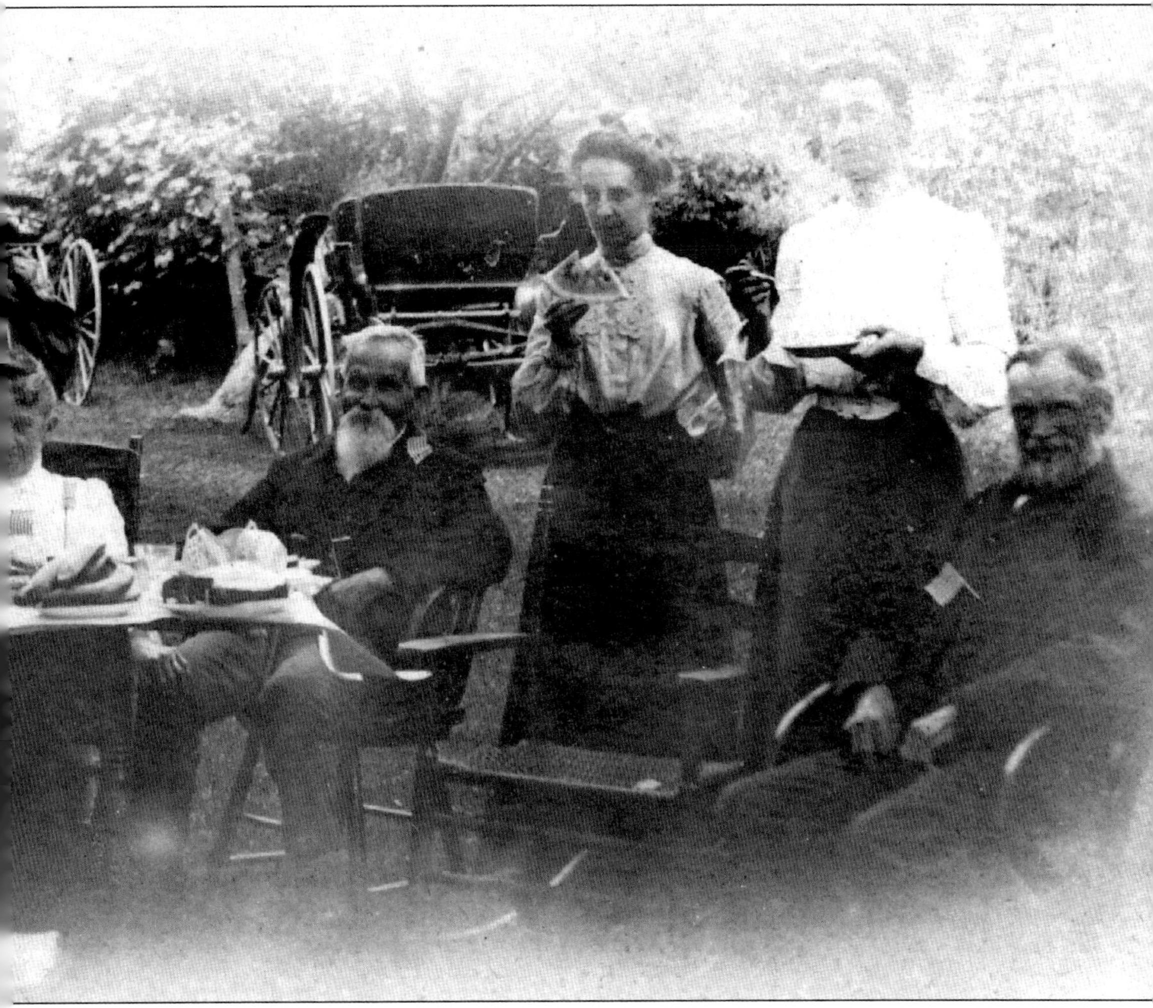

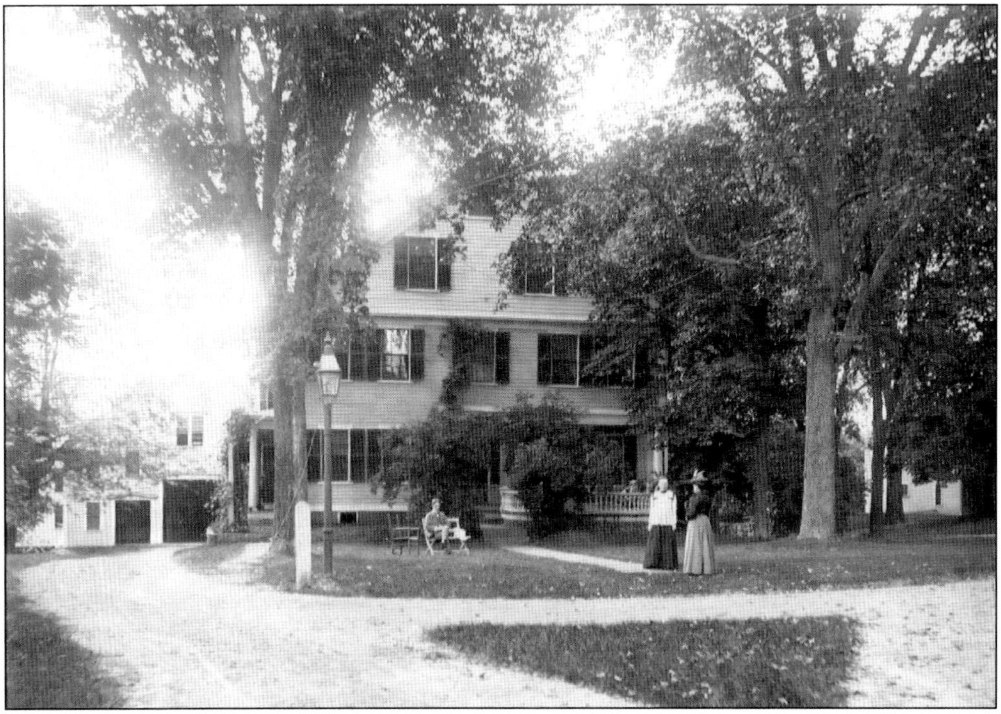

The Whitney House is pictured in a photograph taken by John Barnes of Plymouth *c.* 1910. Barnes was visiting his sisters Mrs. Goddard and Mrs. Atwood at the time.

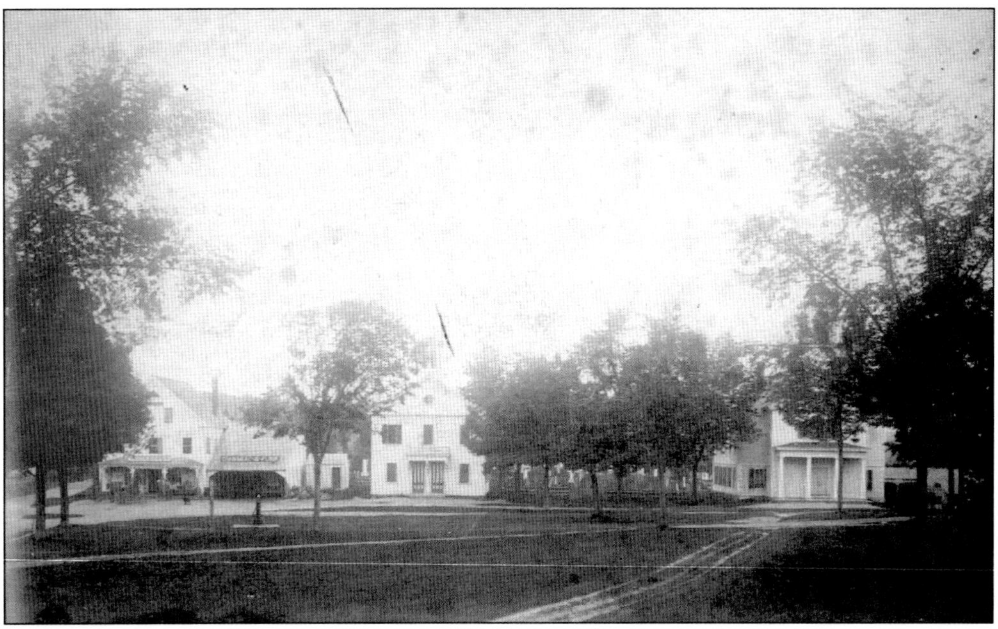

The center of Harvard is pictured in a view looking south *c.* 1890. Notice the general store on the far left. Barely discernable in this image is a horse and wagon pulled up to the front and a dog to the right.

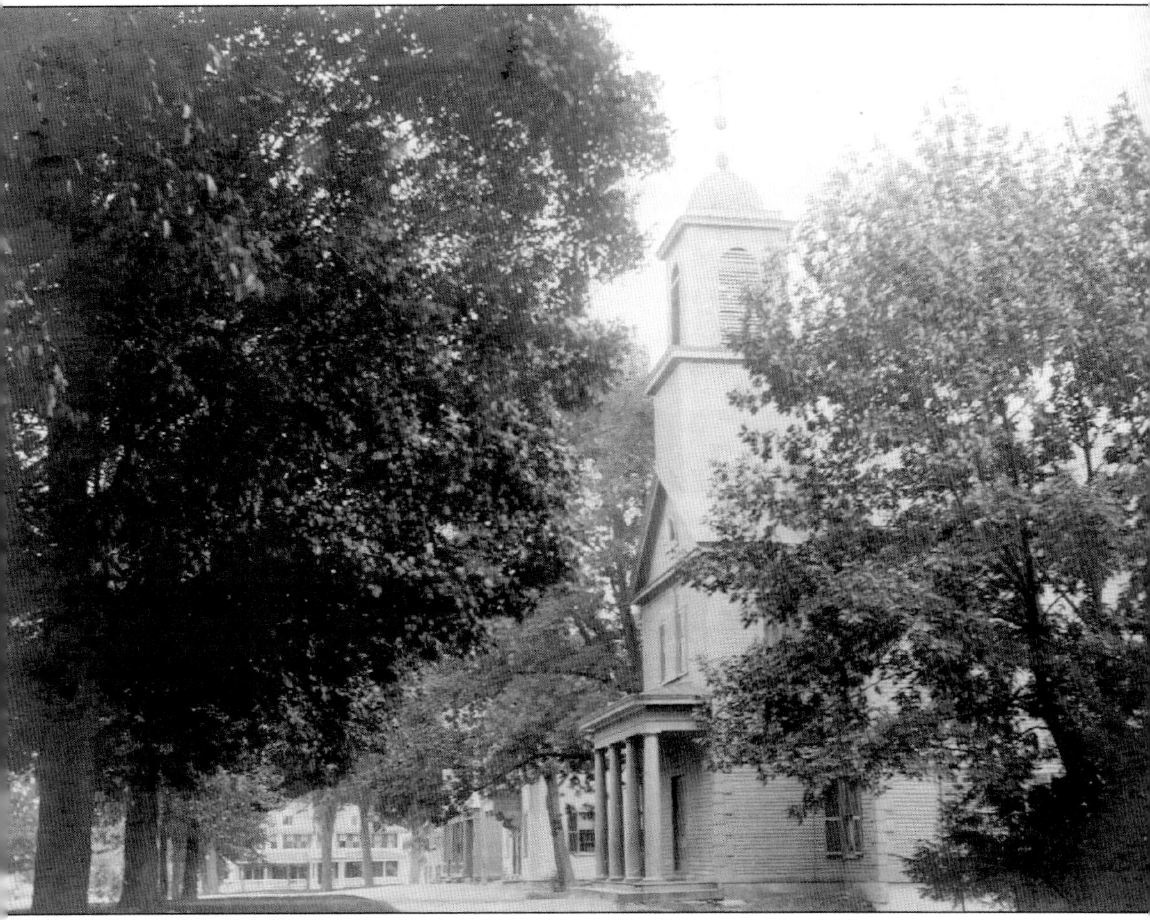

The Evangelical Congregational Church in Harvard is shown c. 1900. Also pictured are the school, store, and the Farwell House (left eastern side).

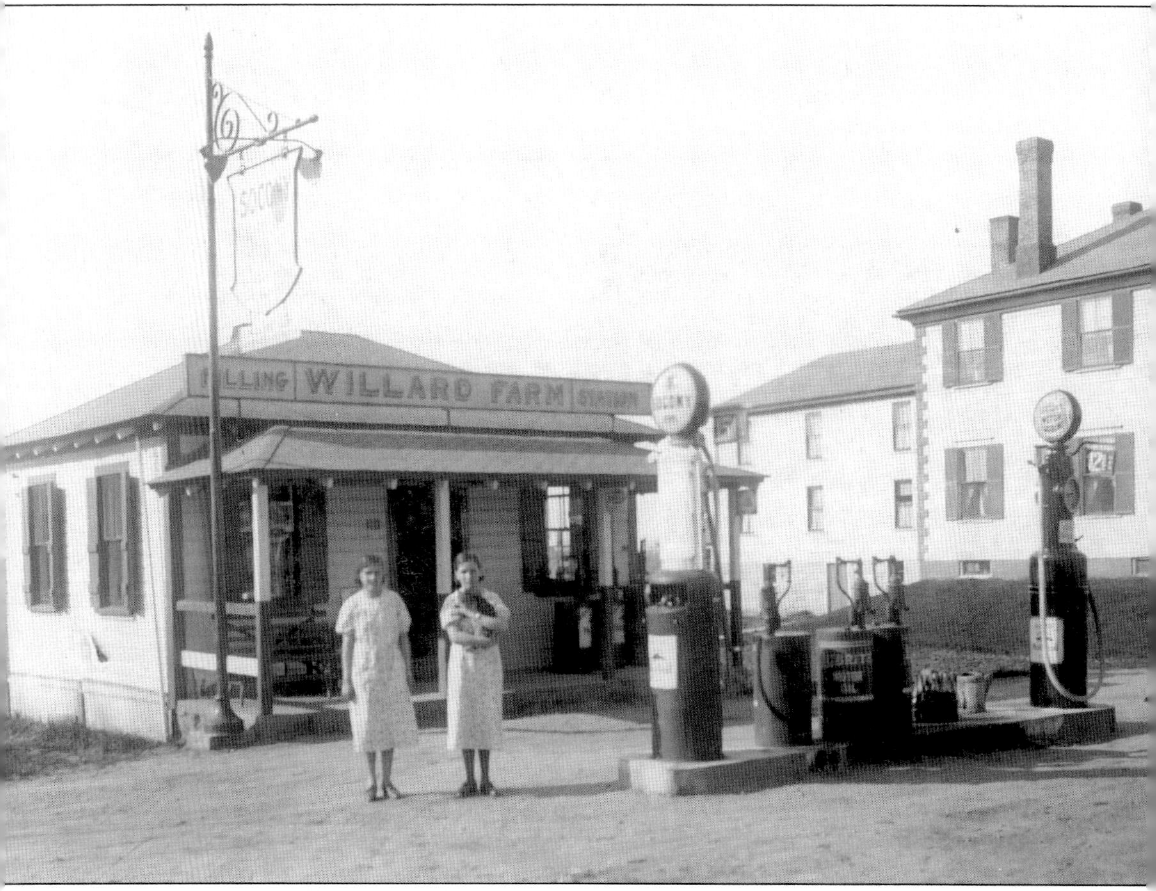

Here we see the Willard Farm filling station c. 1920. Places like this began to crop up to meet the growing needs of automobile travelers. Notice the road is still not paved.

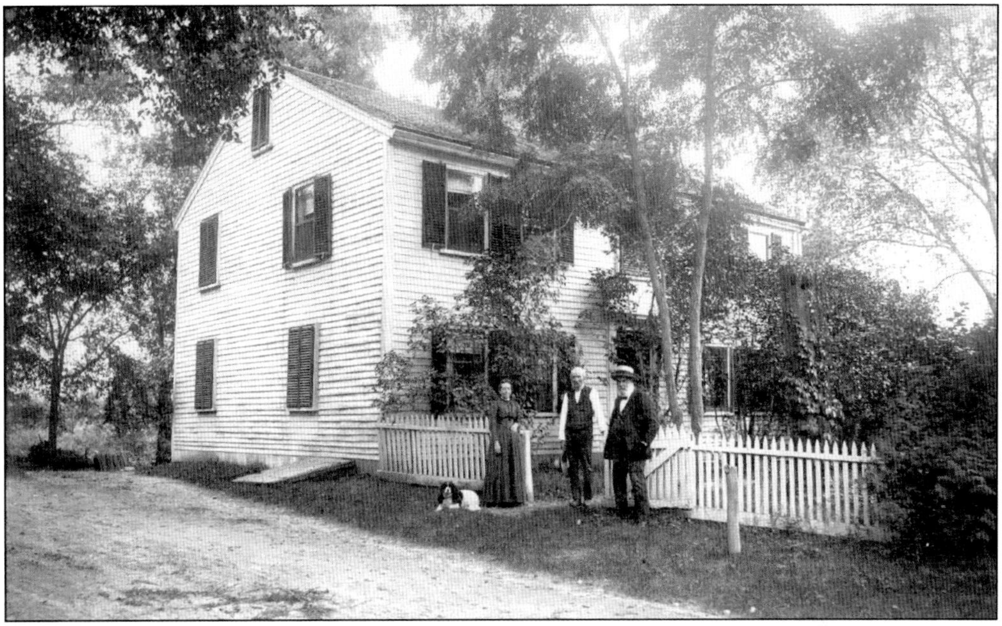

Anabella W. Prescott, John B. Prescott, and Charles H. Prescott are shown *c.* 1900.

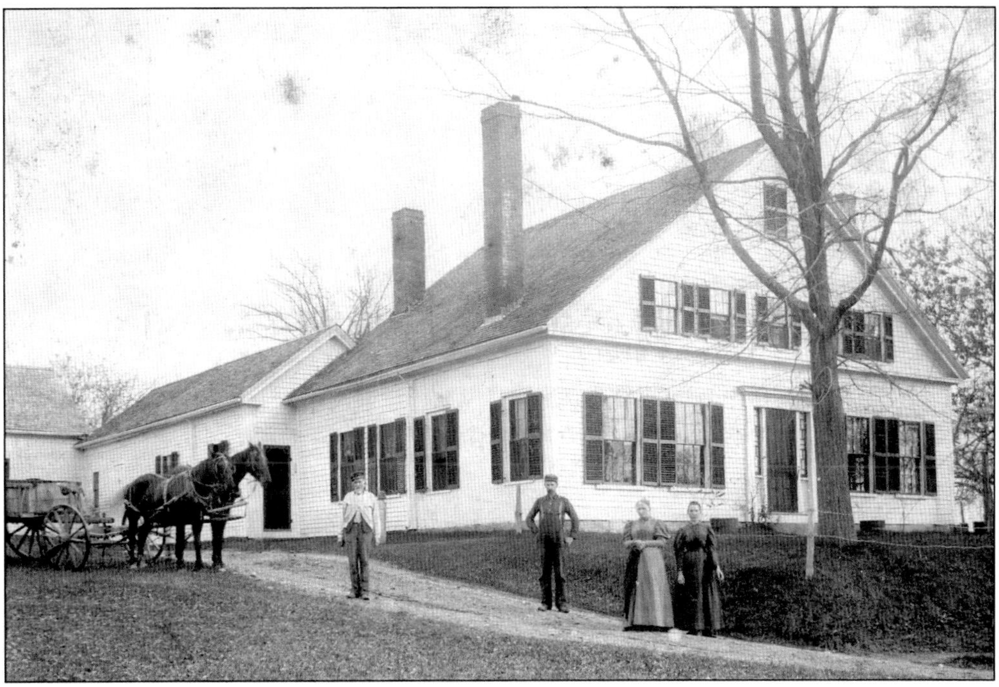

Old-style New England architecture is a prominent feature in central Massachusetts. This house exhibits the distinctly 19th-century arrangement of a main house attached to a smaller edition that, in turn, links to a barn. This enabled people to do their winter work without going outside, but it also increased the risk of fire—an ever-present danger during the days when most homes were heated with fireplaces and woodstoves that connected to unlined chimneys.

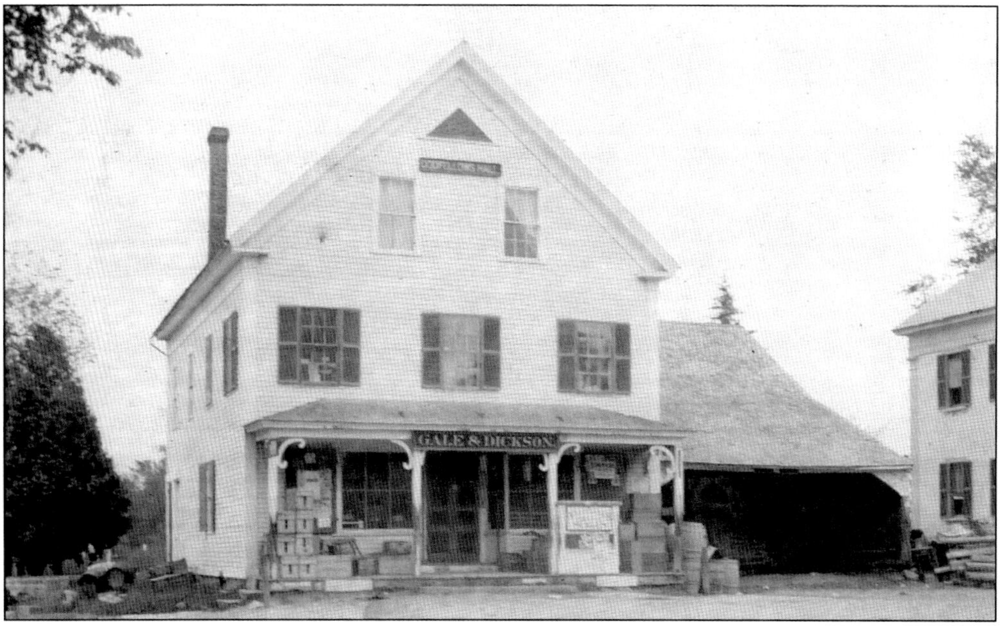

The Gale & Dickson General Store, on the green in Harvard, is shown prior to renovation c. 1890.

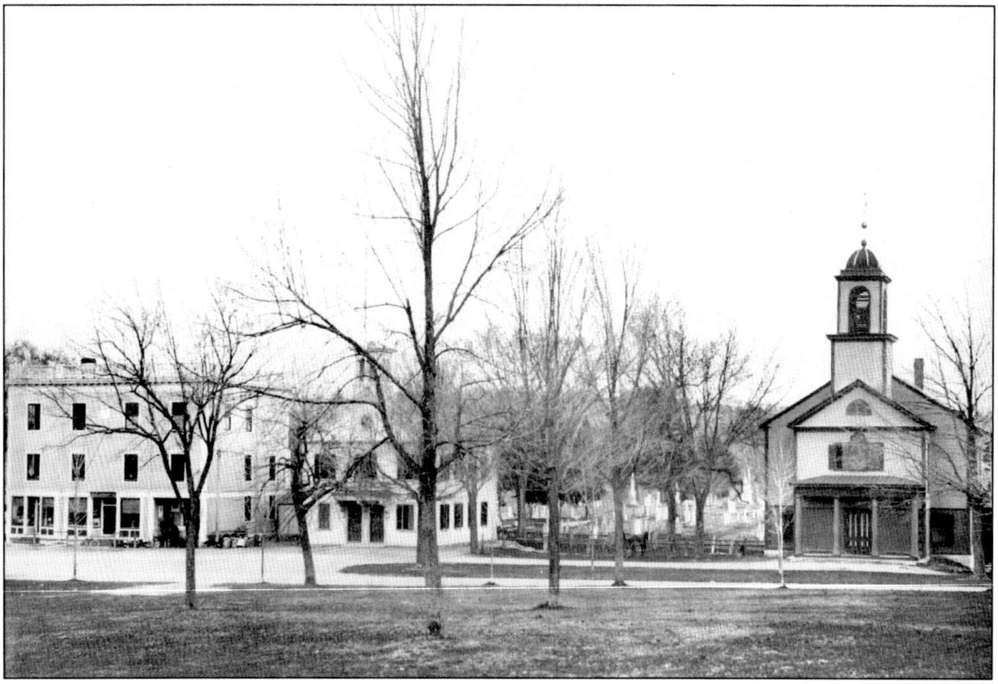
The general store is shown in 1897 after its renovation. The church to its immediate right has subsequently been removed.

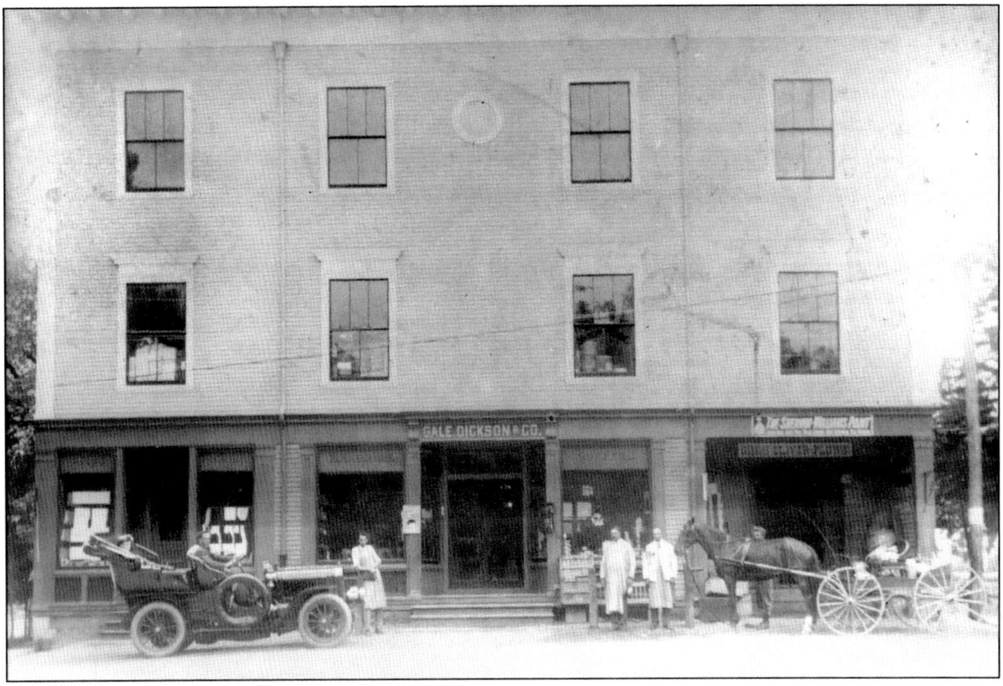

For a period of time following the renovation of the general store, patrons would occasionally meet there using a variety of modes of transportation. This scene captures the spirit of the age.

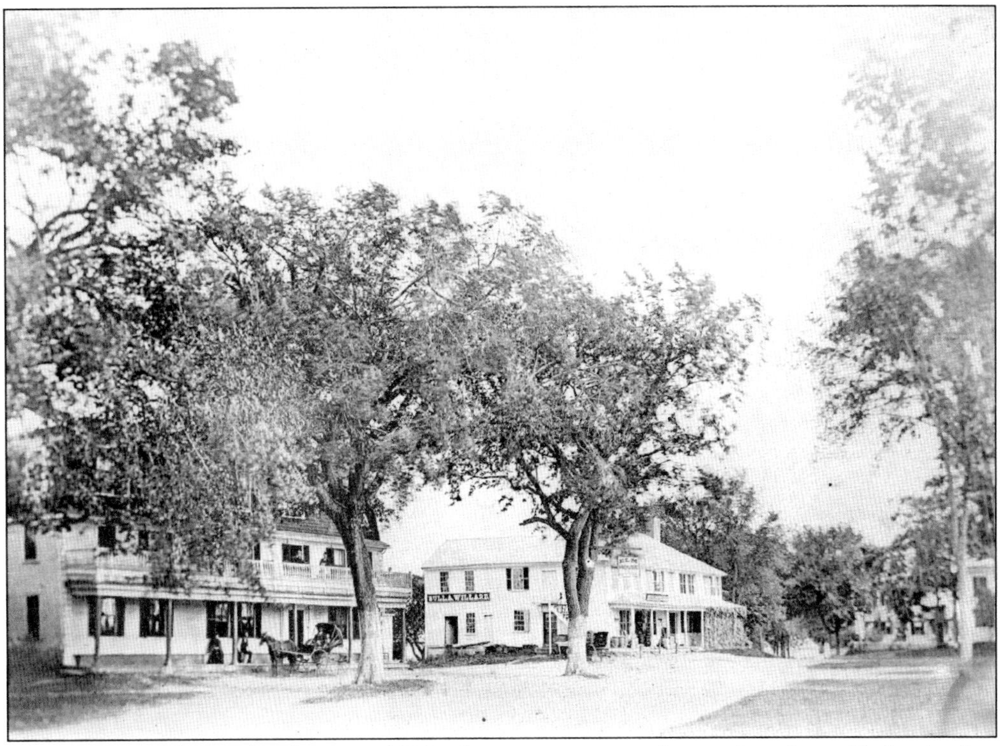

The Elm House (center) is shown *c.* 1890, when it was a general store that also stabled animals.

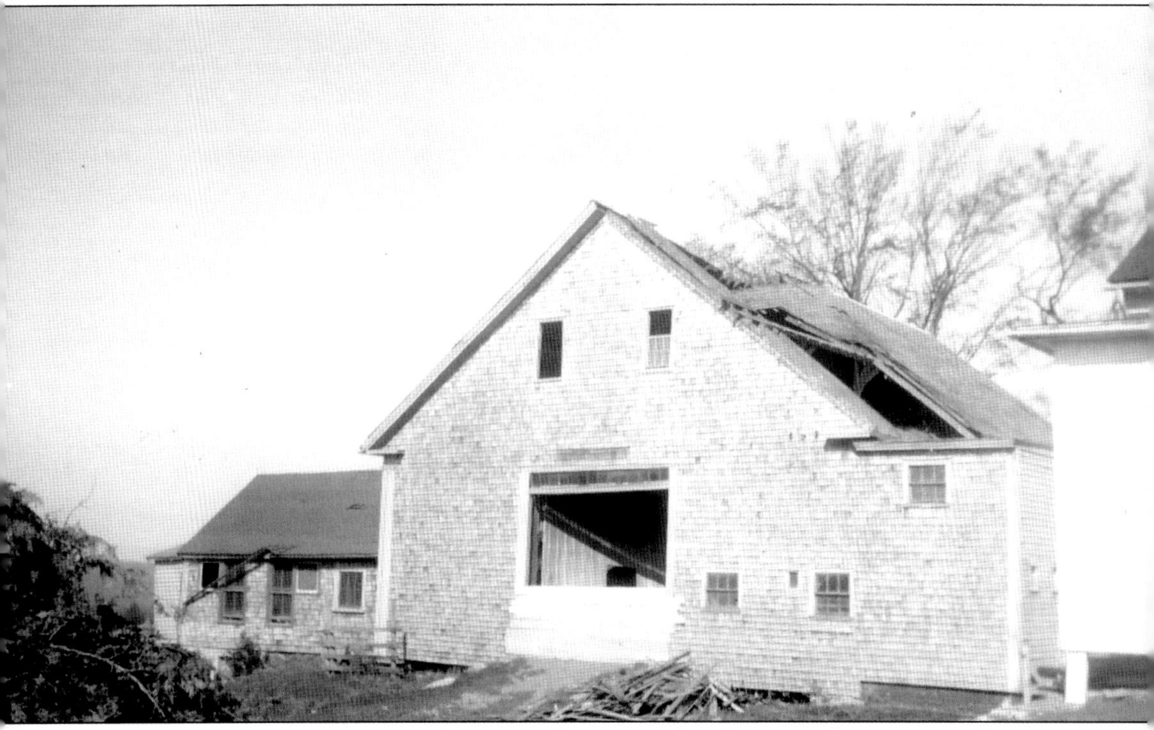

One of the most dramatic transformations for Harvard, and many other towns in the region, was the 1938 hurricane. Pictured here is the damage done to Howard Stone's barn.

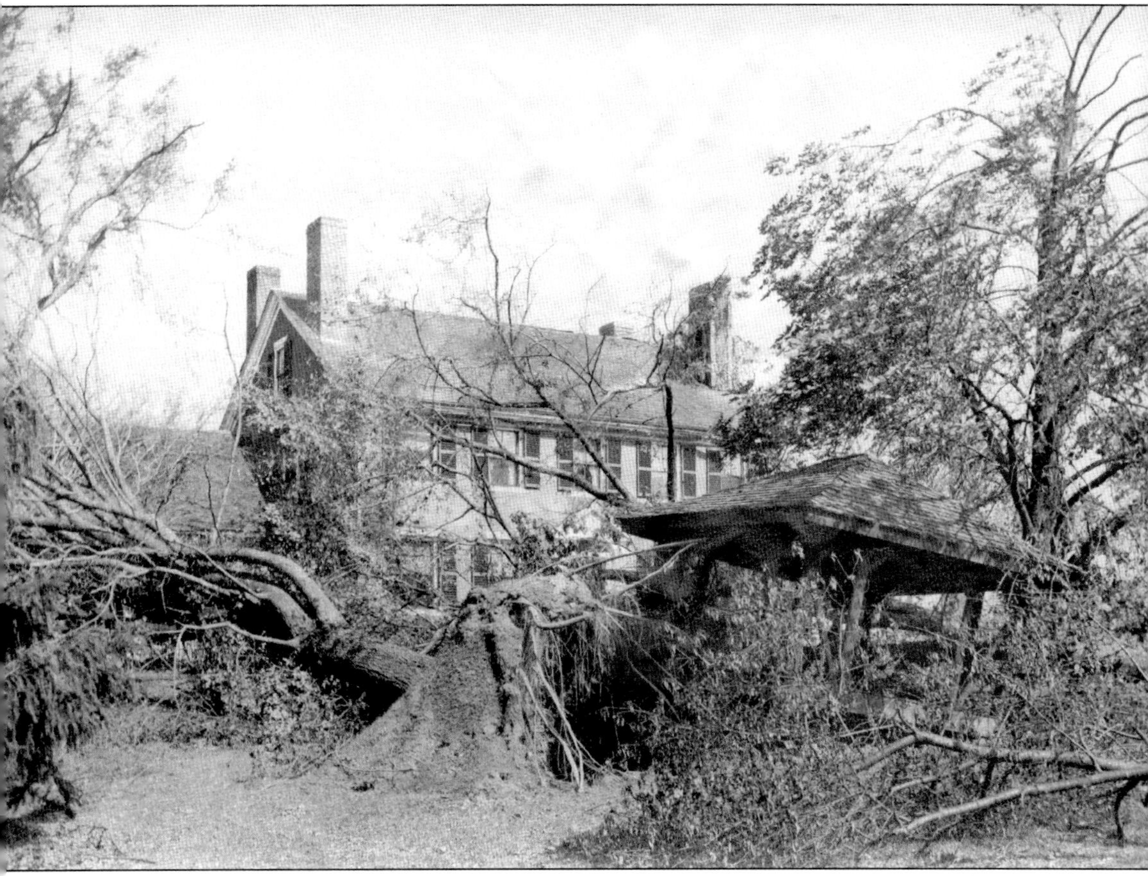

This image shows the damage suffered by the estate of Mrs. Franklin Watson from the 1938 hurricane. The number of large trees blown down by the hurricane was so great that the lumber market was saturated for years after the storm.

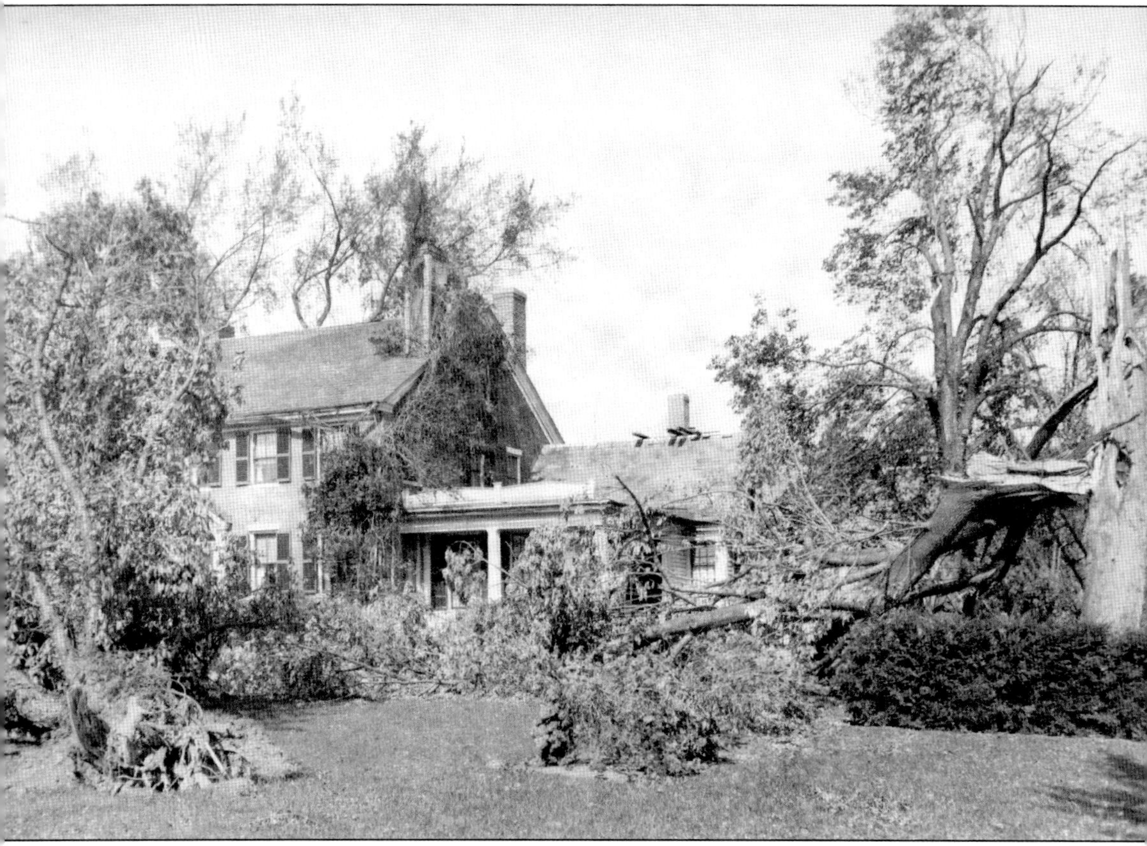

This is another view of Mrs. Franklin Watson's estate after the 1938 hurricane.

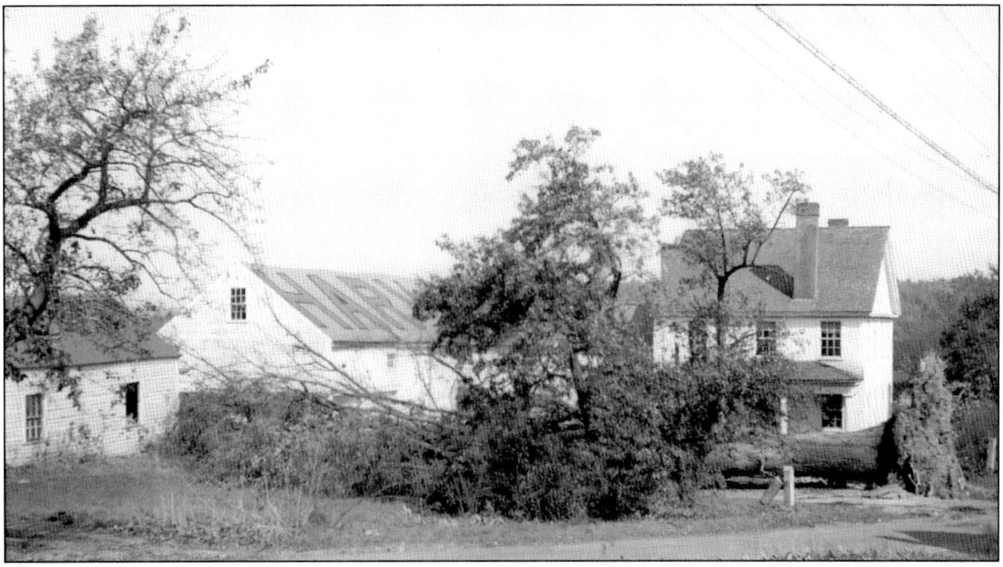

A back-door view shows the hurricane damage to the Whitney elm tree. The roots of this tree extended into the air some 20 feet.

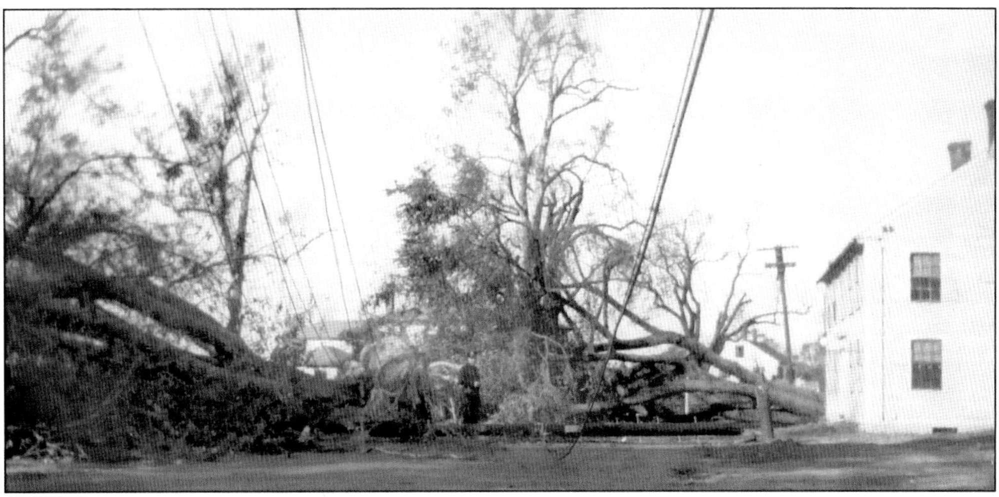

This is Still River center after the 1938 hurricane. The corner of the post office is visible at the far right.

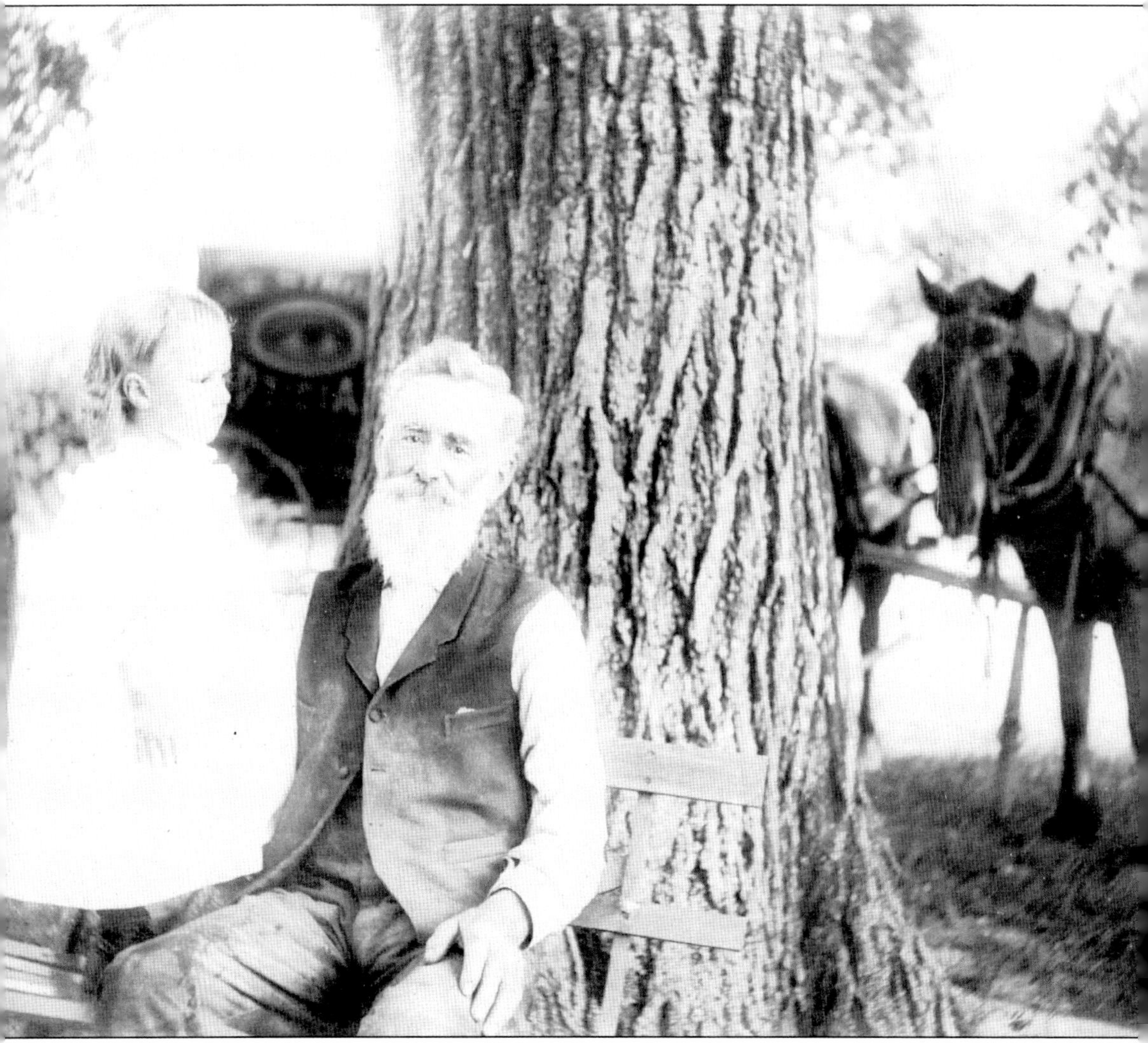

This is Luther Willard and his granddaughter Ruth of Still River c. 1900.

Two

Shaker Village

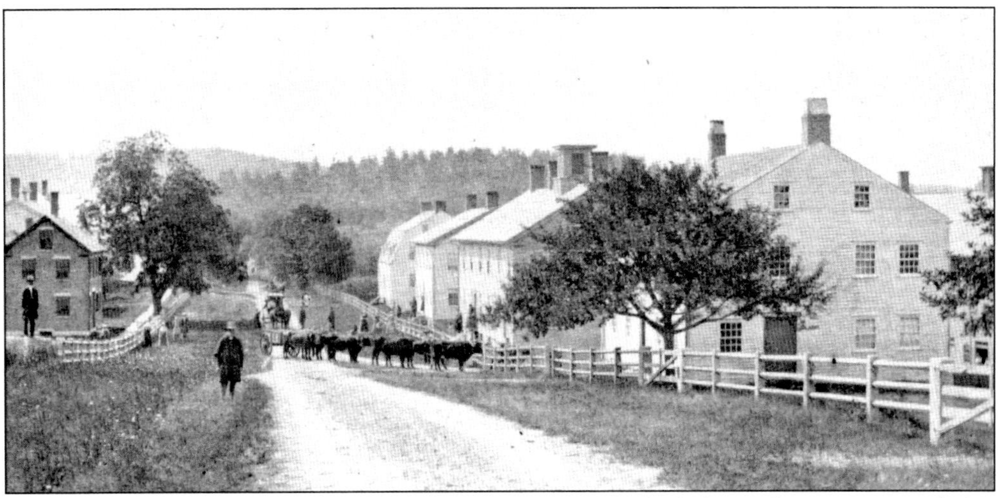

This photograph shows the Church Family of the Harvard Shaker village *c.* 1870. Shaker villages were divided into families, their basic communal economic unit. Several large dwellings are visible on the right, and the brick ministry shop is on the left. A large wagon being pulled by eight oxen is in the center of the road.

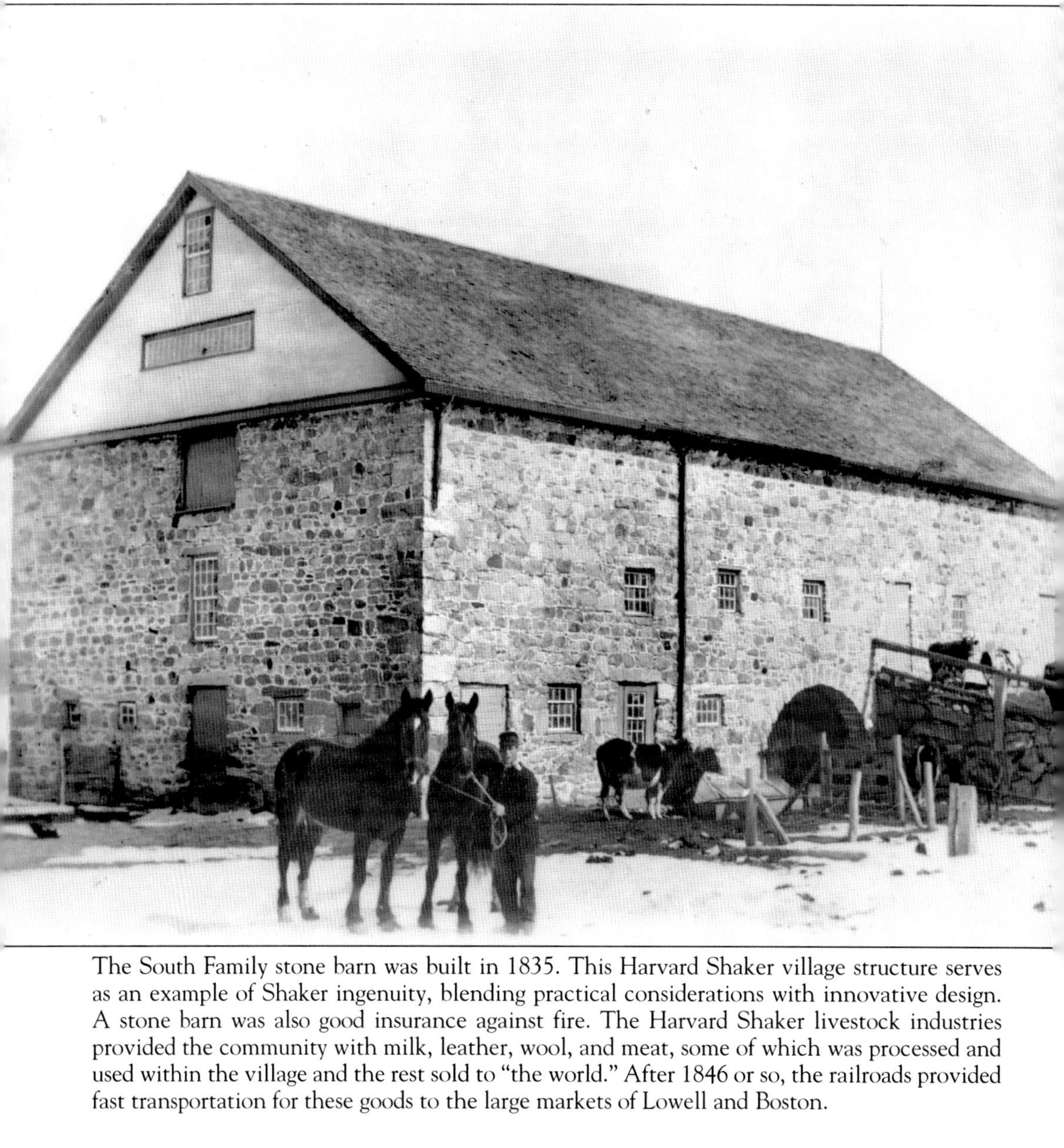

The South Family stone barn was built in 1835. This Harvard Shaker village structure serves as an example of Shaker ingenuity, blending practical considerations with innovative design. A stone barn was also good insurance against fire. The Harvard Shaker livestock industries provided the community with milk, leather, wool, and meat, some of which was processed and used within the village and the rest sold to "the world." After 1846 or so, the railroads provided fast transportation for these goods to the large markets of Lowell and Boston.

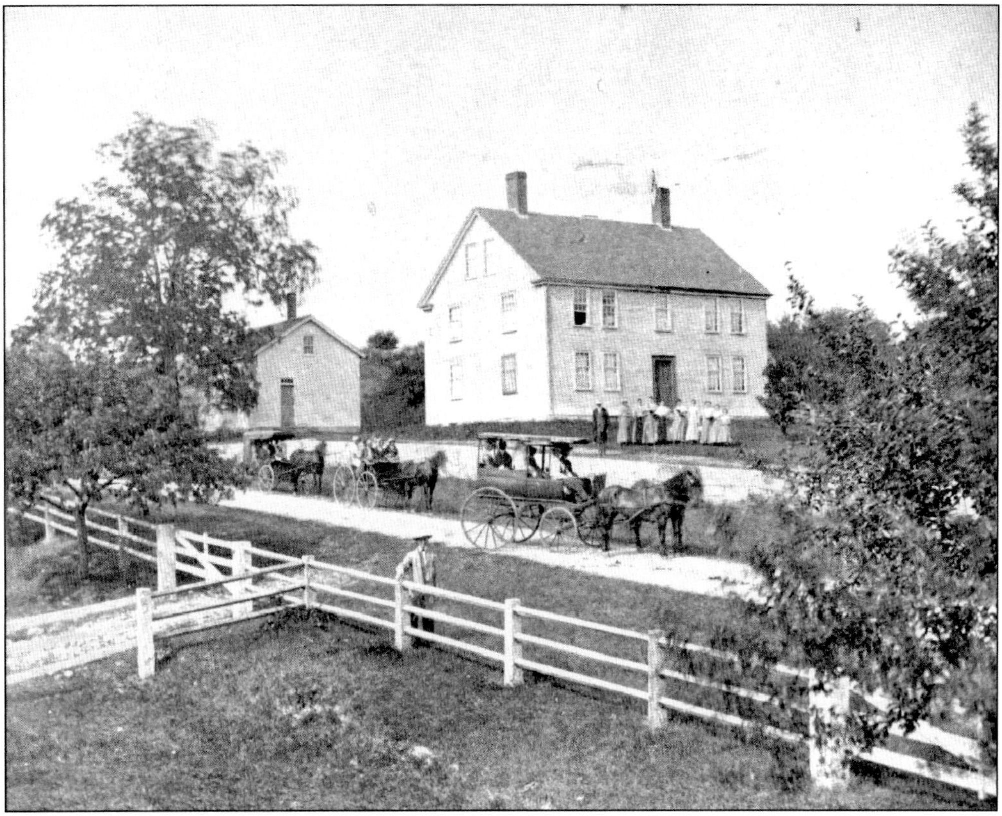

The Church Family Square House of the Harvard Shaker village was built in 1769 by a group of New Light Baptists led by Shadrack Ireland. It was the first house occupied and eventually purchased by the Shakers in the early 1780s. Mother Ann Lee, the founder and spiritual leader of the Shakers, lived in the Square House while in Harvard between 1781 and 1783. This photograph, probably taken in the 1860s or 1870s, shows a group of Shakers in wagons and standing in front of the house.

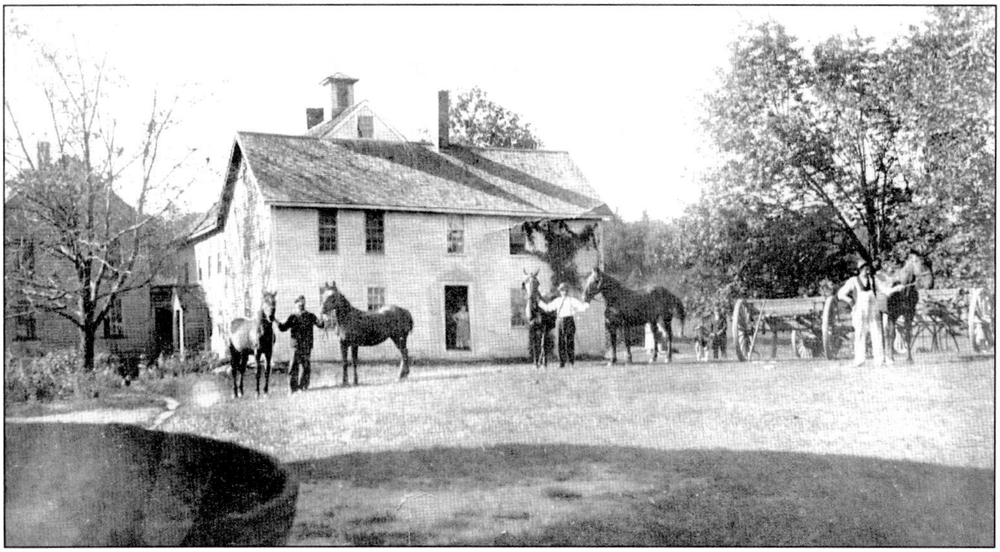

This is the only known image of the East Family of the Harvard Shaker village. The image was probably taken in the 1890s after East Family property was sold.

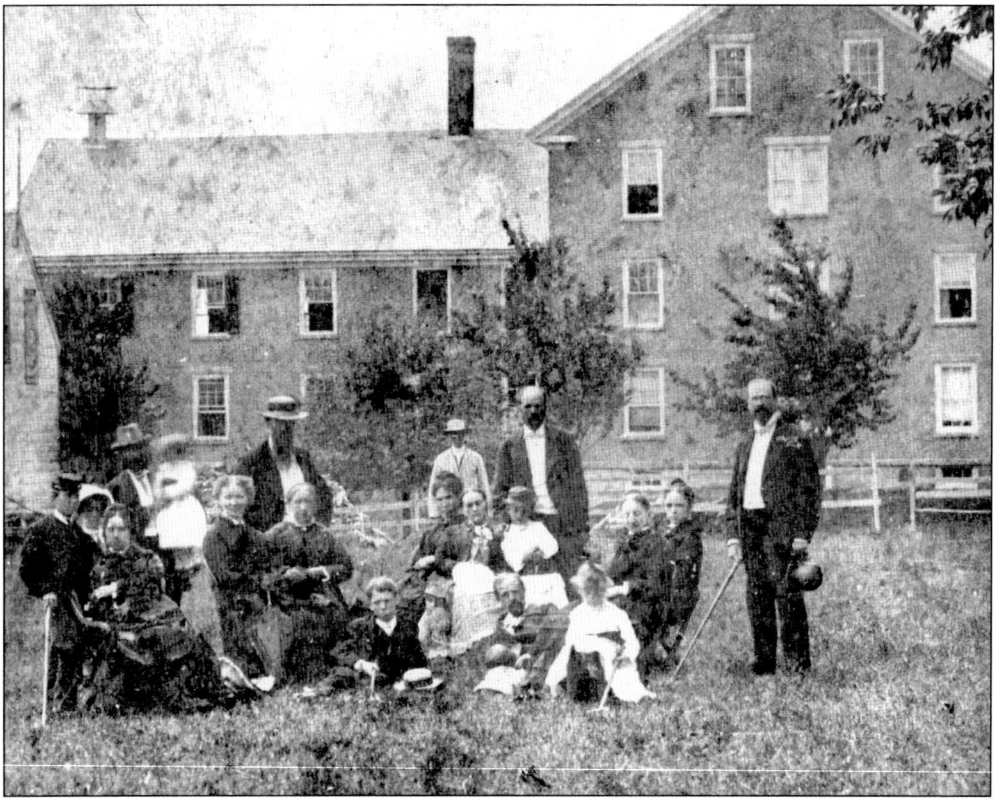

A group of people is gathered by the side of the Rural Home. Built in 1854, the Rural Home served as the main dwelling house for the North Family of the Harvard Shaker village. At least one man on the left is wearing a Union army uniform, suggesting this image dates from the 1860s.

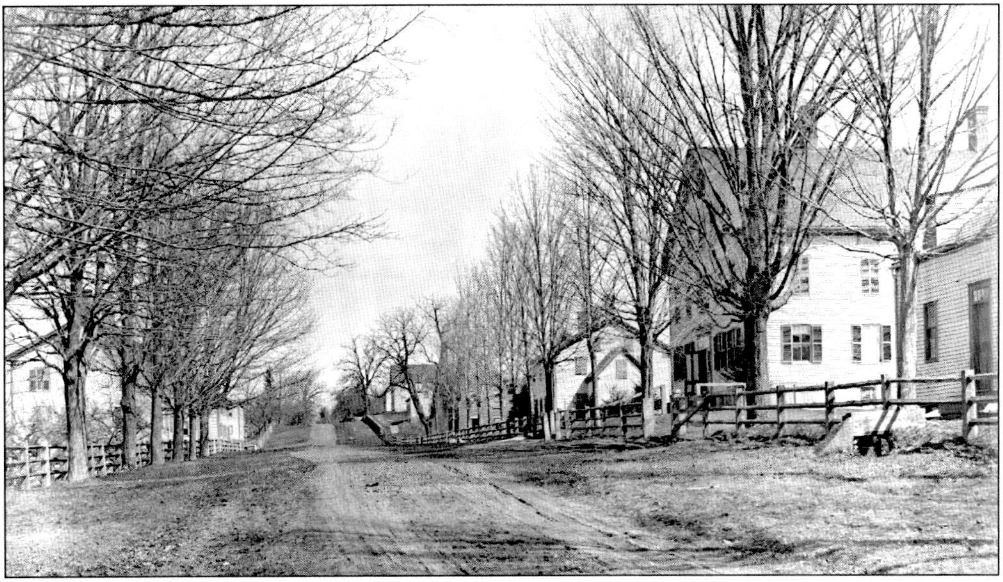

This north-facing image shows the Church Family of the Harvard Shaker village. On the right are the old office (built in 1794), the new office (built in 1841), and the meetinghouse (built in 1792). The old office was moved to Fruitlands Museums in 1920. The other buildings survive in their original locations as private residences.

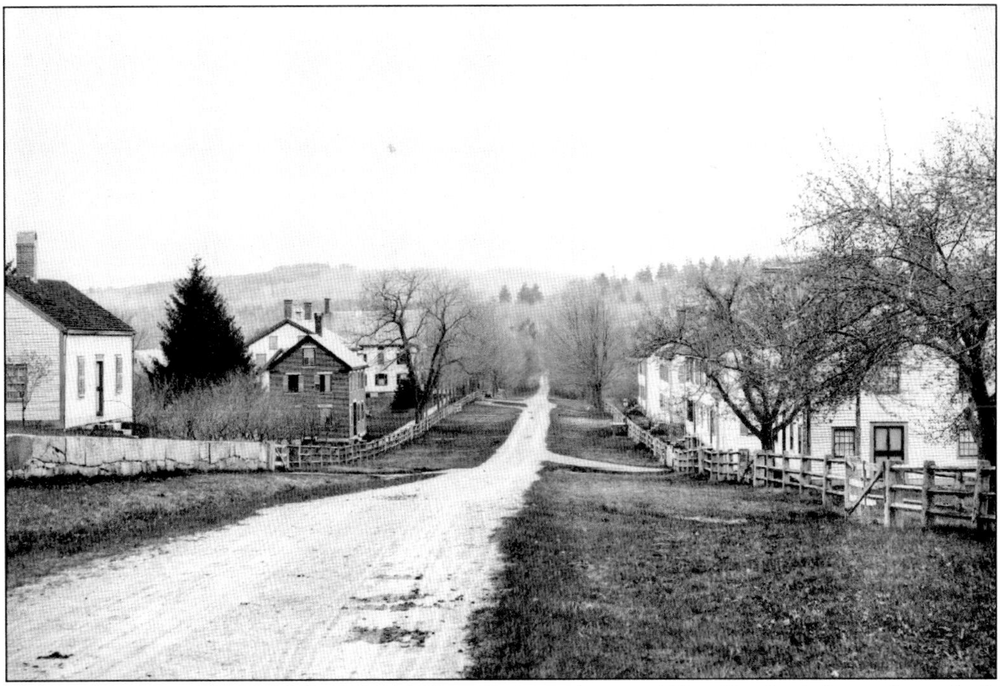

This south-facing image of the Church Family was taken in 1896. To the left are the tailor's shop, the ministry shop, the meetinghouse, and the new office. Buildings on the right include the Brethren's Shop, the First House, the Sister's Shop, and the Second House.

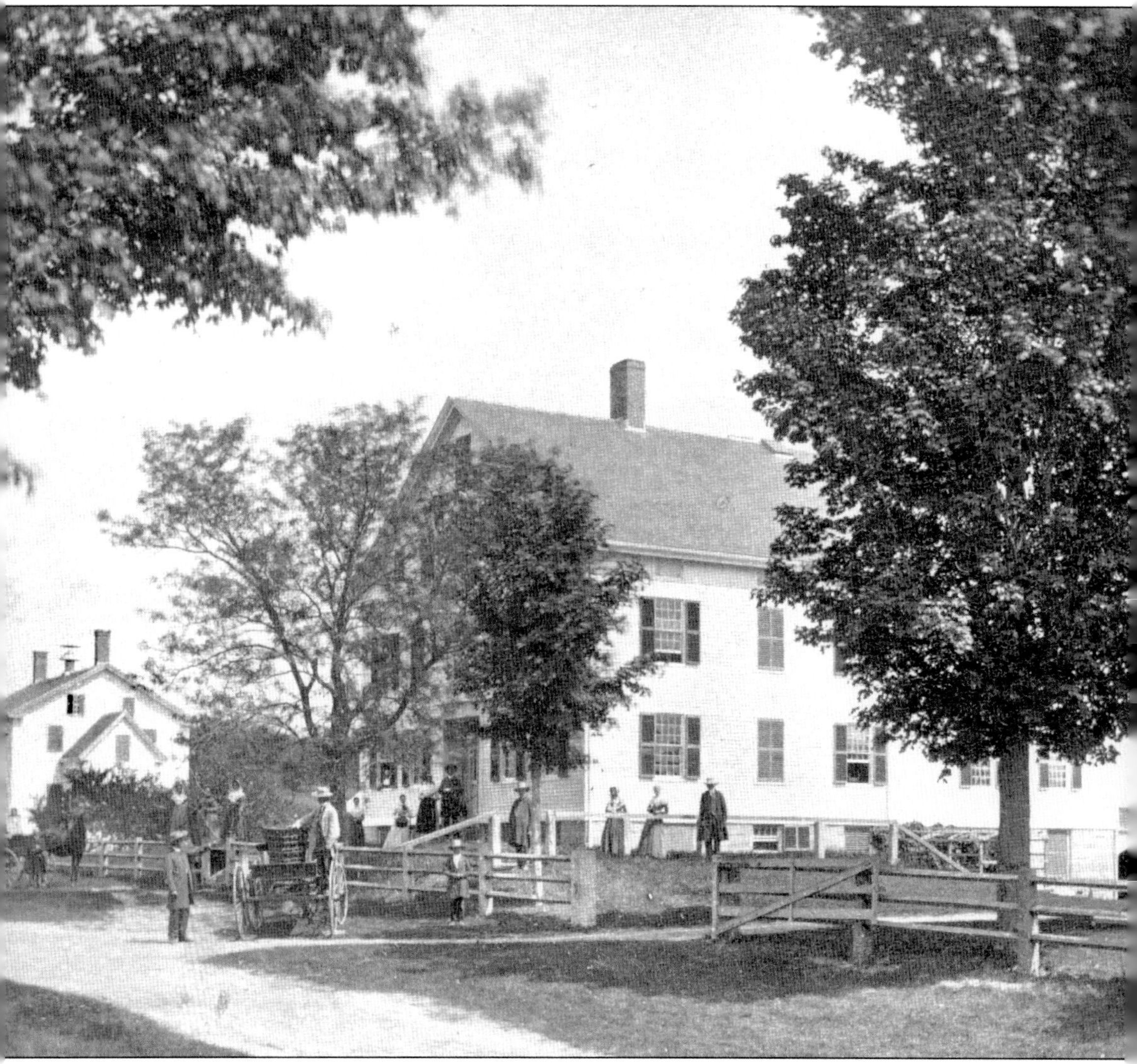

The new office in the Church Family of the Harvard Shaker village was built in 1841 to meet the growing demand for Shaker goods. In the foreground, a number of Shaker people in their distinctive style of dress are visible. In the distance to the left, the meetinghouse is visible. This image probably dates from the 1870s.

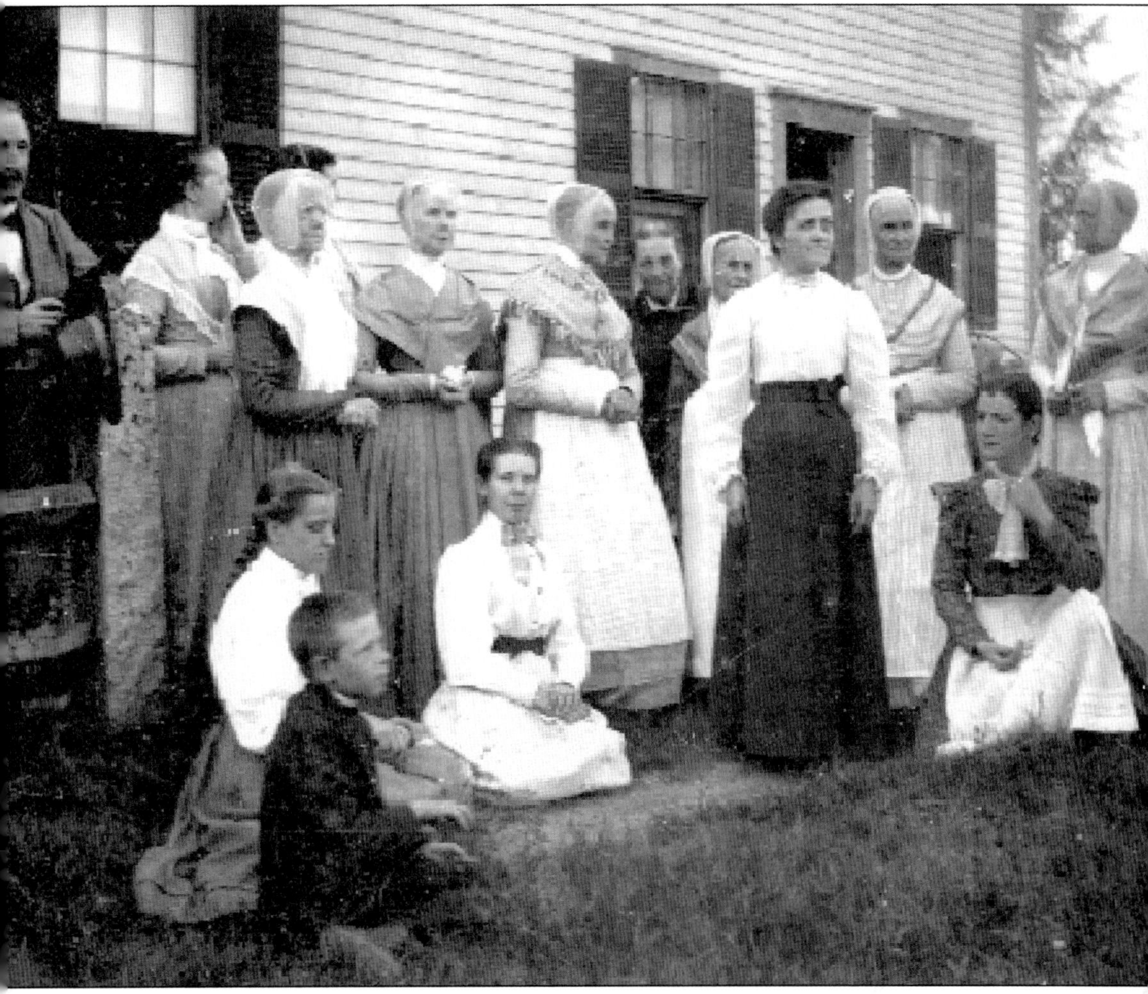

This is an image of a group of Harvard Shakers c. 1905. By the early 20th century, the population of the Harvard Shaker community had been declining for several decades. The clothing shown in this view indicates that several Shakers are grouped with a number of the non-Shaker people. Eldress Ann Walker is the first woman standing on the far left. The woman standing next to her is Olive Hatch. Barely visible behind Olive Hatch is Hattie Maynard. Louisa and Ellen Green are on the far right. This photograph is from the collection of Arthur West, who grew up in the Harvard Shaker village and maintained personal ties to the last sisters in the community, especially Ann Walker.

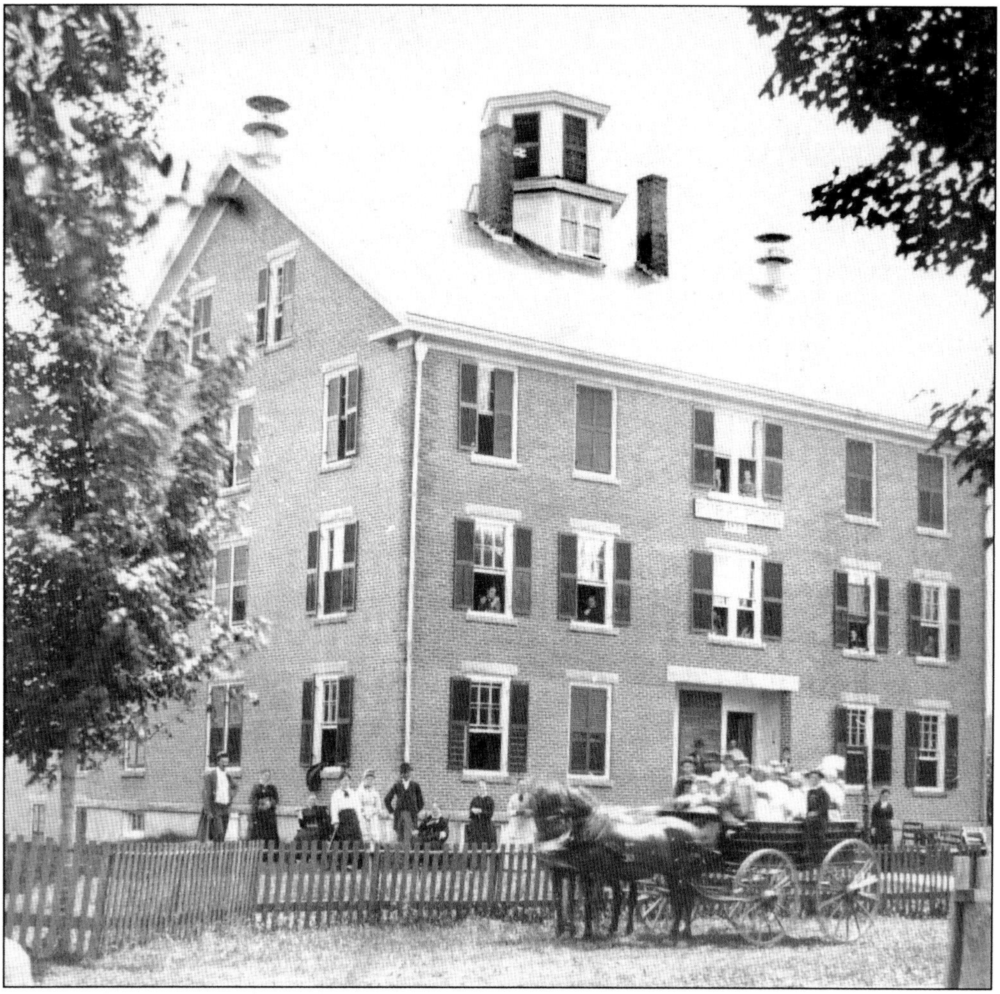

The Rural Home was a large dwelling house built in the North Family of the Harvard Shaker community. It was originally intended to be a dormitory for that family. However, they overspent during its construction, and the society went into debt. This photograph, which probably dates from the 1870s or 1880s, shows a number of non-Shakers in and around the building. These may be guests staying in the Rural Home, which served as a hotel of sorts for a period of time.

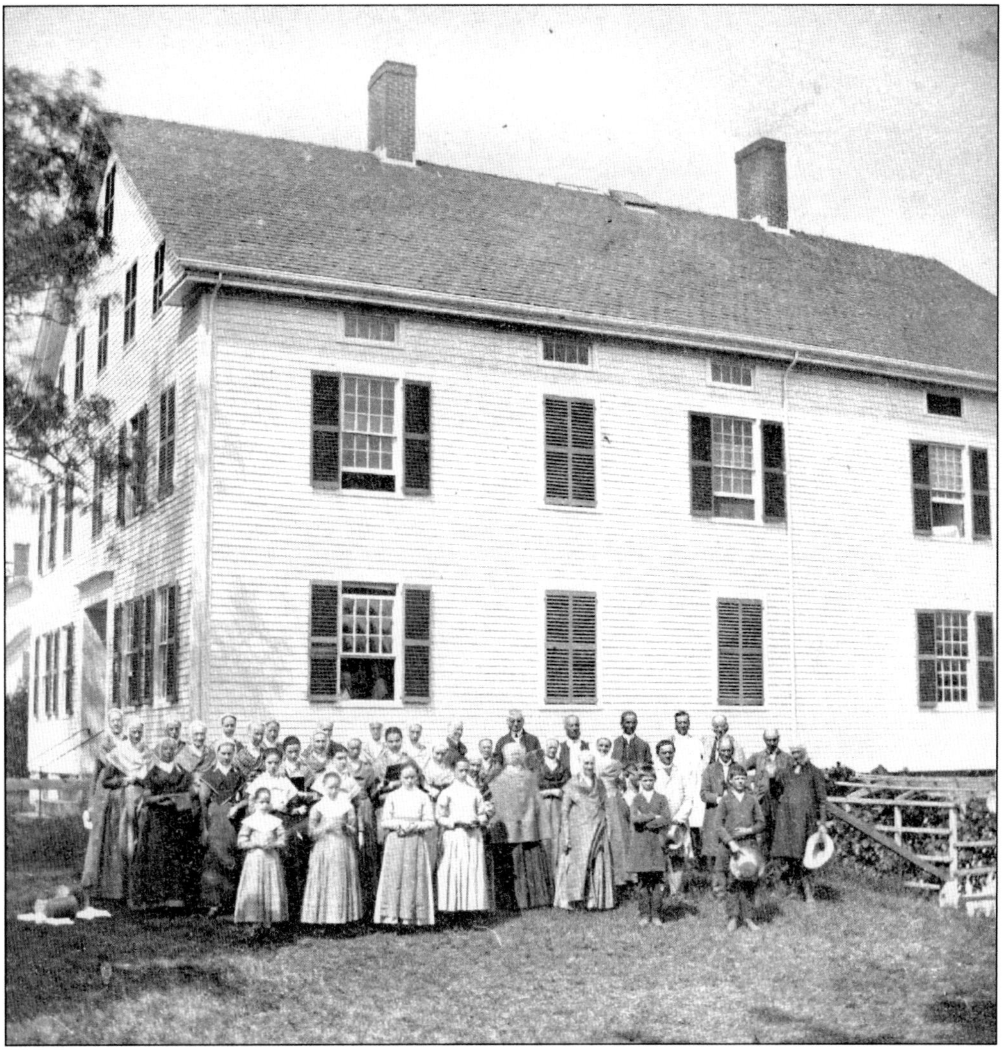

The Church Family of the Harvard Shaker community is seen standing in front of the new office c. 1870. The Harvard Shaker community was a group of families and individuals who devoted their lives to God. They lived communally, practiced equality between the sexes, and developed distinctive agricultural and manufacturing practices, architecture, and forms of worship. The brethren and sisters of the village lived, worked, and worshiped together but generally lived separately, with men on one side and women on the other.

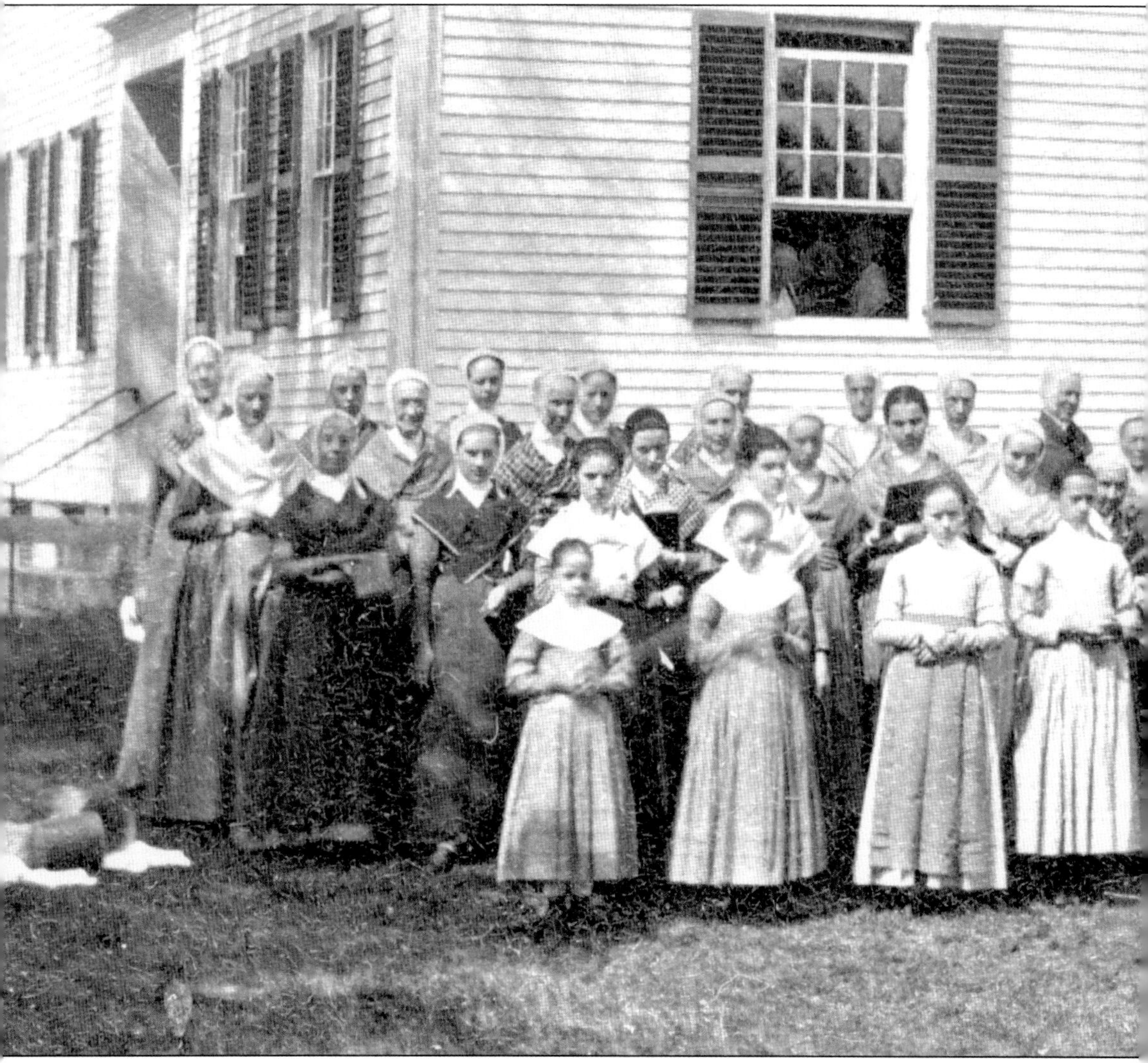

This image offers a closer view of the Church Family standing in front of the new office. The distinctive style of dress for the sisters and the brethren is readily apparent. The sisters of the Harvard village were almost always more numerous than the brethren and, as such, they formed

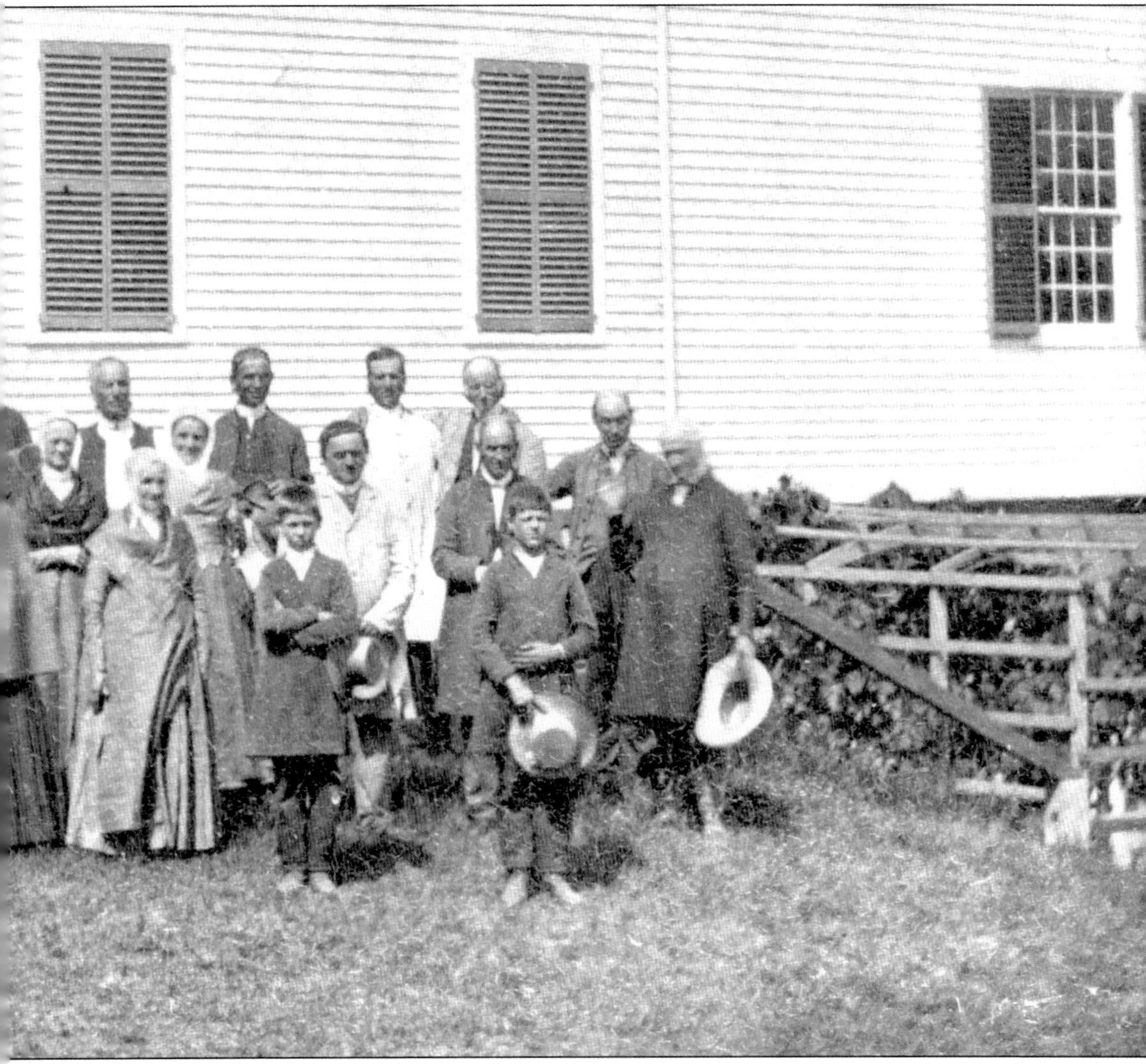

the core workforce of the village. The sisters performed many different functions to support village life.

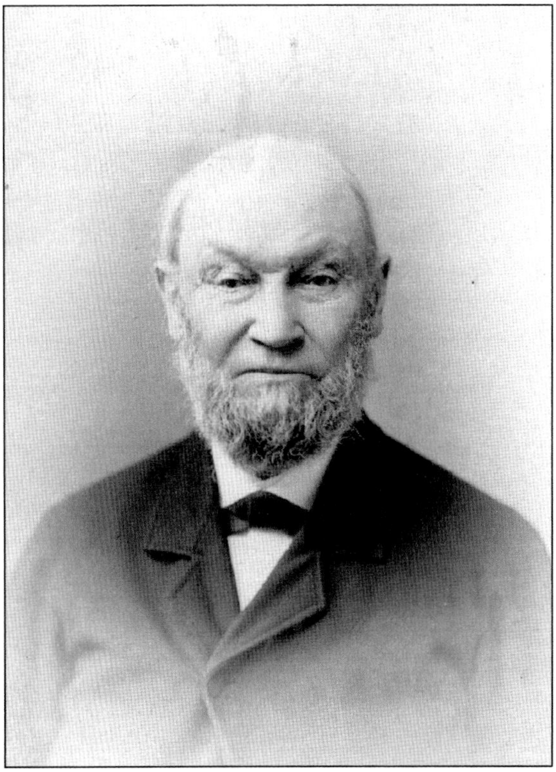

Simon Atherton was admitted into the Harvard Shaker Church Family in 1808 at the age of five. He served as trustee for 47 years, finding markets for Shaker products and looking after Shaker business interests in Boston. Atherton died in 1888.

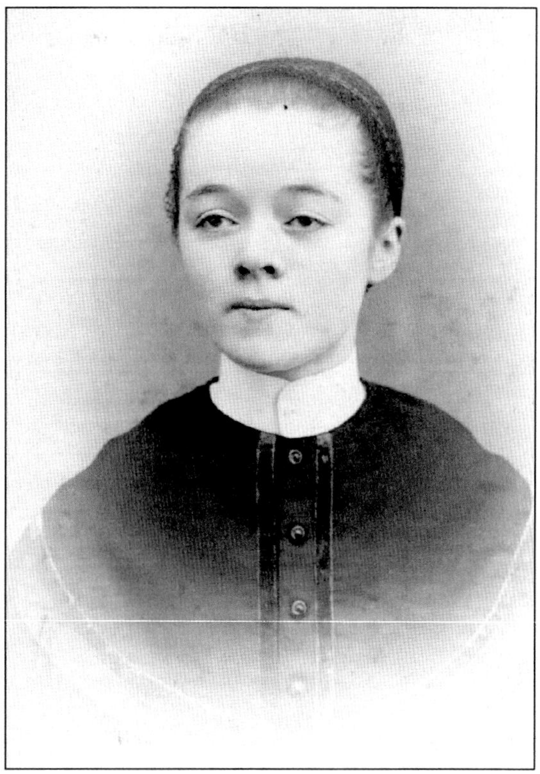

Sister Francis Dempsey was a Shaker during the early part of her life but left the village in 1893.

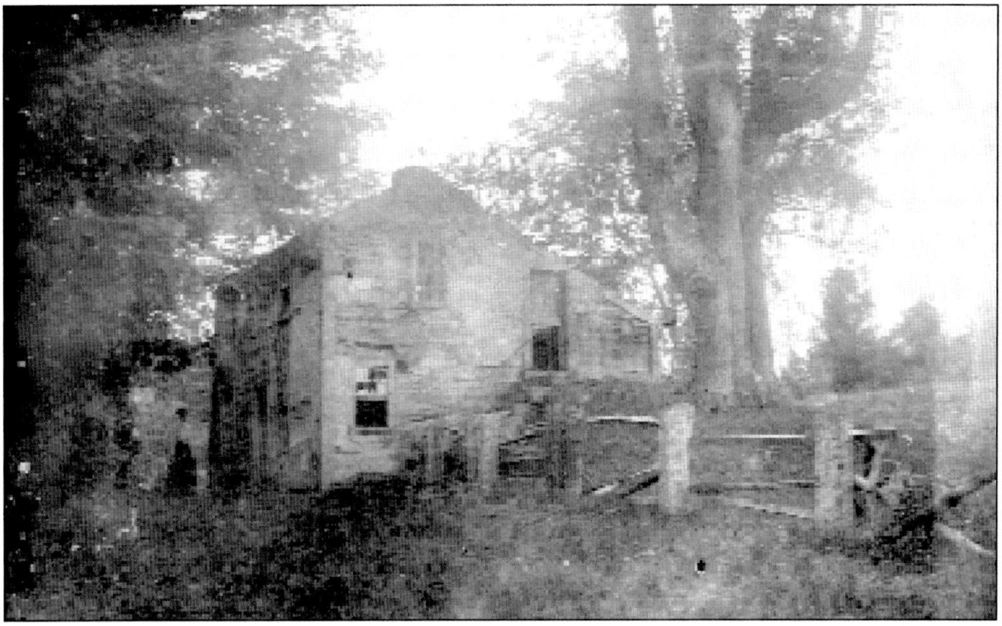

The Jeremiah Willard House and surrounding farmland in the South Family of the Harvard Shaker village provided the budding community with a core area to build their village around.

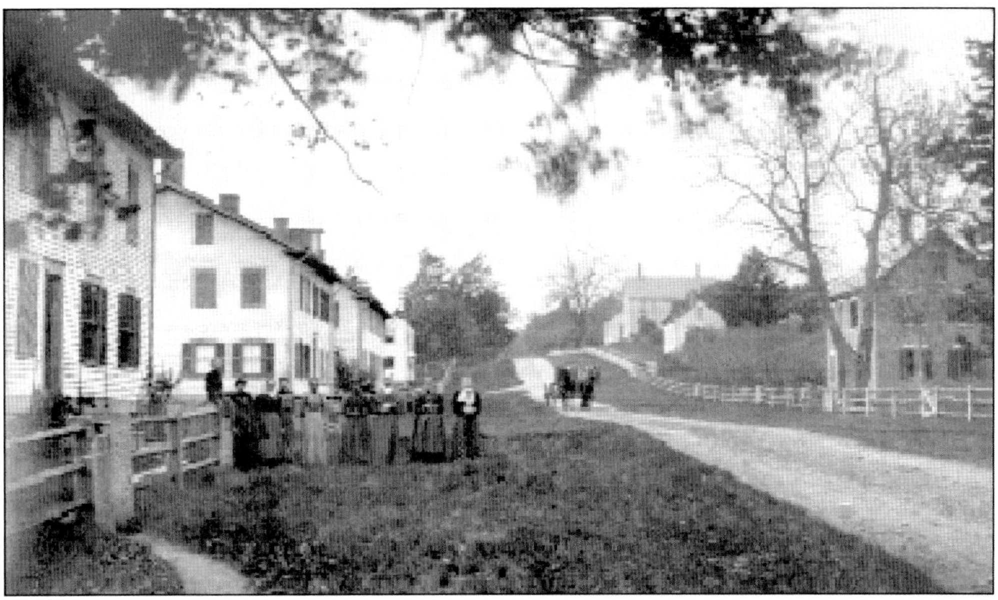

This view of the Harvard Church Family looks north. Dwelling buildings and shops are visible to the left. Up the street on the right, the tailor's shop and Square House are also visible.

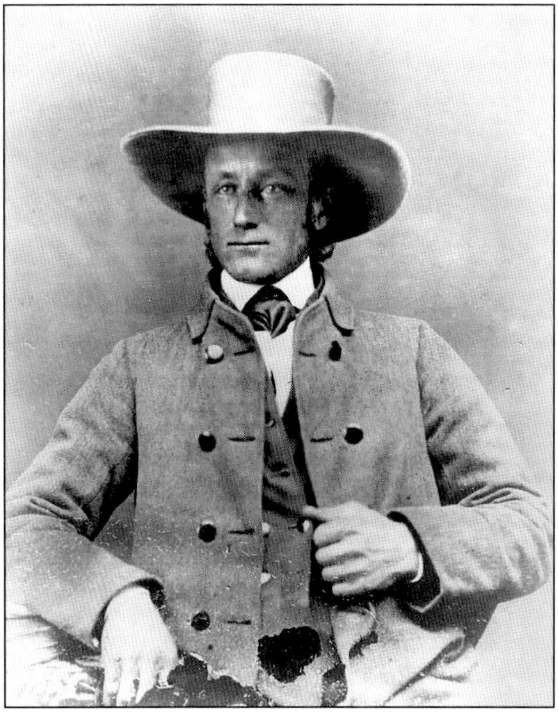

Elijah Myrick is shown as a young man c. 1855. Myrick and his family joined the Harvard Shaker community in the 1820s. He remained a Shaker all his life and was an important leader in the Shaker village and the town of Harvard.

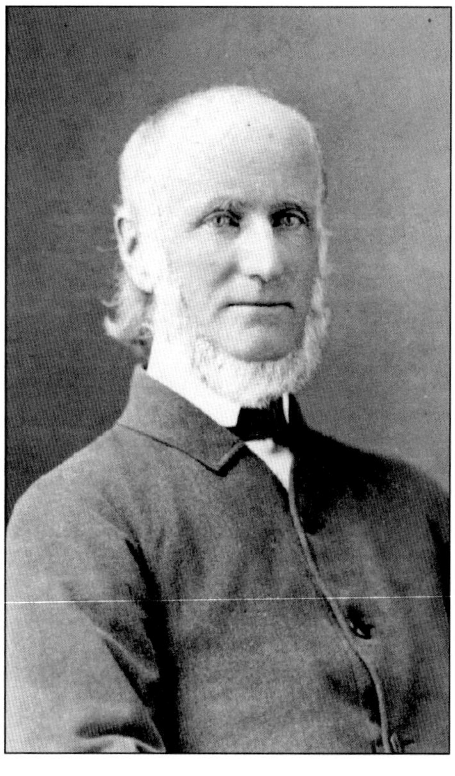

Seen here later in life, Elijah Myrick was a talented trustee and elder. An accomplished engineer, inventor, and educator, Myrick understood the benefits of modernization, especially as it might benefit the well being of the Shaker community.

Catherine Walker joined the Harvard Shakers in 1847 after walking many miles, pregnant in a snowstorm. Her daughter Ann is one of only a few people ever born a Shaker.

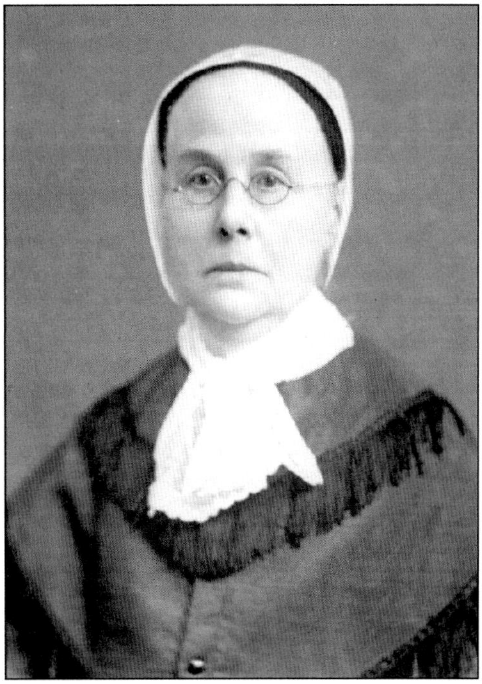

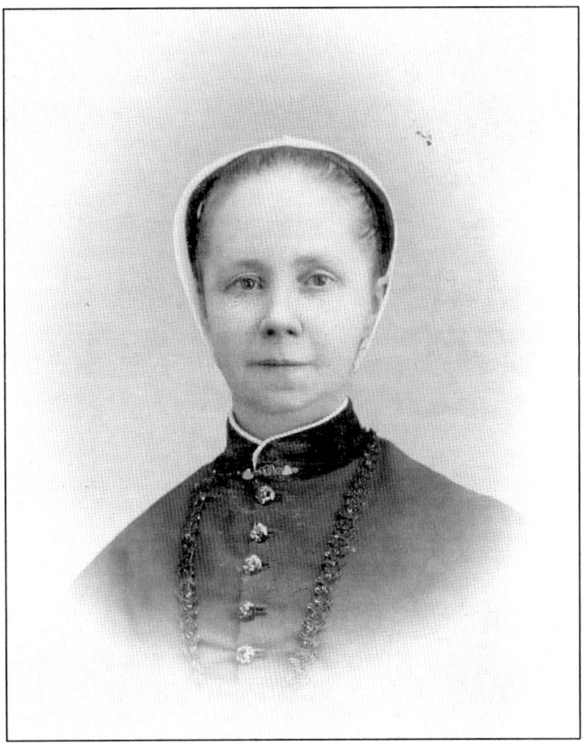

Ann Lucy Walker was born a Harvard Shaker in 1847. She became an important leader in the community during the closing decades of the 19th century. When the ministry at Mount Lebanon sent Shakers to Harvard to increase their numbers, Ann was one who disliked their influence on village life. She died in 1909, nine years before the Harvard village closed.

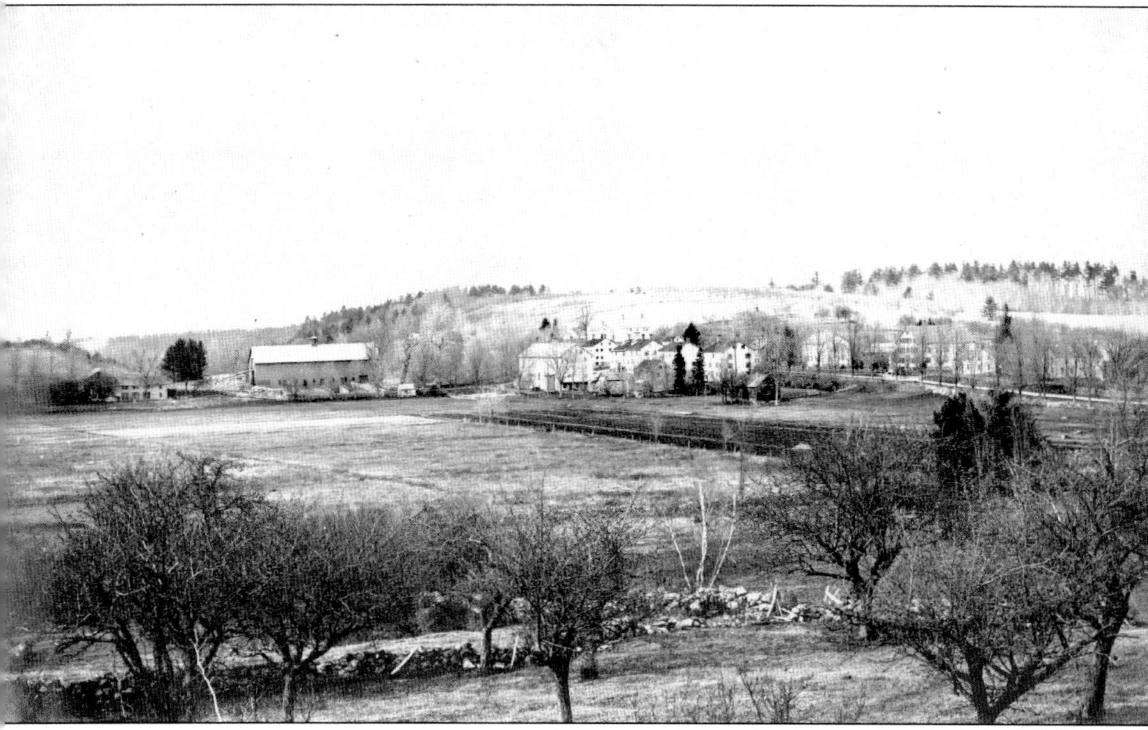

This north-facing view of the Harvard Shaker village shows the Church Family. The Church Family was the central family within the Harvard Shaker community. The barn to the left barn was built in the 1840s and was once the largest barn in the state. It burned down in the 1890s.

Sister Maria Foster from Harvard is wearing a heavily fringed bertha, characteristic of a sister's clothing after the 1870s. She worked for many years as the schoolteacher and was also an excellent weaver of palm products and horsehair sieves.

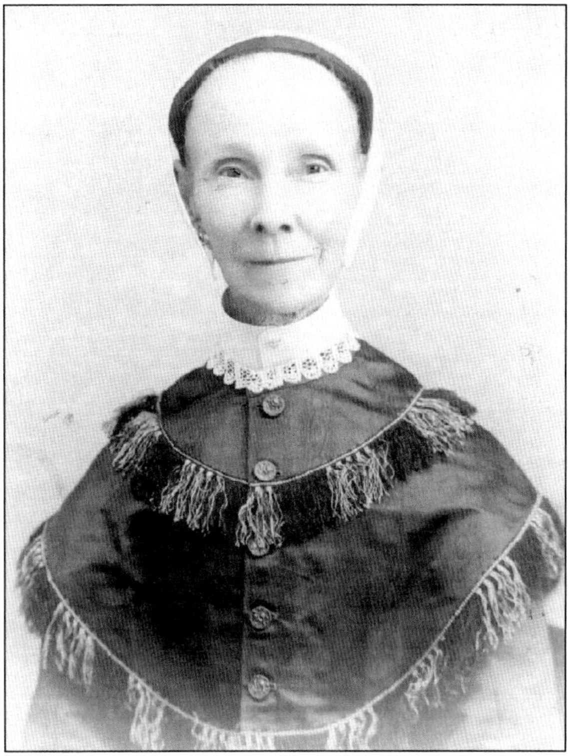

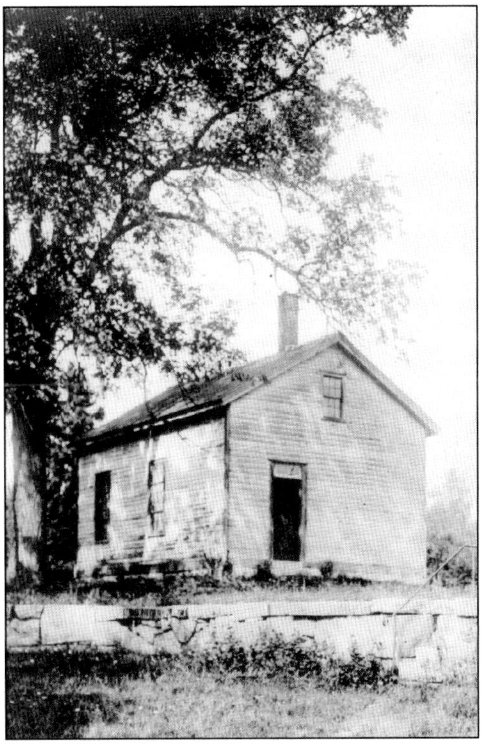

For many years, Shaker children were educated here at the schoolhouse in the Harvard Shaker village. When the school was finally closed, some believed it marked the beginning of the end for the Shaker village.

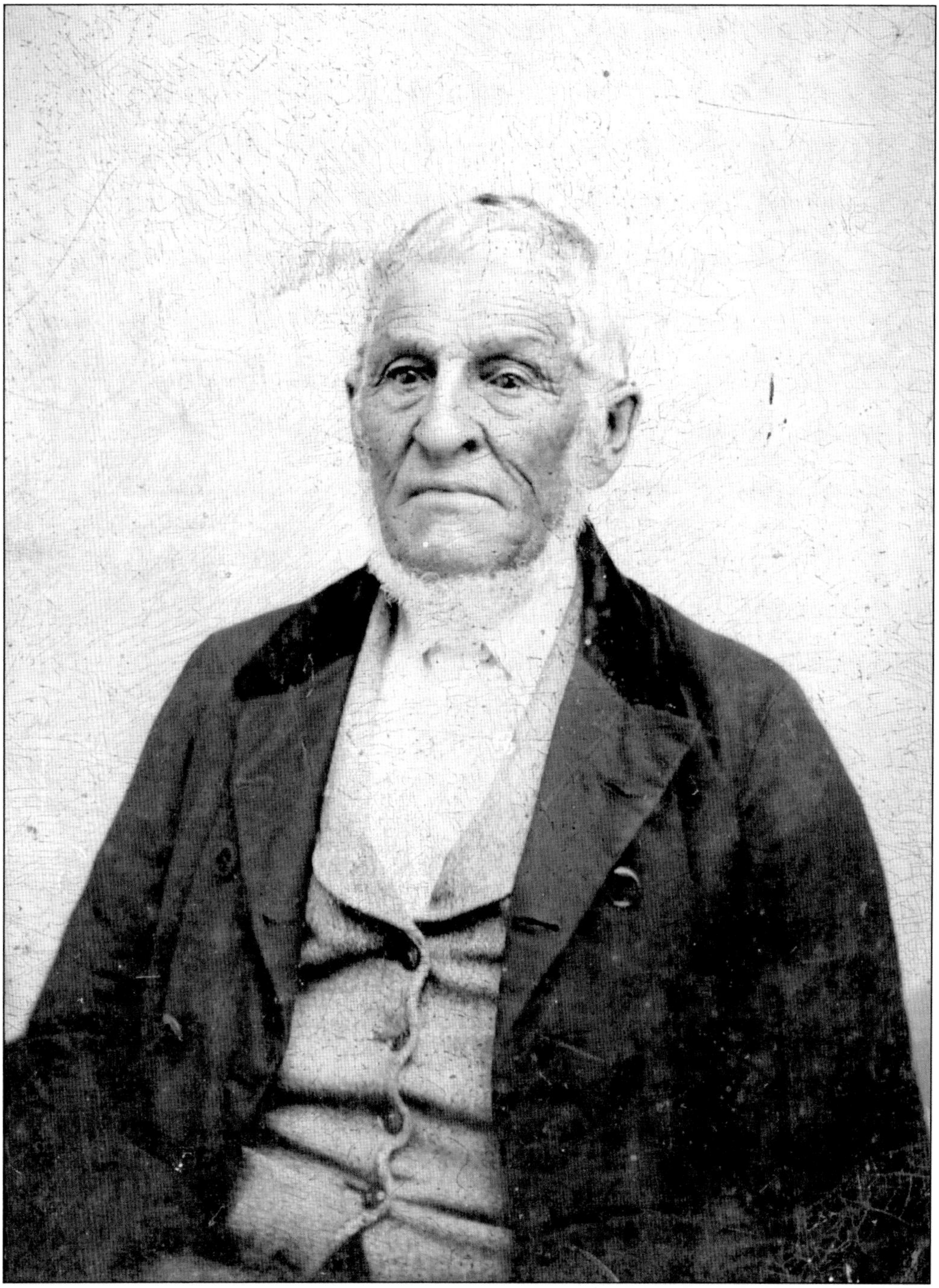

Elder John Cloutman was an important member of the Harvard Church Family. He was admitted in 1817 at the age of nine and lived the rest of his life as a Harvard Shaker. He died in 1883. At that time, Elijah Myrick eulogized him as "the salt of the earth." His main occupation was farming, but like all Shakers, he did a variety of jobs. The journals indicate that Elder John was always helping to maintain the economic and spiritual foundations of village life.

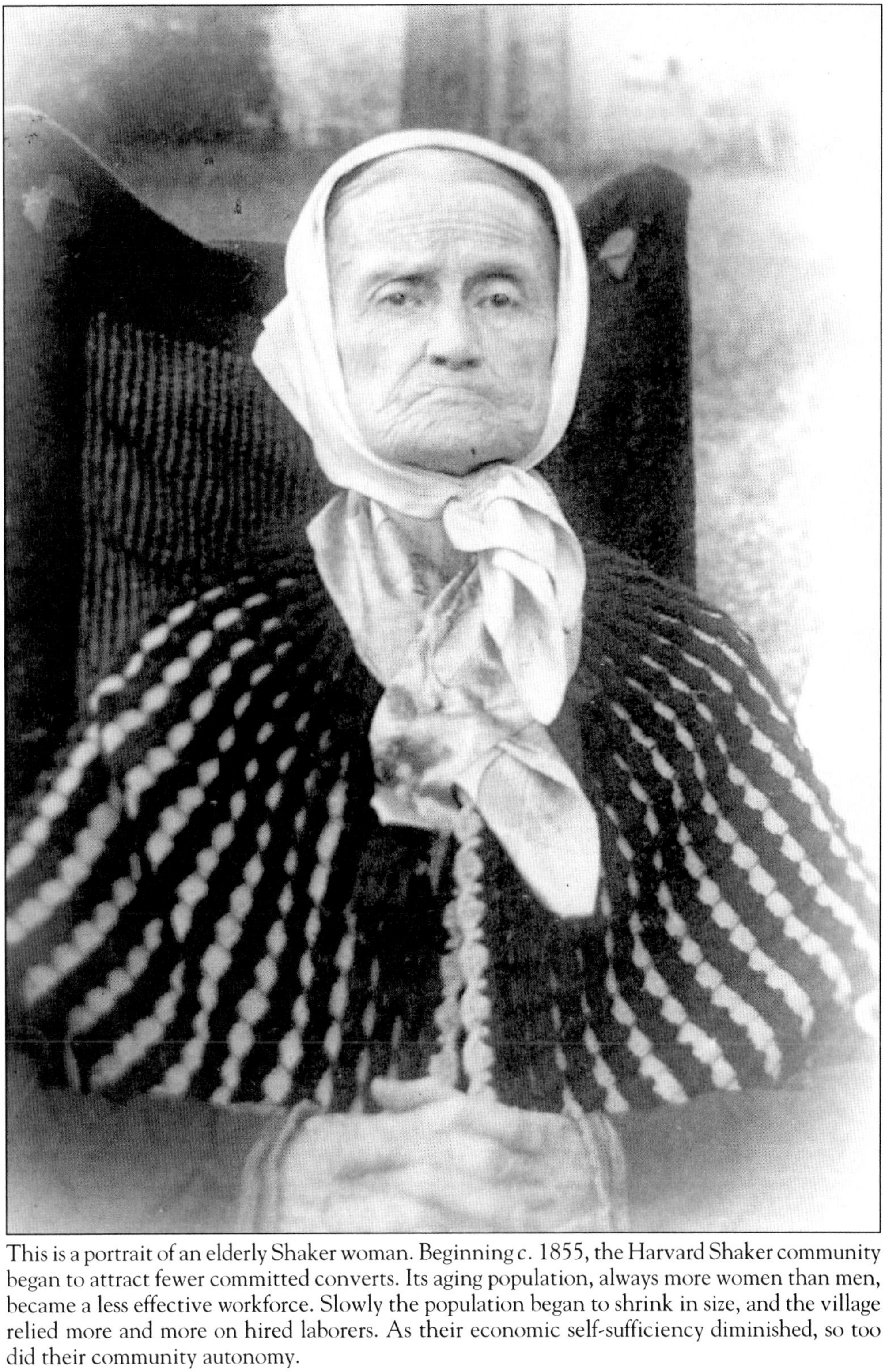

This is a portrait of an elderly Shaker woman. Beginning c. 1855, the Harvard Shaker community began to attract fewer committed converts. Its aging population, always more women than men, became a less effective workforce. Slowly the population began to shrink in size, and the village relied more and more on hired laborers. As their economic self-sufficiency diminished, so too did their community autonomy.

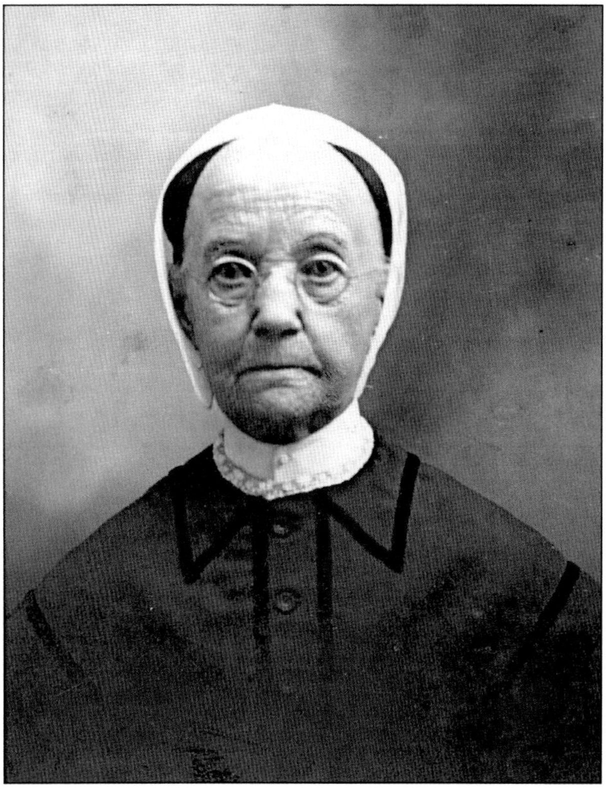

Olive Hatch was born in 1808 and was admitted into the Harvard Church Family at the age of 18. She had previously lived in the Shirley Shaker village and served in both villages throughout her life. She helped produce and market the sisters' sieves, palm leaf bonnets, mats, and fans in neighboring towns and cities.

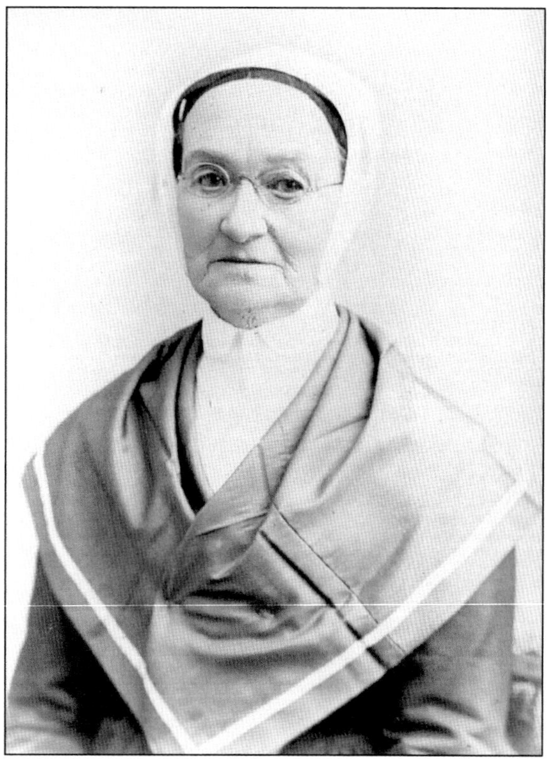

Eliza Babbit entered the Harvard Shaker community at the age of 13 in 1820. She was an important community leader and a skilled administrator. Under her guidance, the society cleared the debt incurred from building the Rural Home. Sister Eliza was the ministry's elder sister for 40 years.

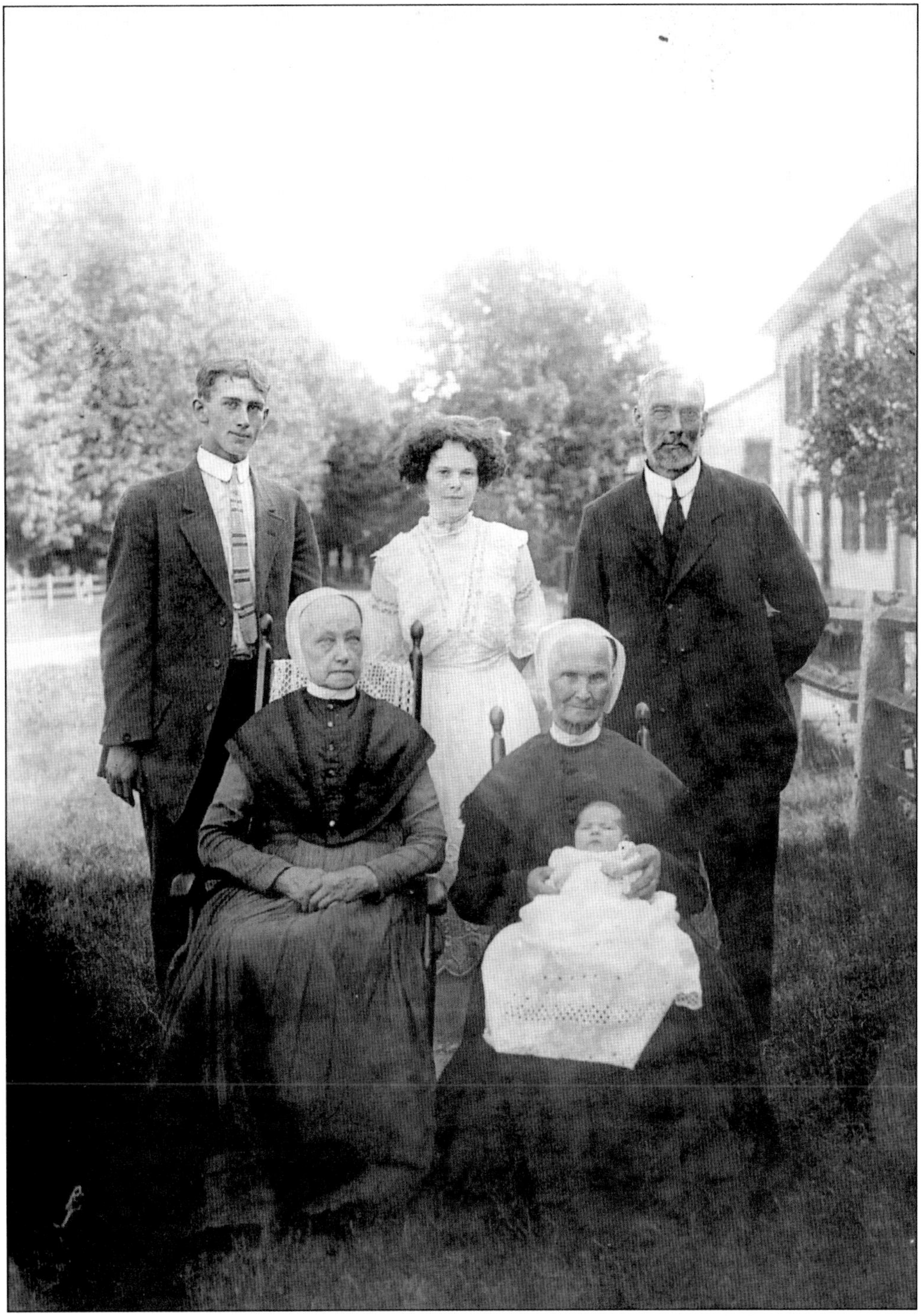

Louisa Green, along with her two children, entered the Mount Lebanon Shaker community to escape an abusive husband. She was transferred to Harvard with about 12 others in 1880. From left to right are the following: (front row) Ellen (Louisa's daughter) and Louisa (holding a baby girl); (back row) Rupert, Gertrude, and Newcomb.

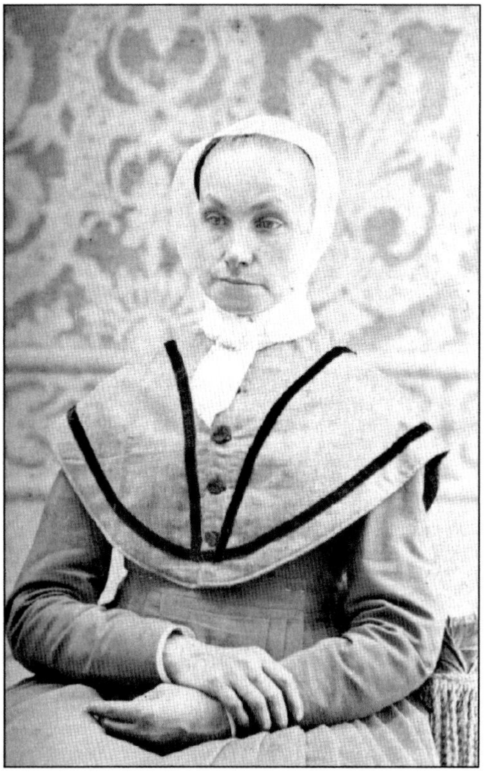

Ellen Green, daughter of Louisa Green, is one of the Canaanites sent by Mount Lebanon to Harvard in 1880. Declining membership in both Harvard and Mount Lebanon prompted the Shaker leadership to send about 12 people from their community to Harvard. Ellen and her mother both died Harvard Shakers.

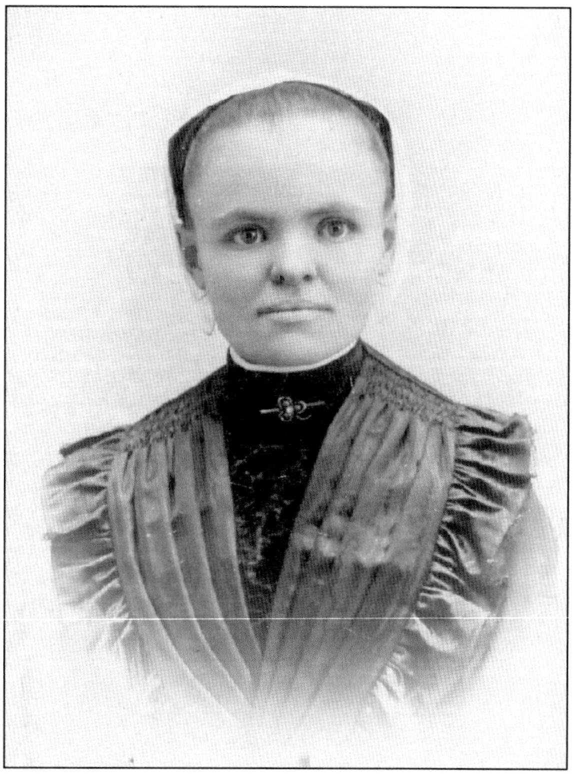

Anne Bell Tuttle, born in 1867, entered the Shirley Shaker village in 1876. She moved to Harvard when the Shirley village closed in 1908 and then to Mount Lebanon after Harvard closed in 1918. She remained at Mount Lebanon until her death in 1943.

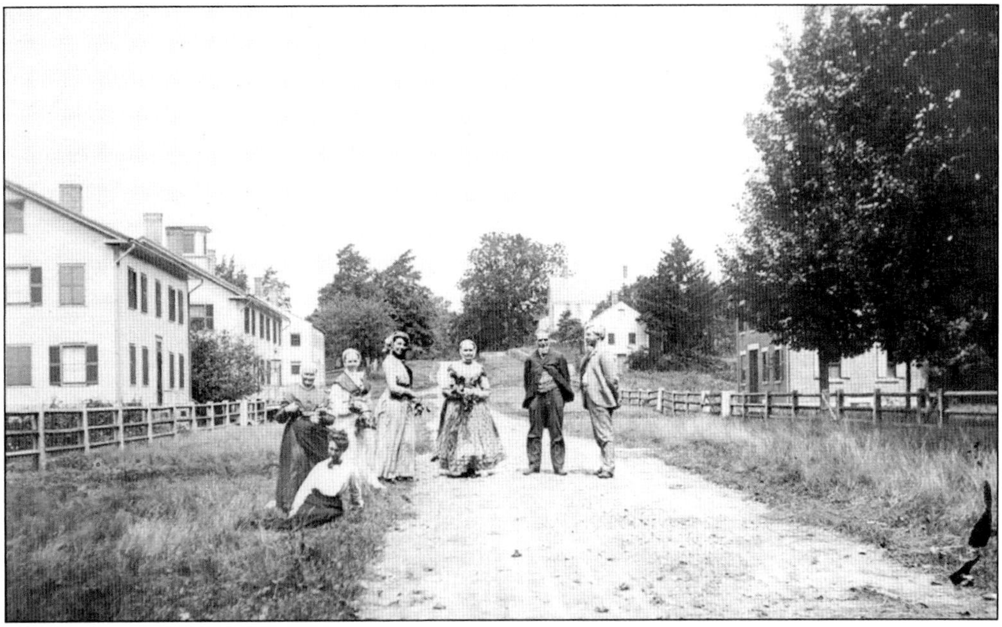

This photograph of the Church Family in Harvard probably dates from the first few years of the 20th century. From left to right are Sisters Louisa Green, Ann Walker, unidentified, Elizabeth Grover, Bliss Goss, and unidentified.

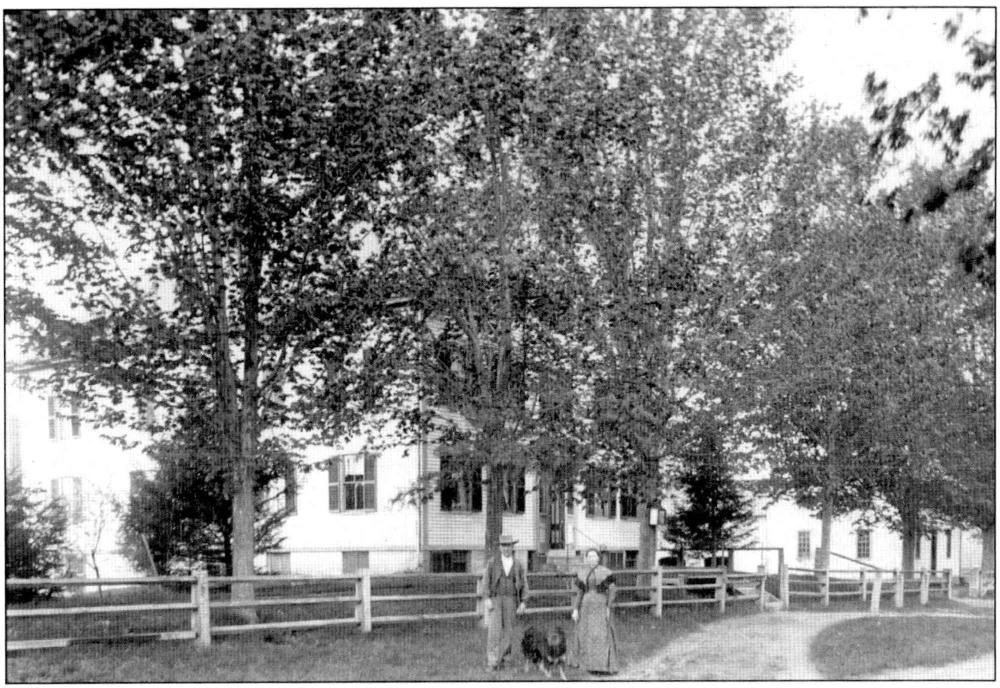

The Shakers practiced celibacy, relying on converts to maintain their numbers. Prior to the Civil War, they also received a number of orphans and children from disadvantaged homes. Within the community, the brethren and sisters lived generally separate lives, using different entrances, sitting on opposite sides of the room at meals, and so on. Ann Walker is on the right.

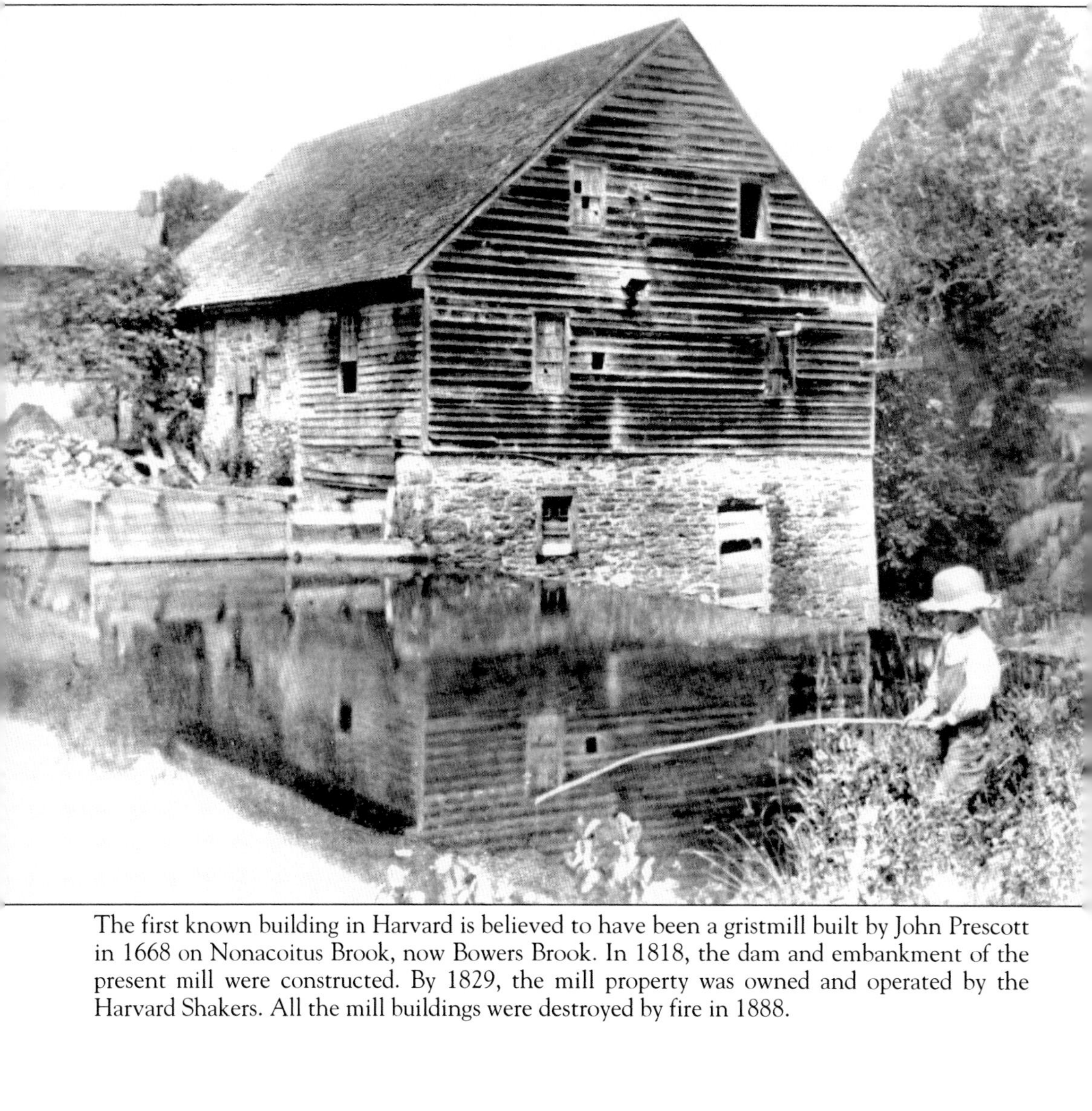

The first known building in Harvard is believed to have been a gristmill built by John Prescott in 1668 on Nonacoitus Brook, now Bowers Brook. In 1818, the dam and embankment of the present mill were constructed. By 1829, the mill property was owned and operated by the Harvard Shakers. All the mill buildings were destroyed by fire in 1888.

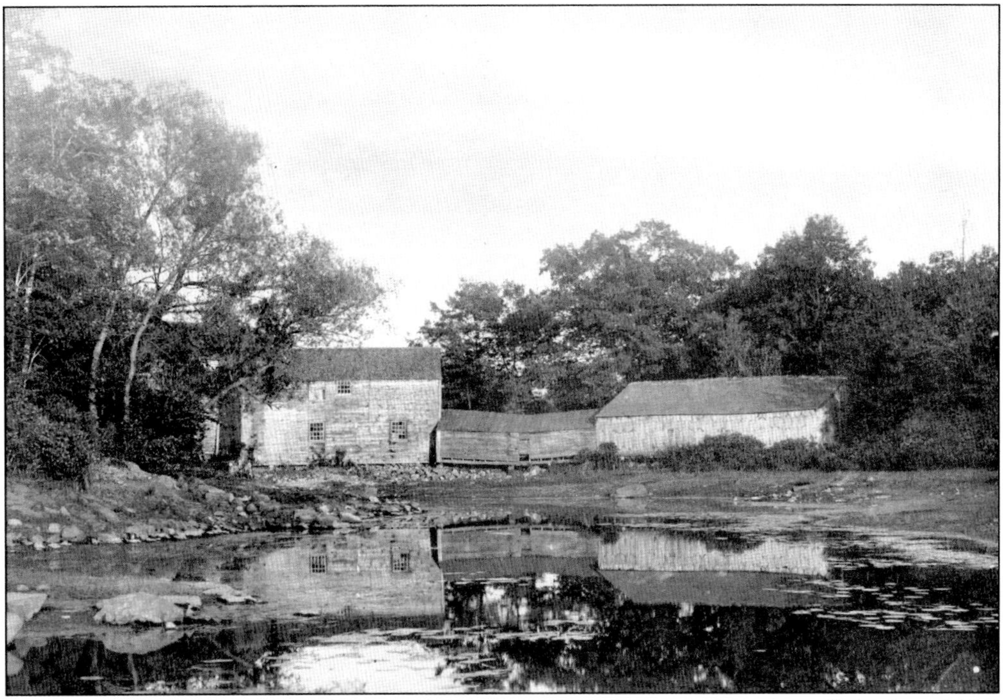

One of the most important industries of the Harvard Shakers was their sawmill, built in 1808. Sister Tabitha Babbit, a Harvard Shaker, invented the circular saw—an invention that was probably first used in this mill.

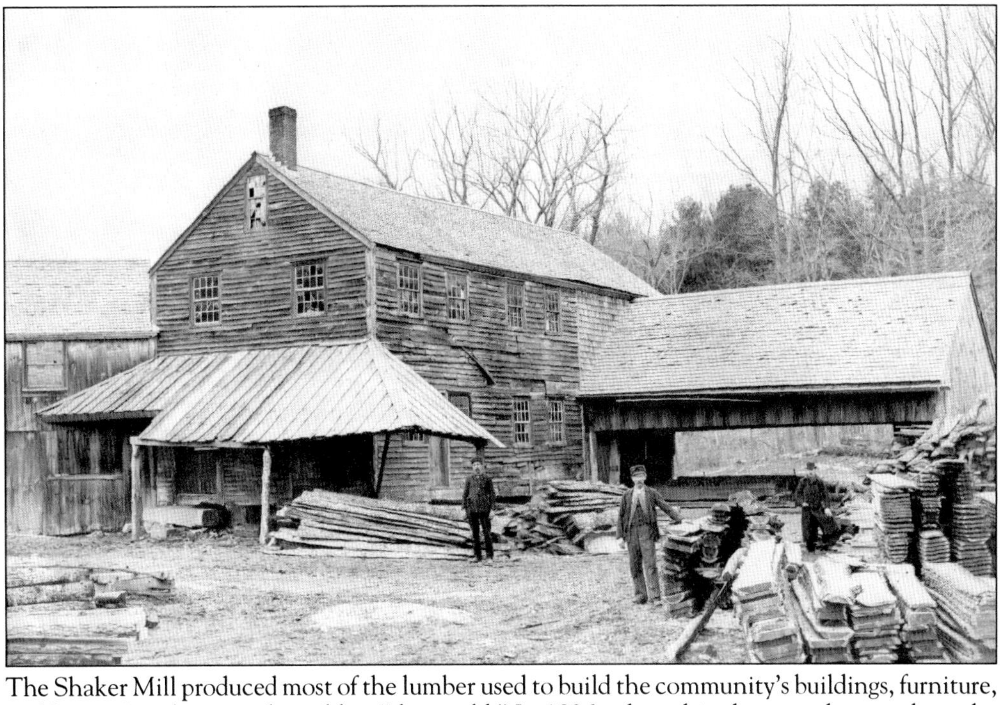

The Shaker Mill produced most of the lumber used to build the community's buildings, furniture, and boxes. Lumber was also sold to "the world." In 1896, when this photograph was taken, the mill was run by hired men.

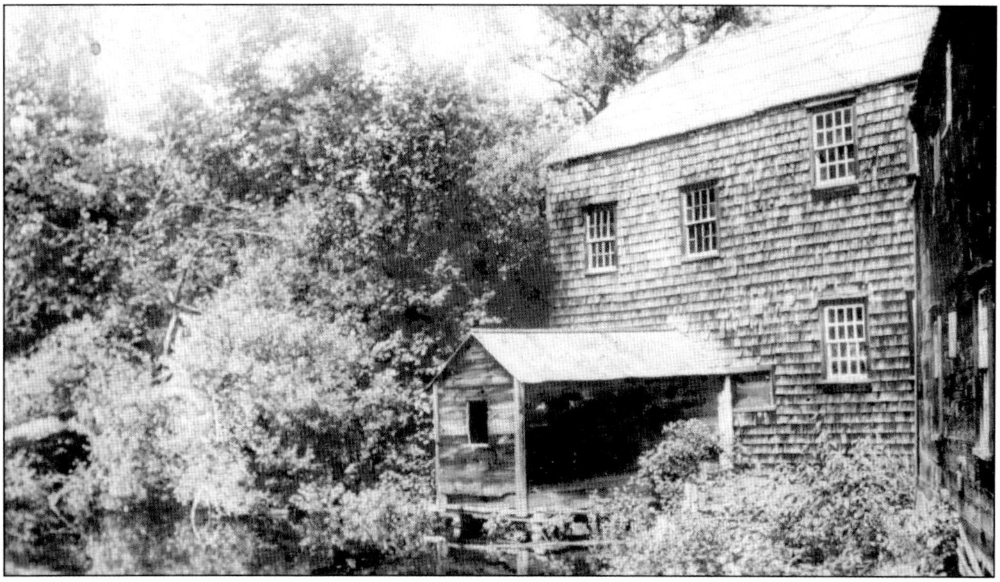

Besides making goods for their own use, the Harvard Shakers manufactured seed boxes, matchboxes, brooms, and some furniture for sale to "the world." For example, between 1841 and 1842, the Shakers produced 339 chairs, 92 of which were for sale.

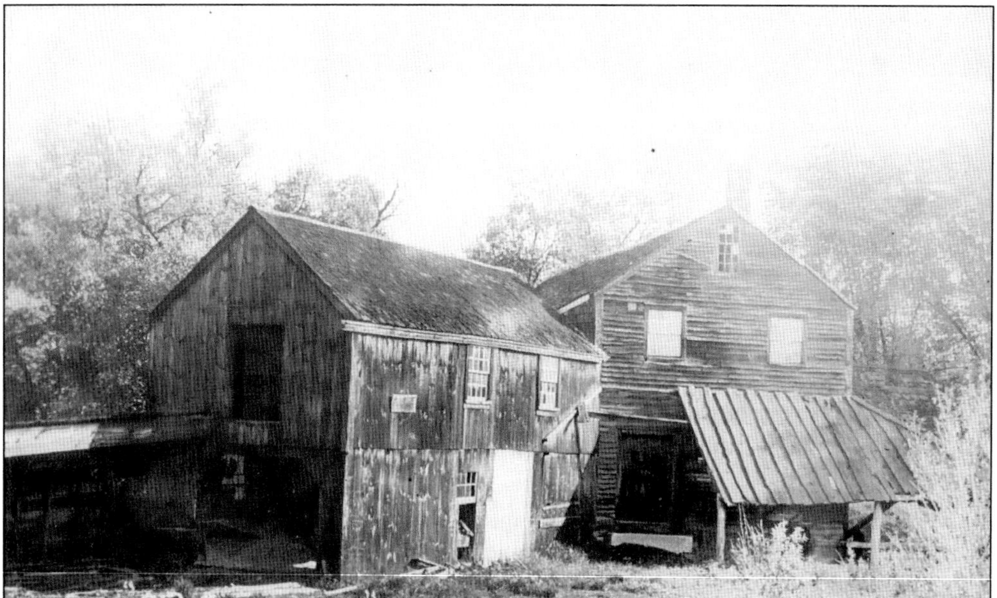

Besides manufacturing lumber, the Shaker sawmill produced broom handles, fence posts, shingles, and herb boxes. In January 1860, the stone milldam and millrace were repaired and improved. The following December, the wheel and machinery were replaced.

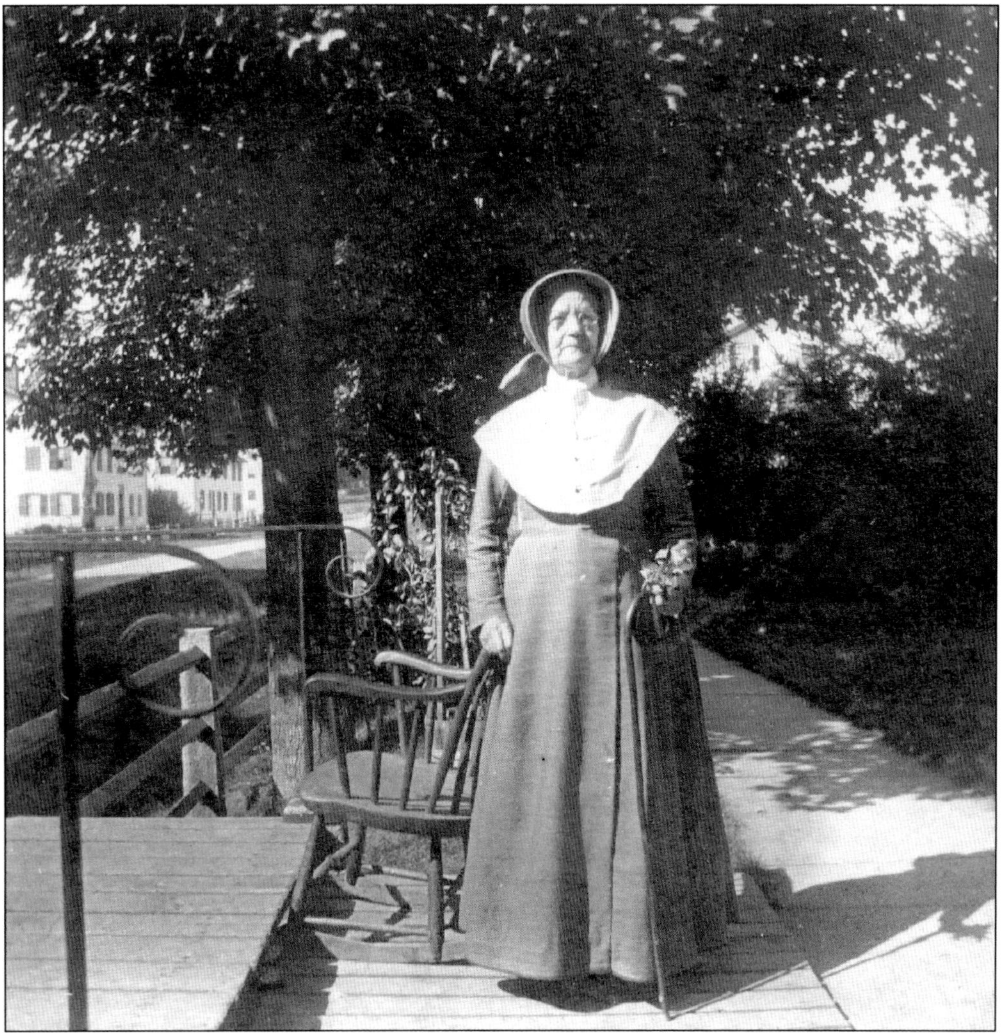

Olive Hatch is pictured here standing on the street in the Harvard Shaker village with Mother Ann's chair. This Colonial-style chair, modified by the Shakers into a rocker, is believed to be one of the few relics from the early days of Shakers in the 1780s to be directly associated with Mother Ann Lee. Ann Lee founded the Shaker religion.

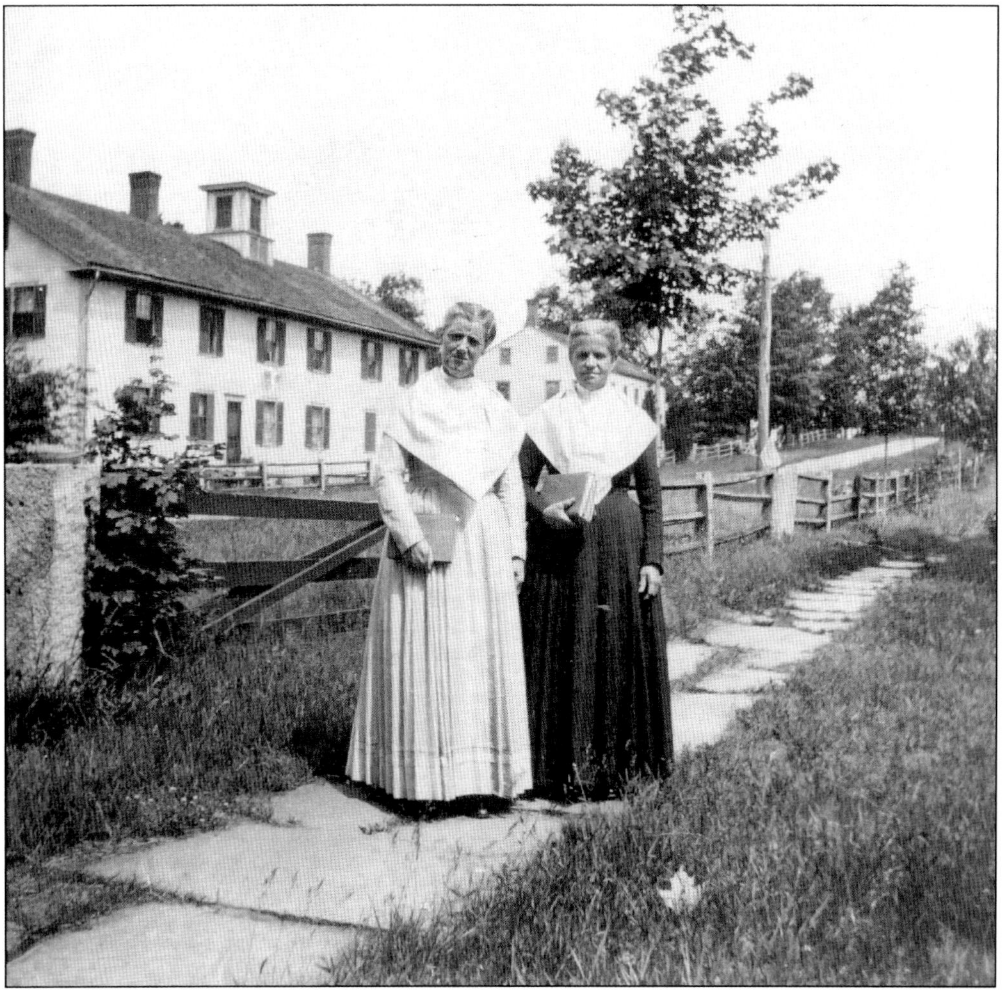

Two Shaker sisters are shown standing on the sidewalk in the Church Family of the Harvard Shaker village.

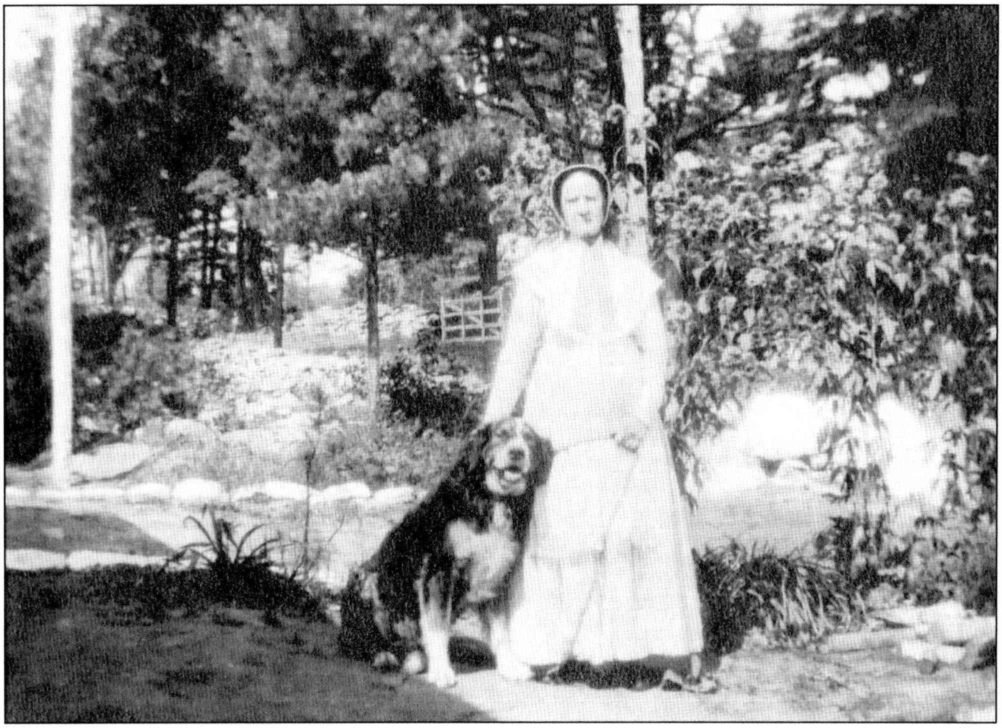

Sister Lottie Tremper entered the Mount Lebanon Shaker village as a child. Louisa Green was her aunt. Tremper joined the Harvard Shakers in 1878 at the age of 18. She attended the funeral of Pres. William McKinley in 1901 with six other Harvard sisters. She was the last Shaker buried in the Harvard Shaker cemetery.

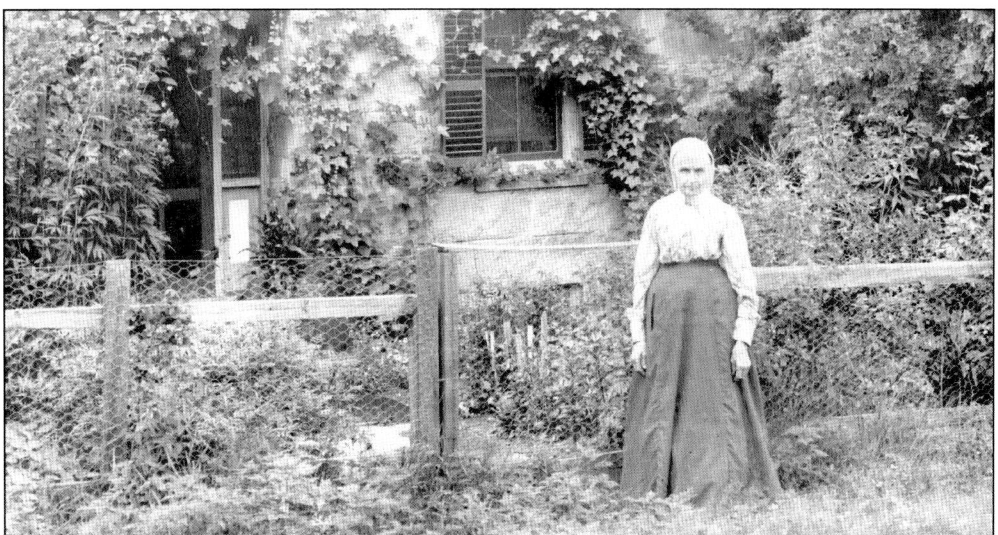

Myra McLean, pictured c. 1910, entered the Shaker community of Harvard late in life, probably after 1890. In 1918, when the village closed, she chose to remain in the area rather than move to Mount Lebanon.

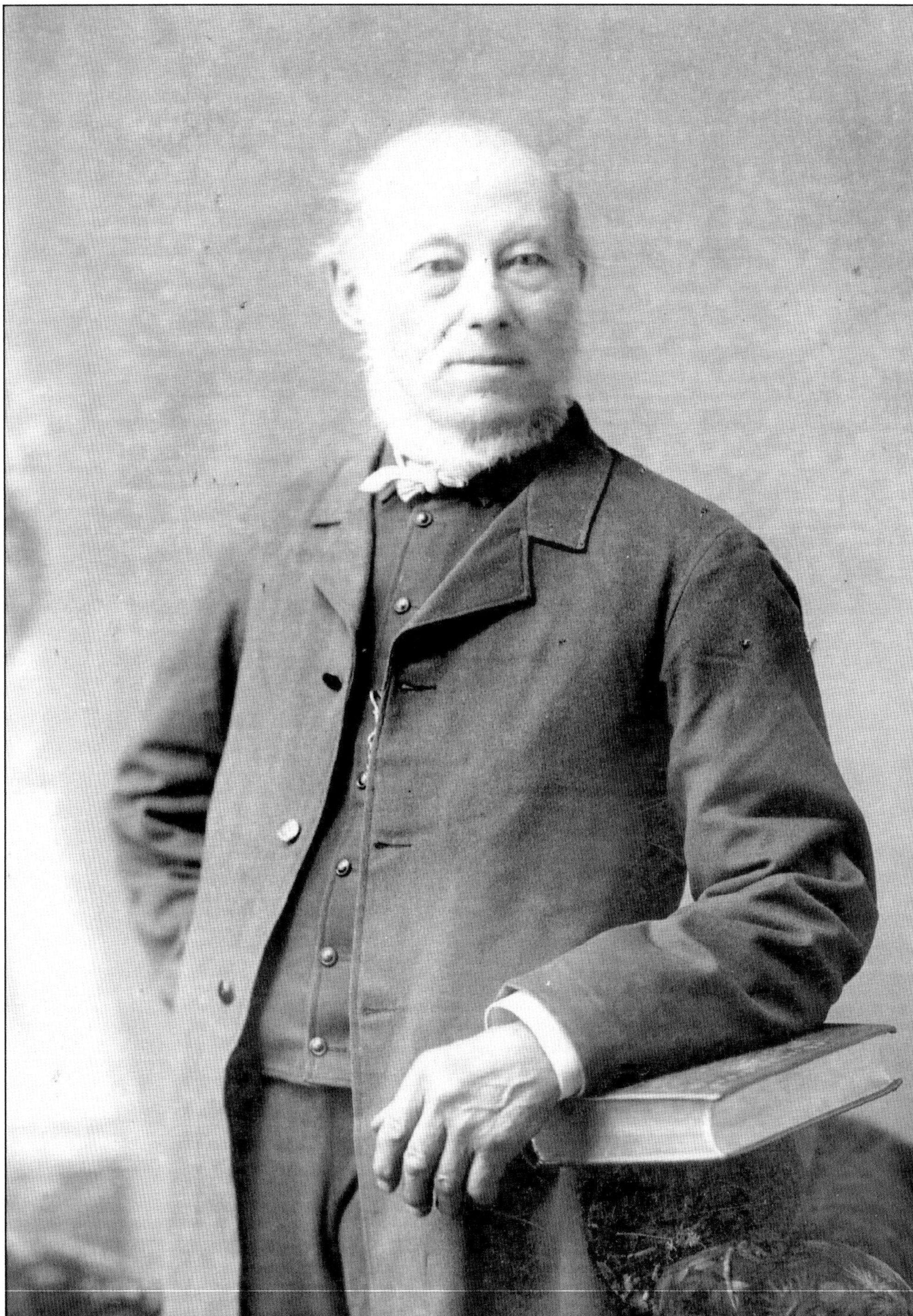

Born in Germany in 1809, Philip Mayer eventually found his way to the Harvard Shakers. He joined in 1863 and was in charge of raising chickens. Curiously, he left the community in 1898 at the age of 89, perhaps to return to Germany.

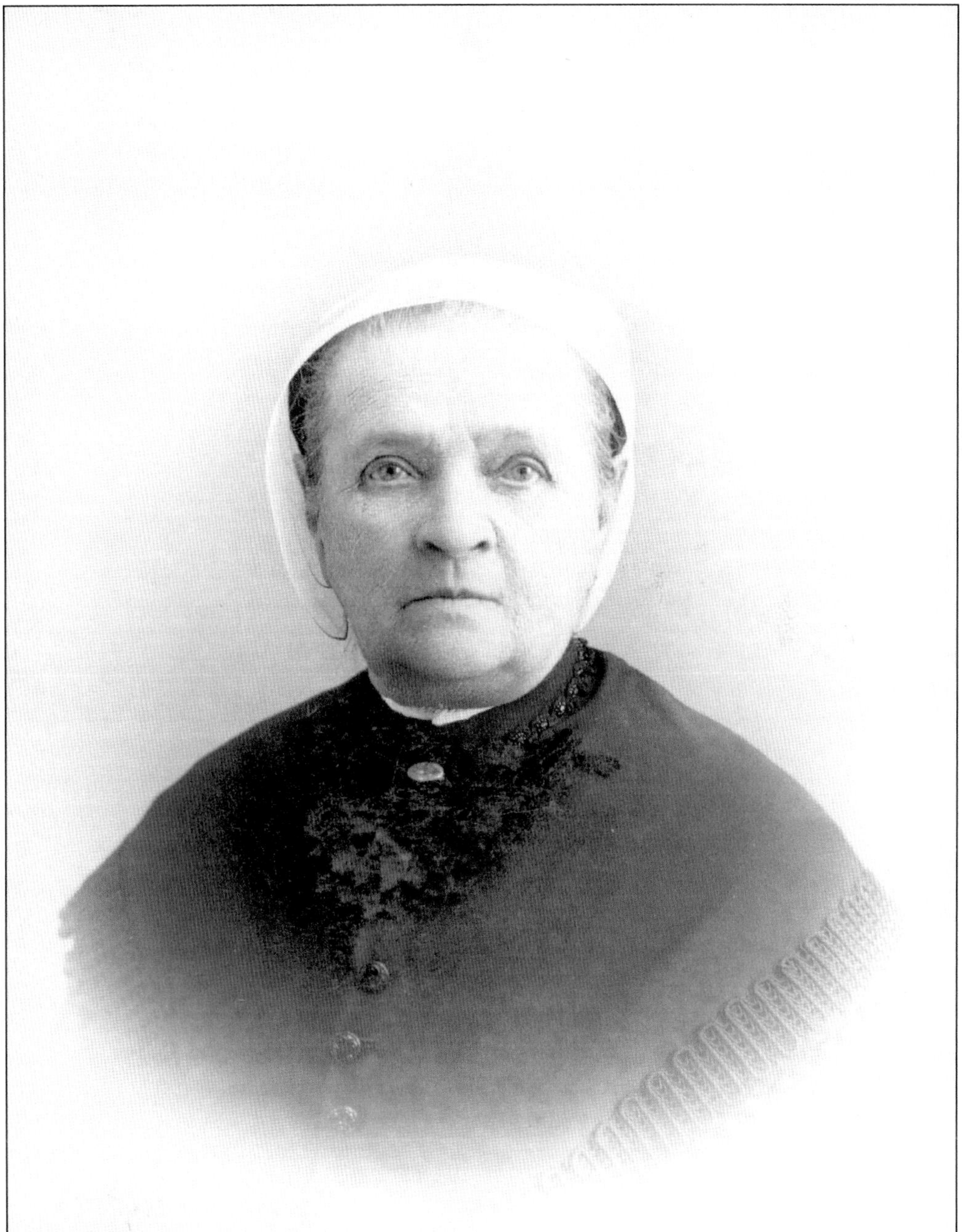

This picture of Myra McLean reveals the interesting details and textures of clothing worn by later Shakers. Like other businesses, the Shakers had to modify their products to appeal to the Victorian tastes of late-19th-century America. Those fashions also influenced Shaker-style clothing.

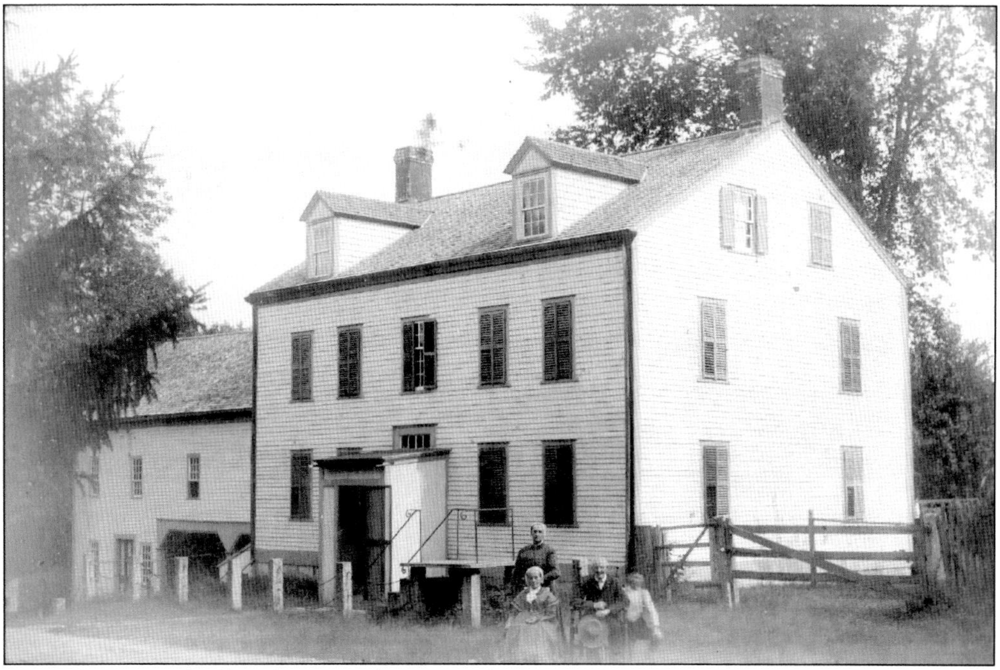

A South Family dwelling house in the Harvard Shaker village is shown c. 1890. In front of the building are, from left to right, Myra McLean (standing), Catherine Walker, Ezra Newton, and an unidentified person. Notice the wagon-mounting platform in front of the door.

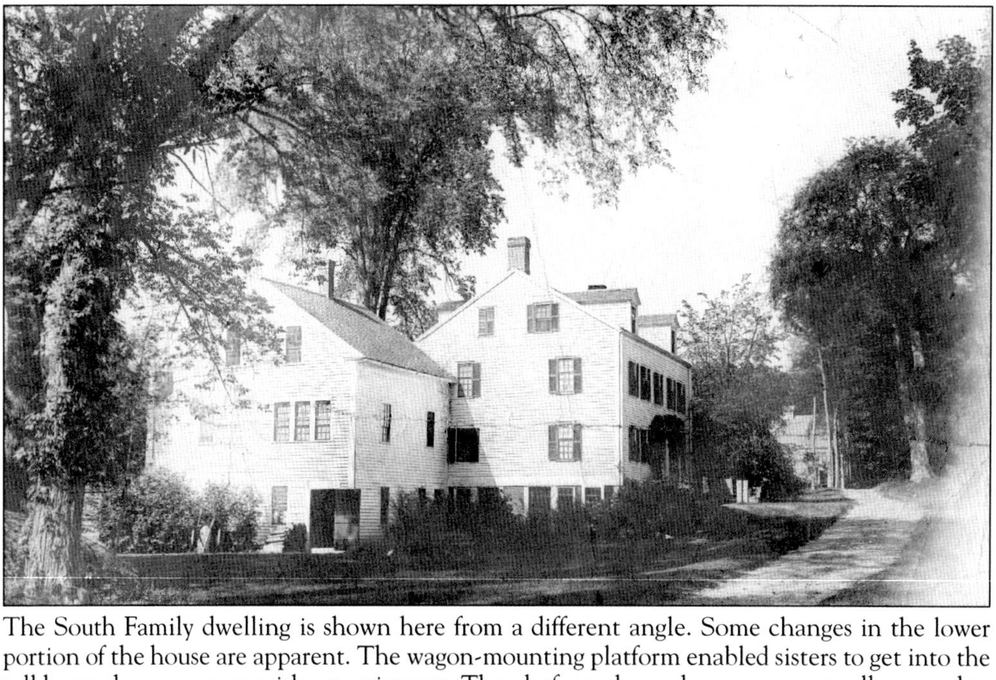

The South Family dwelling is shown here from a different angle. Some changes in the lower portion of the house are apparent. The wagon-mounting platform enabled sisters to get into the tall horse-drawn wagons without assistance. The platform shown here was eventually moved to Fruitlands Museums in 1920.

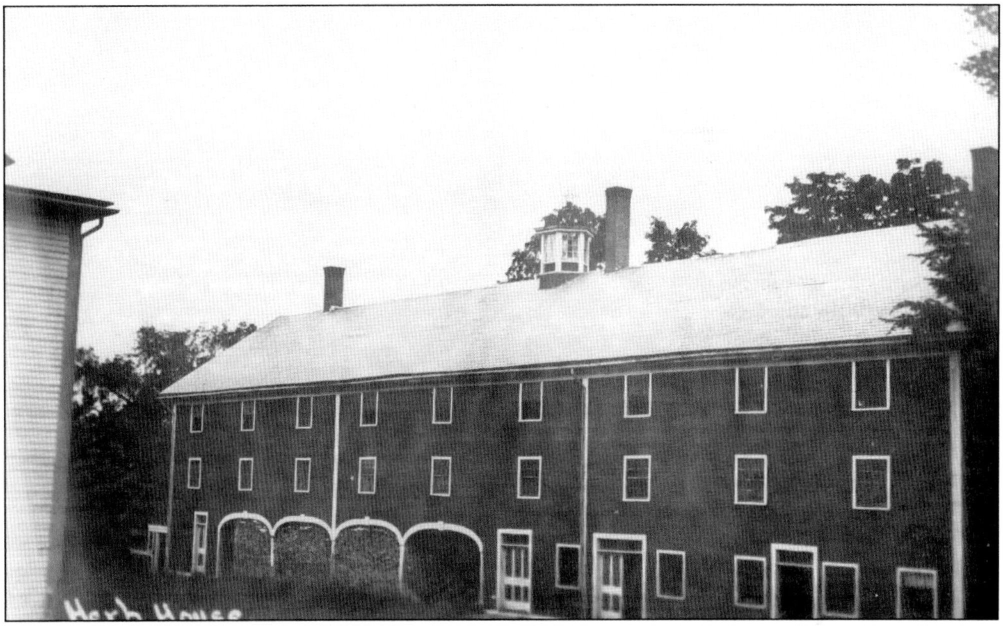

This is the herb house in the Church Family of the Harvard Shaker village. The Shakers were the first group to successfully package and market seeds and herbs. The success of this industry was based on the high quality of the herbs they sold. This large building was needed to accommodate the volume of products they prepared and shipped.

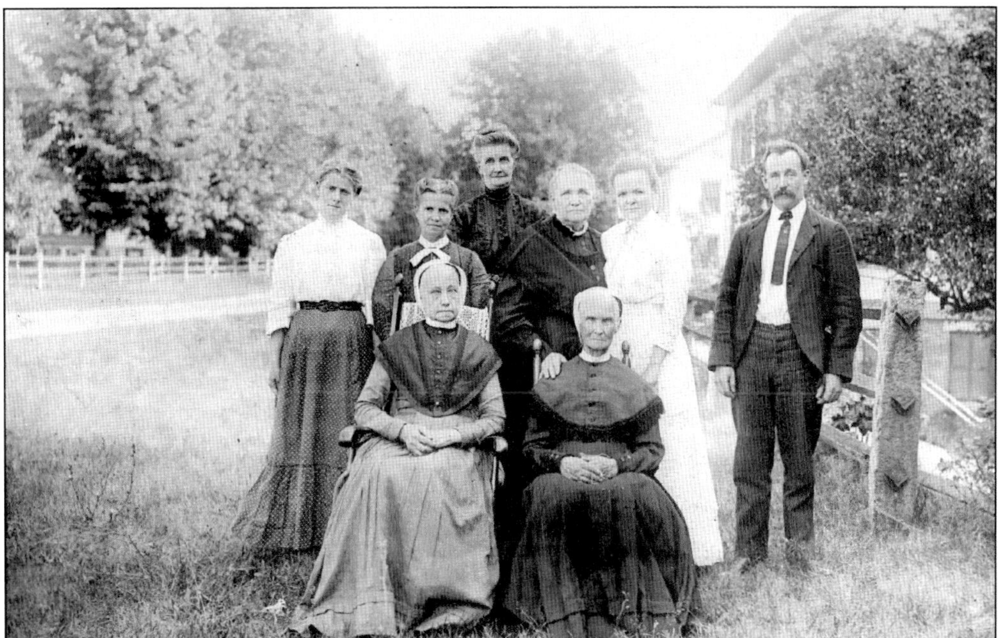

Harvard Shakers are pictured *c.* 1910. Seated are Ellen Green (left) and Louisa Green. Directly behind Louisa are Myra McLean and Anne Bell Tuttle (white dress). The rest are unidentified.

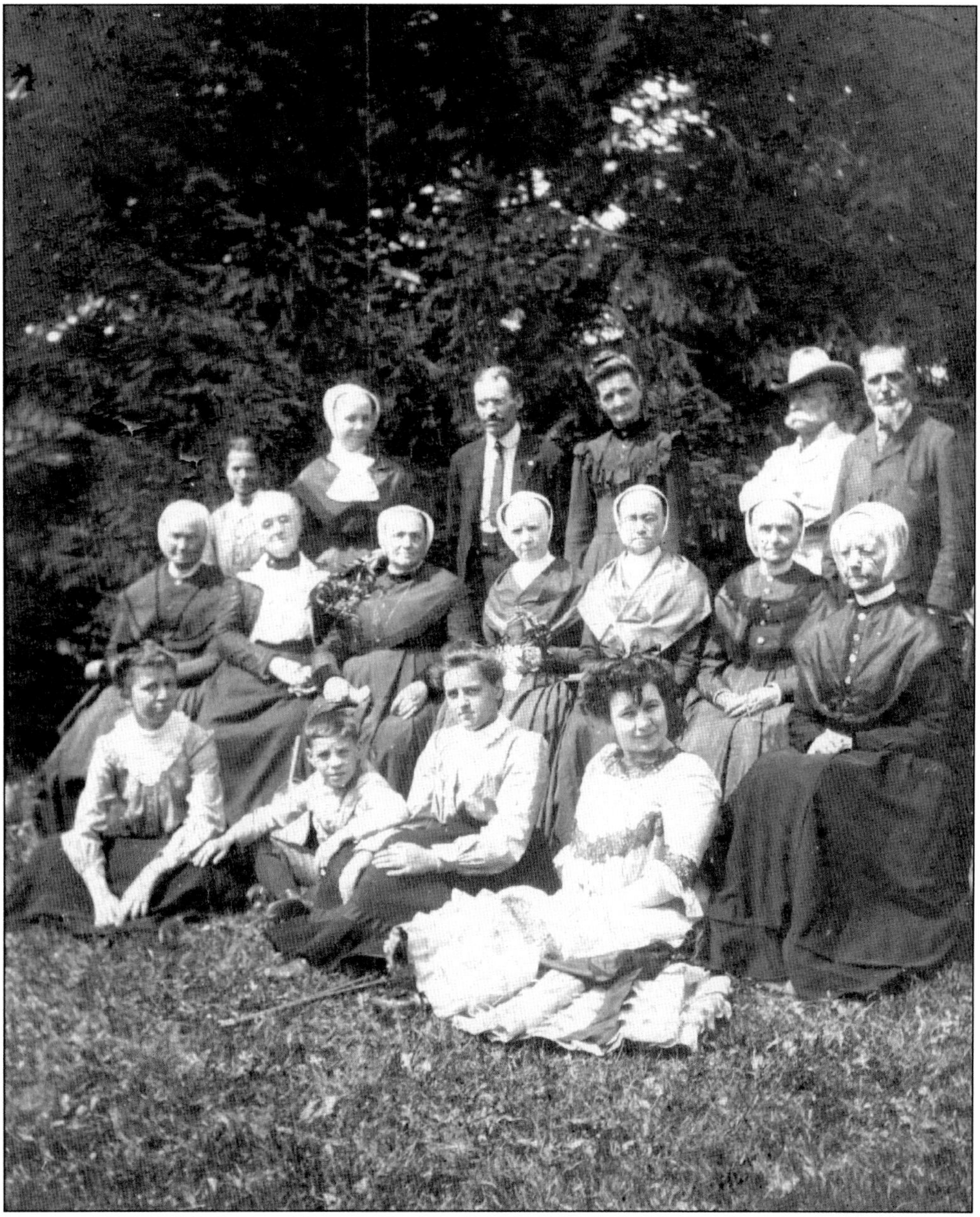

A group of Harvard Shakers photographed before 1908 includes, from left to right, the following: (front row) Edith Hobbs, unidentified, Mary Ashley, and unidentified; (middle row) Louisa Green, unidentified, Myra McLean, Margaret Egelson, Elizabeth Grover, Ellen Green, and Olive Hatch; (back row) Maud Barter, Ann Walker, unidentified, unidentified, unidentified, and Bliss Goss.

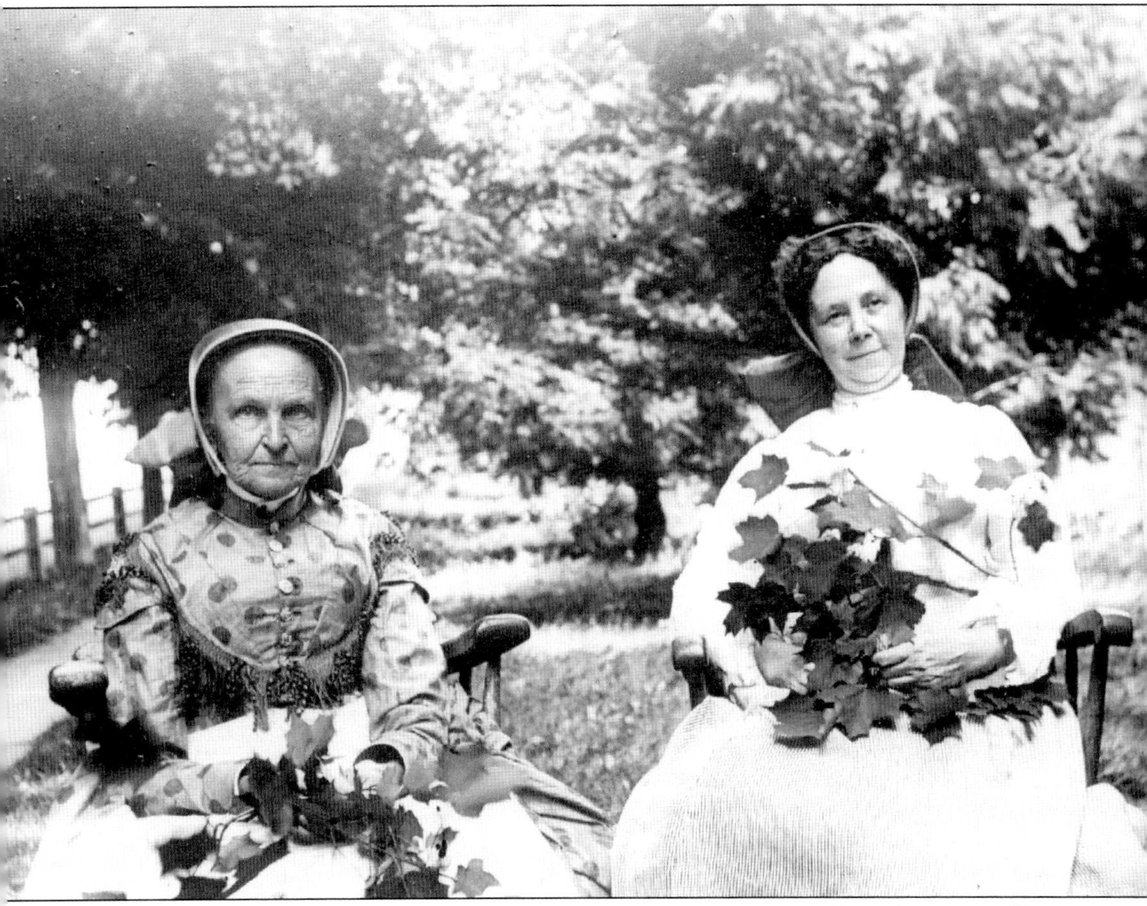

This *c.* 1904 photograph shows longtime friends Elizabeth Grover (left) and Ann Walker, who is apparently wearing a wig. These two women were young during the heyday of the Harvard Shakers.

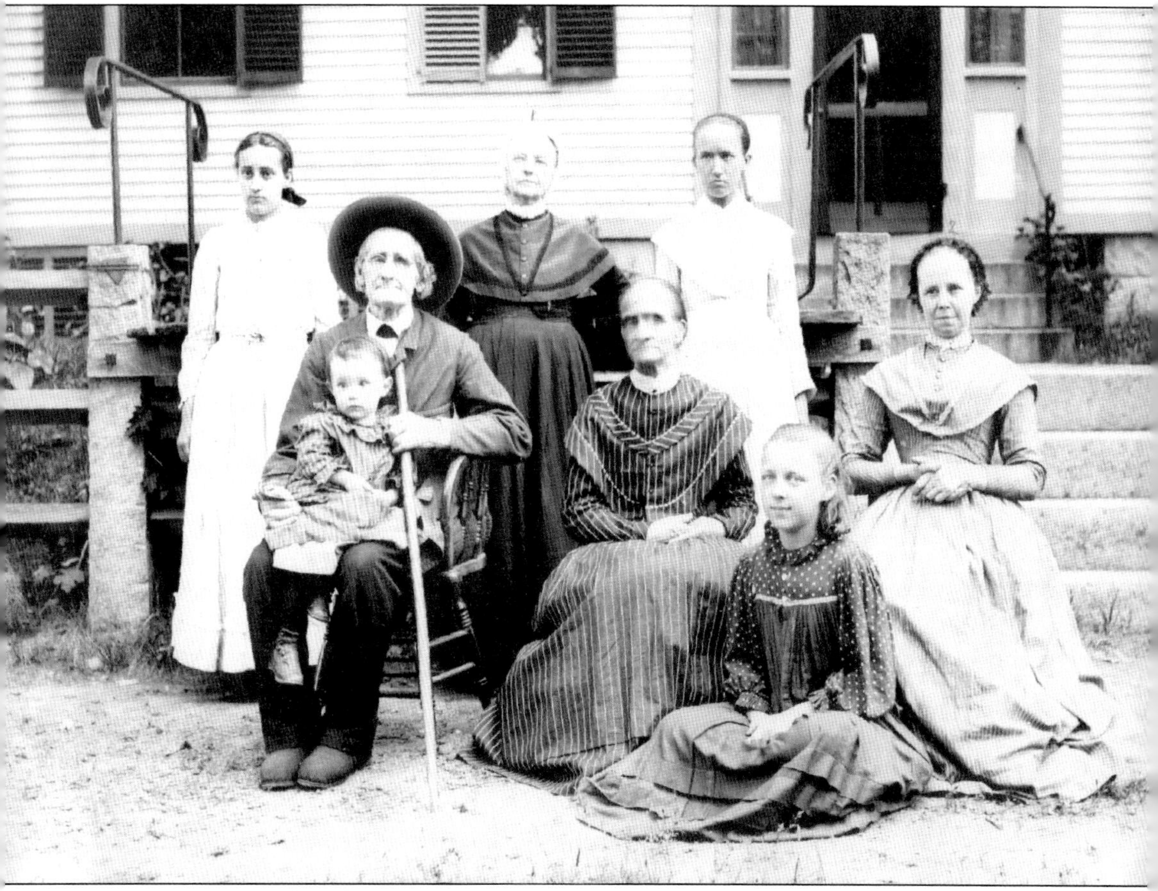

Taken in 1895, this photograph shows some of the last members of the Harvard Shaker community. Seated are, from left to right, Ezra Newton, Marshie Bullard, and Ann Walker. At this point in their history, the Shakers had closed their entire village except the Church Family, which ended in 1918 after 137 years.

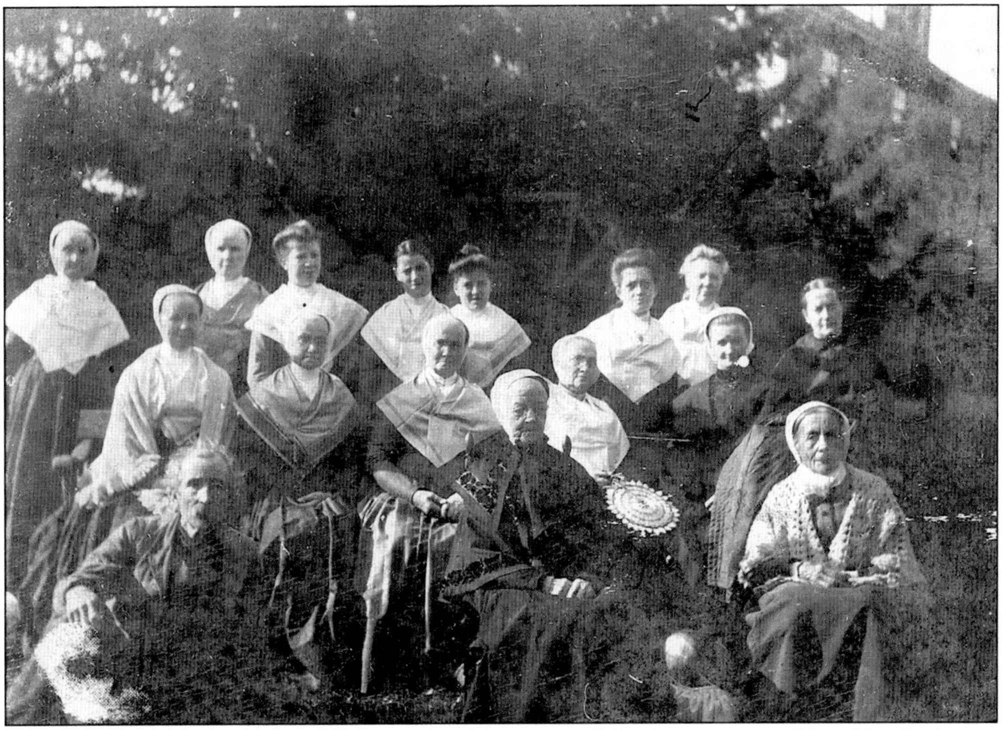

This picture was taken *c.* 1895. Sitting in the center of the front row is Olive Hatch. In the middle row are Ann Walker, Ellen Green, Louisa Green, and Hattie Whitney. Fifth from the left in the back row is Mary Ashley.

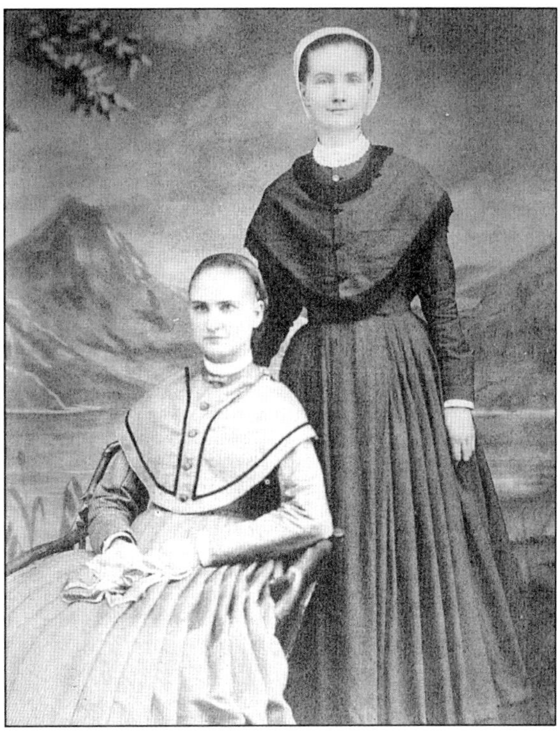

Two unidentified Shaker sisters are shown wearing berthas—large, buttoned collars that were typical of Shaker dress after 1870.

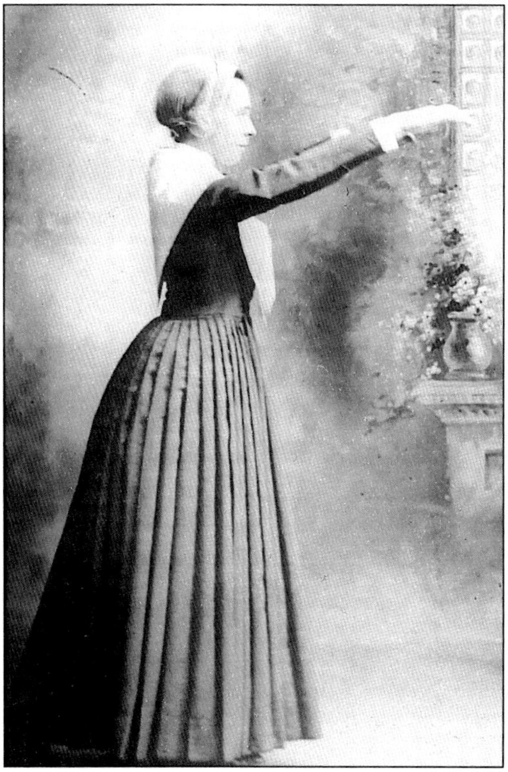

This is one of a three-part series of a Shaker dance called growing and securing brotherly love.

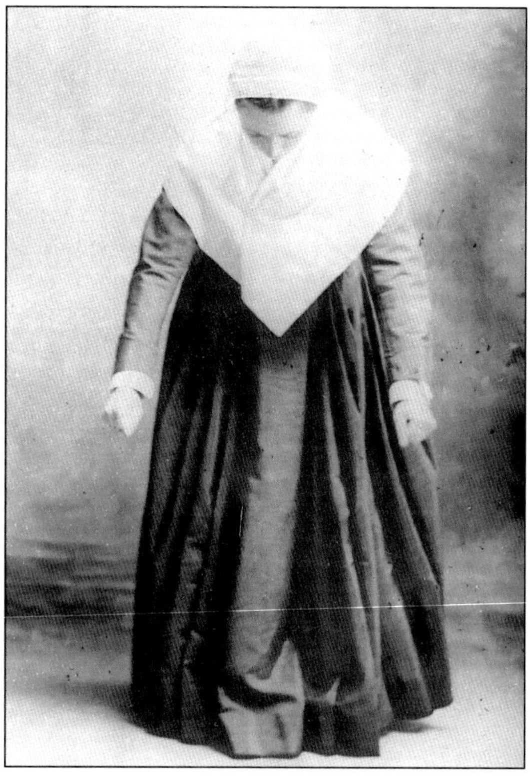

Initially, Shaker dancing was wild spinning and shaking. It was this extemporaneous and sometimes erratic dancing that got the Shakers their name.

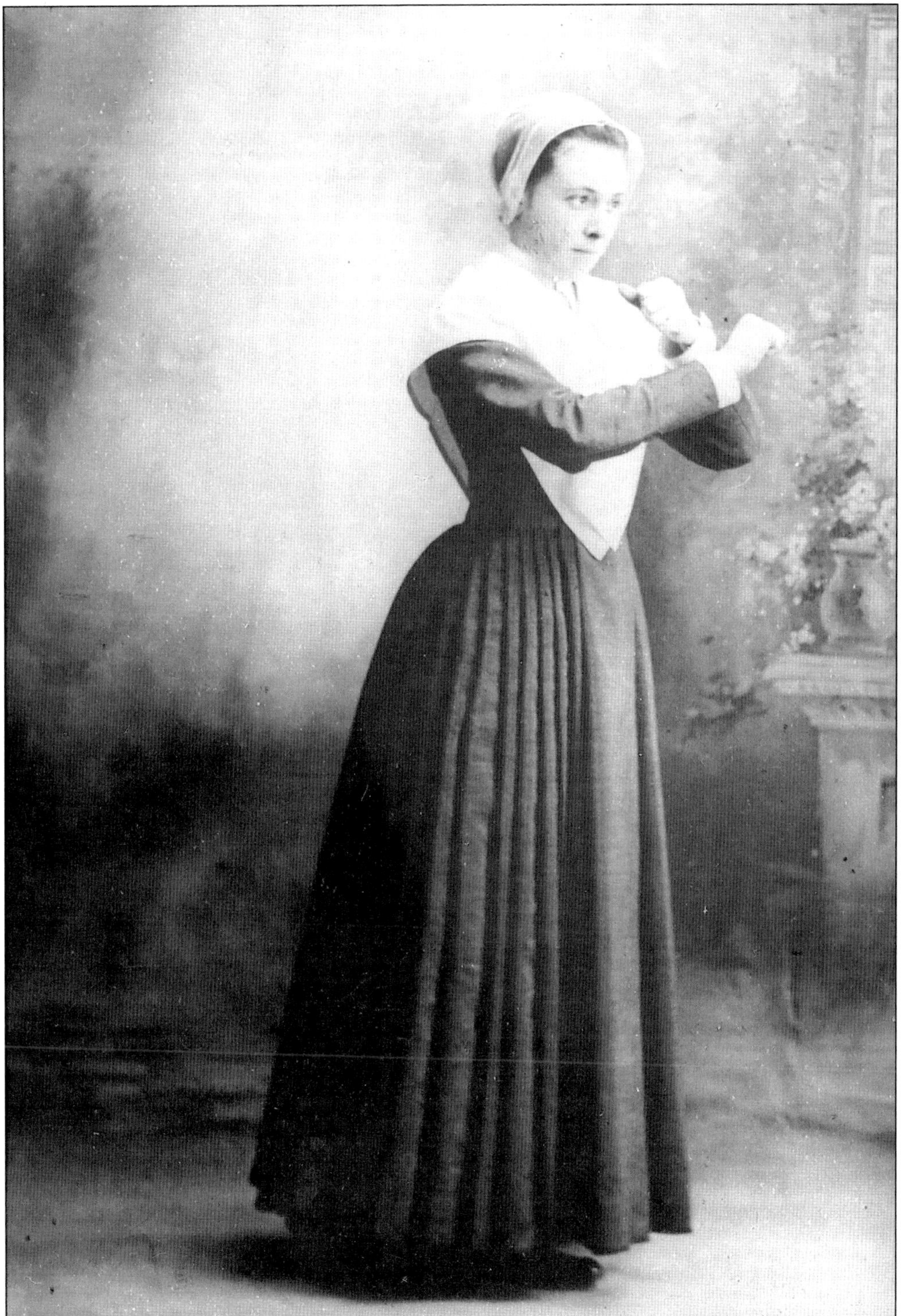

Later, as the religion matured, the Shakers' dancing became highly stylized and choreographed, as illustrated in this series of photographs.

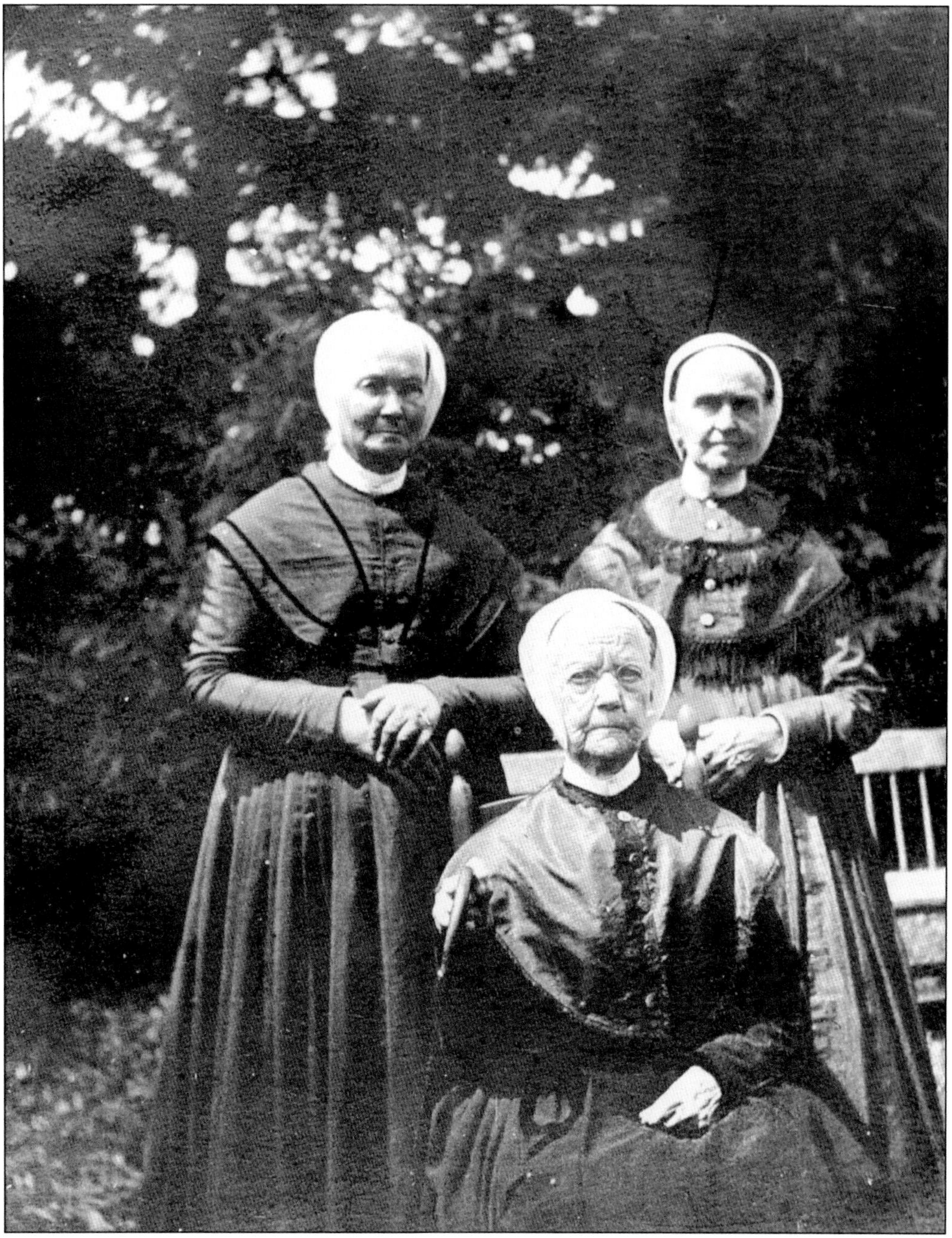

Olive Hatch, Louisa Green, and Elizabeth Grover are shown *c.* 1903. Each sister is wearing a similar bonnet but different berthas.

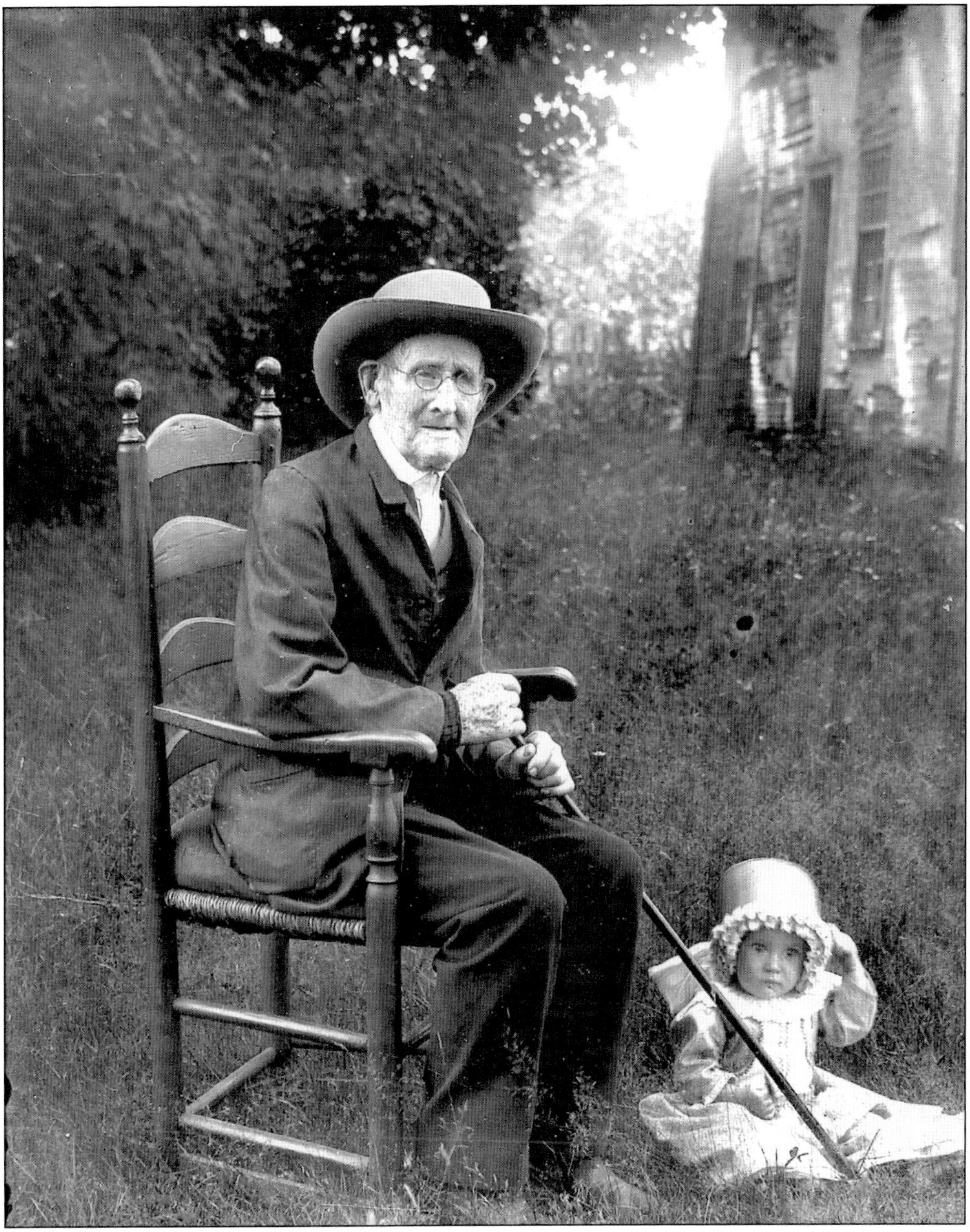

Ezra Newton, shown here with an unidentified child, died in 1897 at the age of 101.

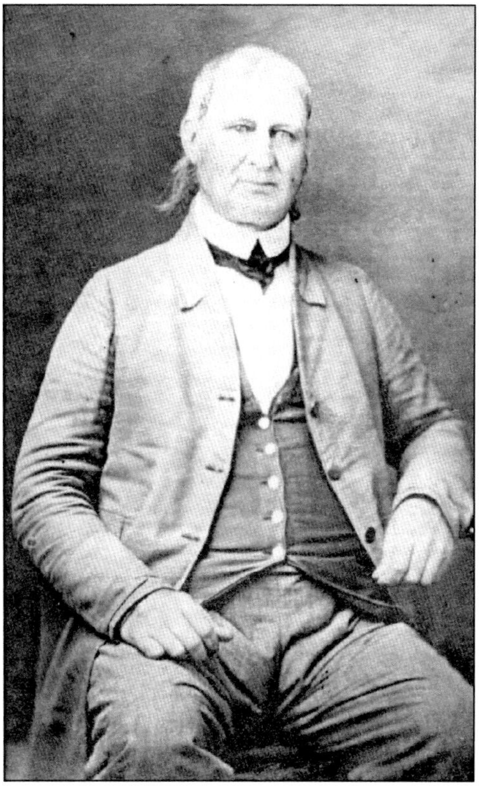

Augustus Grosvenor joined the Harvard Shaker community in 1819 with his parents, brother, and sisters. He held many leadership positions in the village and managed the sawmill for years. He oversaw the building of the Rural Home but ran the society into debt as a result of its construction. Grosvenor died in 1864 of heart failure. An autopsy revealed a three-inch cleft in his heart, which was displayed in the Ayer Drug Store until 1879.

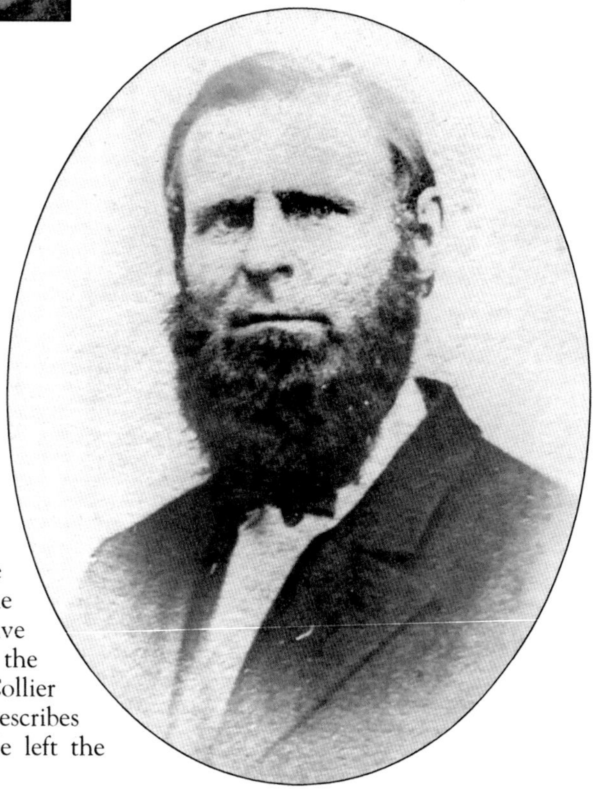

Alfred Collier joined the Shakers in 1831 at the age of eight. During the Era of Manifestations, Alfred was one of Harvard Shakers whose visions gave strength to his faith. He served as the head of the village farm for 20 years. Collier also wrote an insightful journal that describes the farm activities in the village. He left the community in 1864.

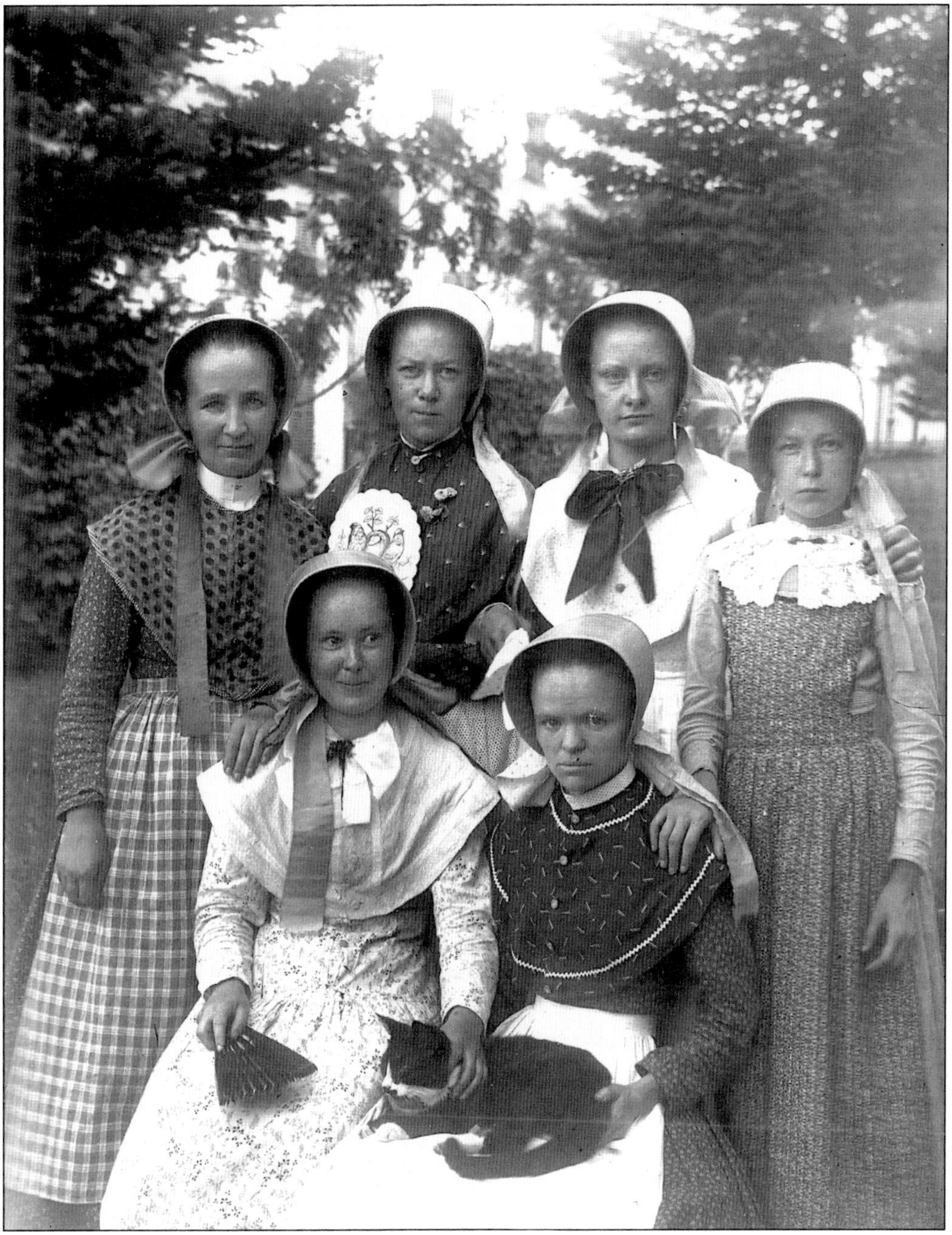

The clothing worn by these six Shaker sisters is typical of the late-19th-century Shaker style of dress for women.

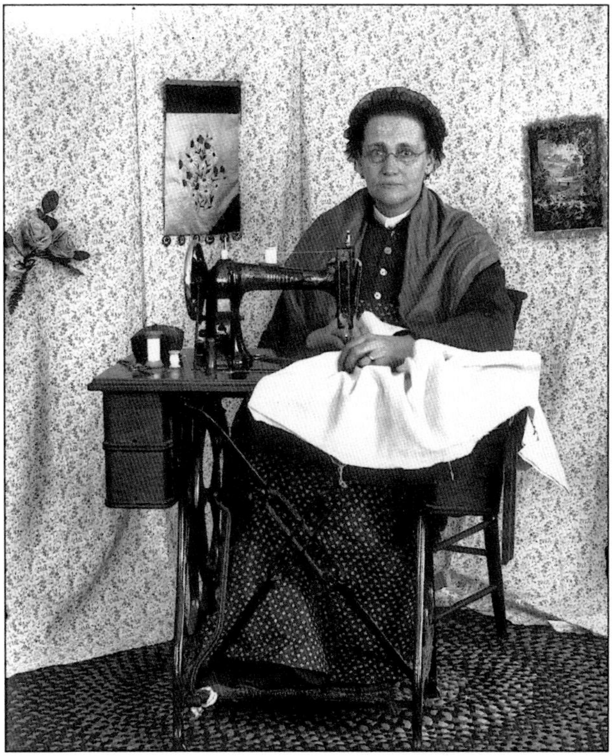

This studio portrait shows Sister Myra McLean with a sewing machine.

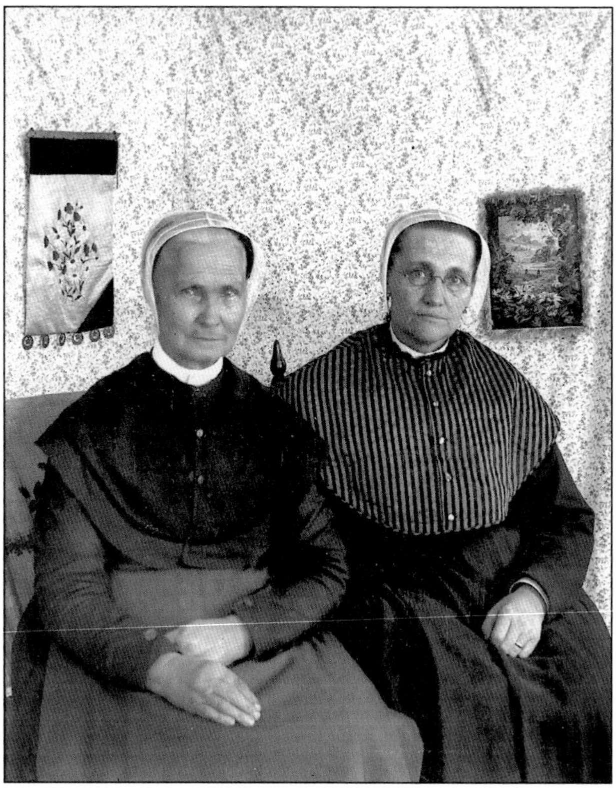

This studio portrait, probably from in the 1890s, shows Louisa Green (left) and Myra McLean. Curiously, Sister Myra is wearing what looks like a wedding ring.

An unidentified Shaker woman poses *c.* 1890.

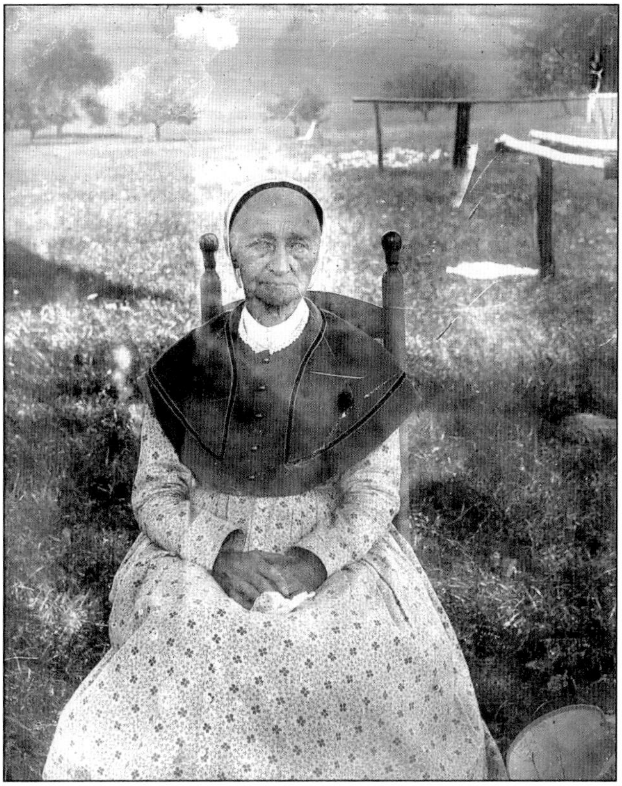

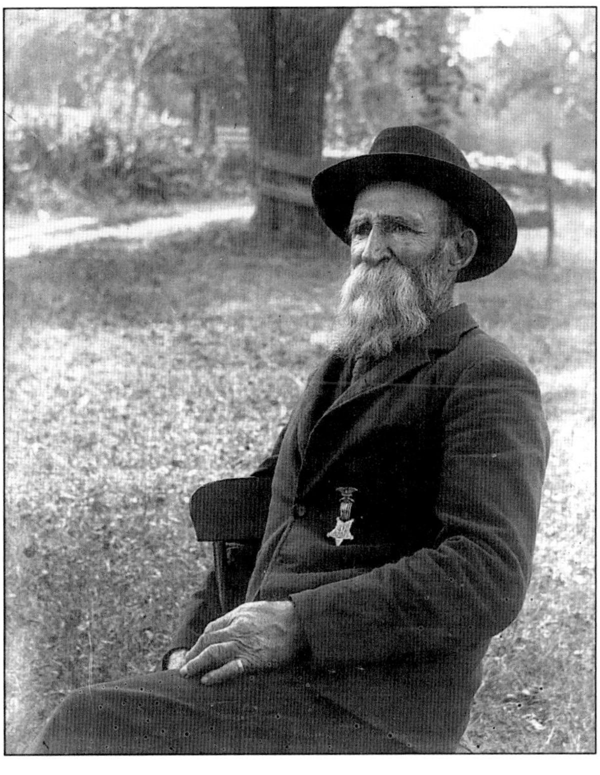

This unidentified man is probably one of the hired laborers who worked for the Shakers.

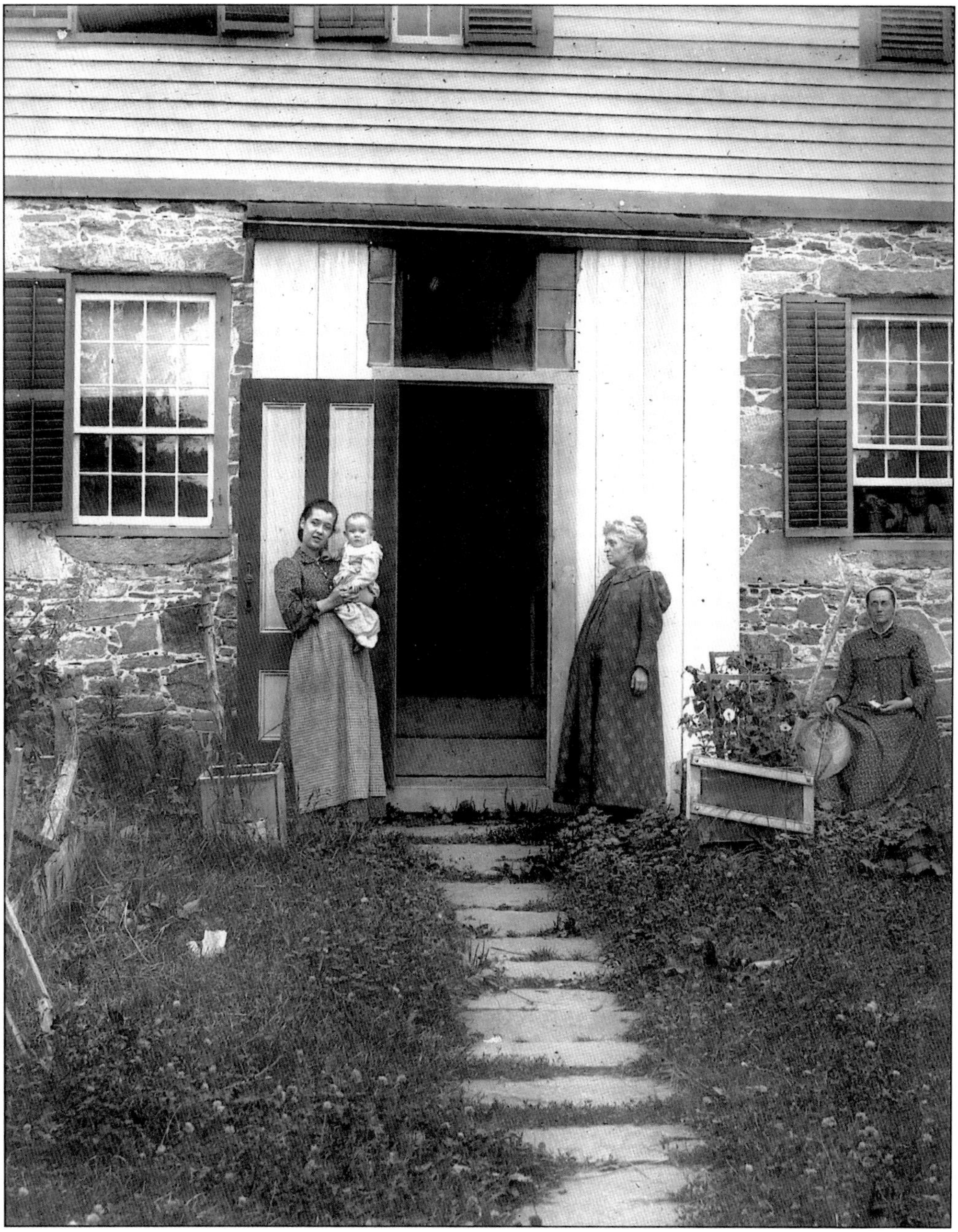

This is a group of Shaker women, probably *c.* 1900. Sister Myra is on the right. The other two women and the child are unidentified. As the population of the Harvard Shaker community diminished, they rented out some of their buildings and rooms to other people.

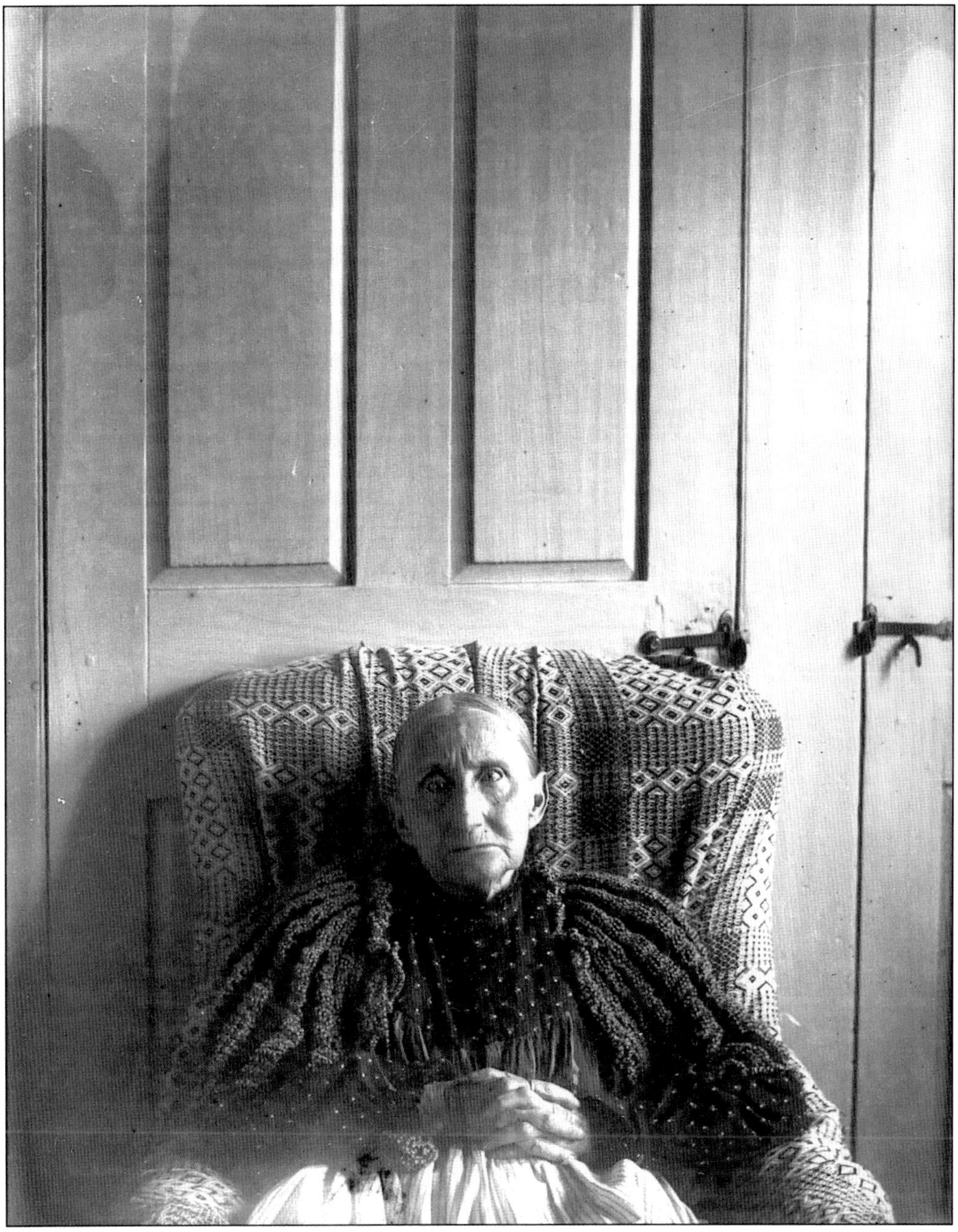

Posing here is an unidentified Shaker woman.

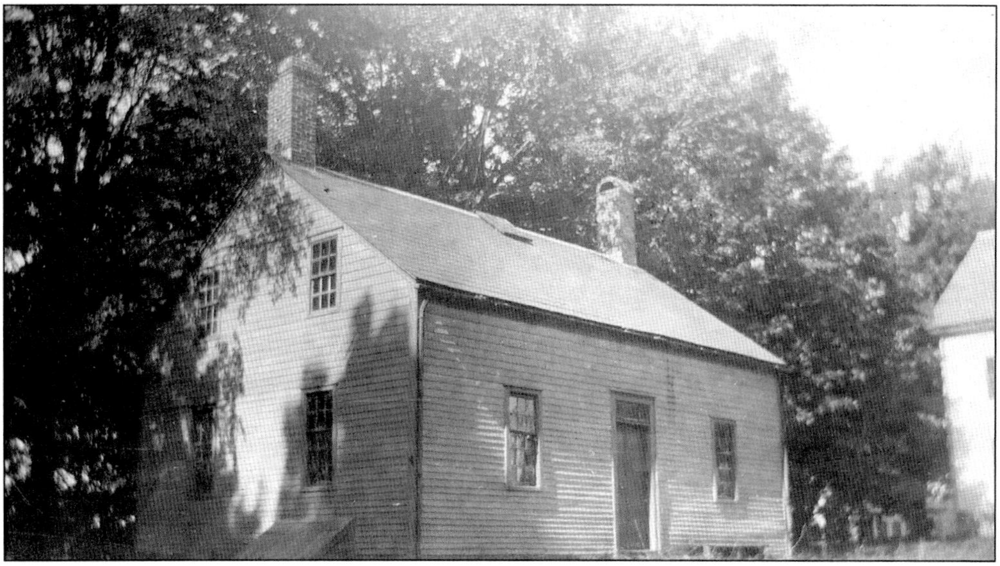

The old Harvard Shaker office was originally built in 1794. This photograph was taken in 1920 before the building was dismantled and moved to Fruitlands Museums.

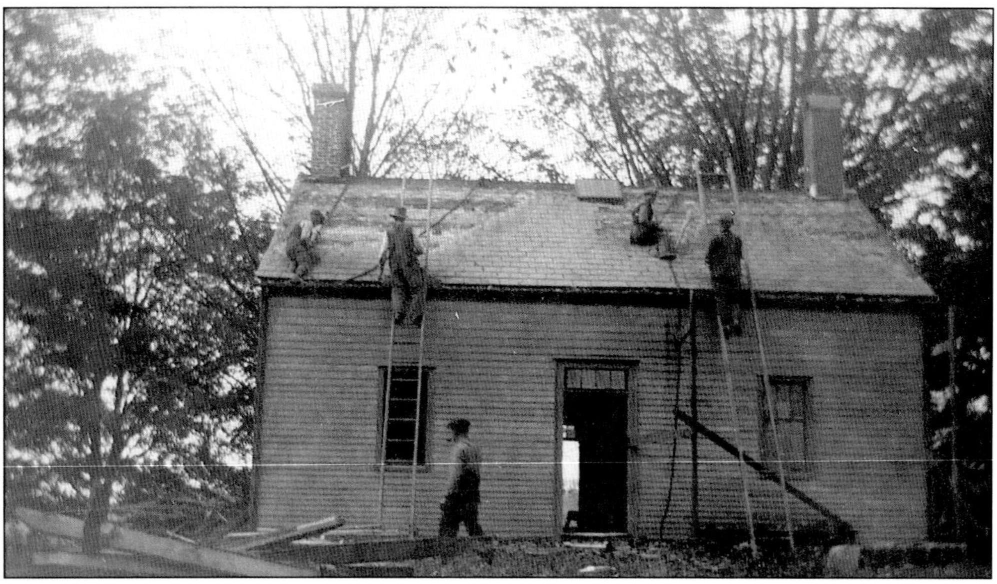

The workers begin to take the old Harvard Shaker office apart.

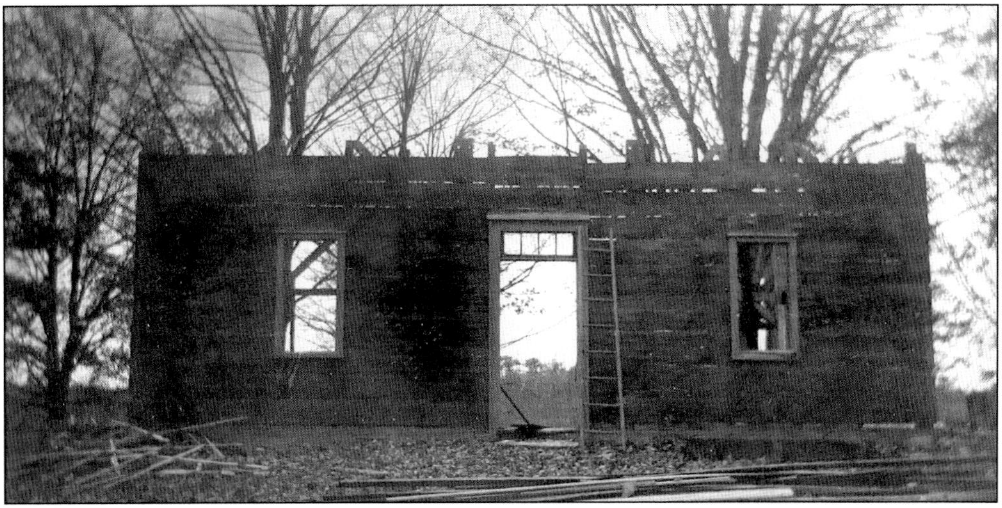
Here is old Harvard Shaker office with the roof and second floor removed.

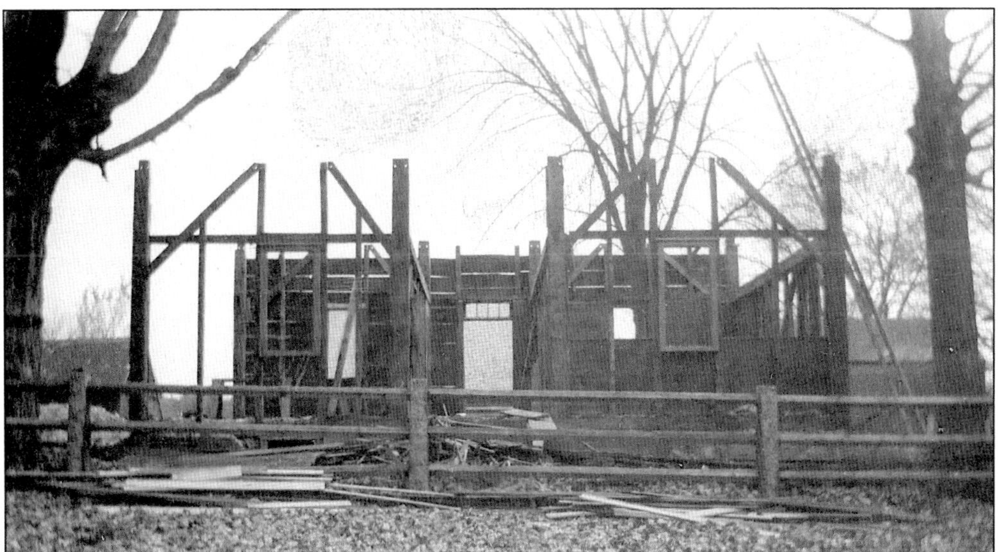
This last photograph shows the timber construction of the walls.

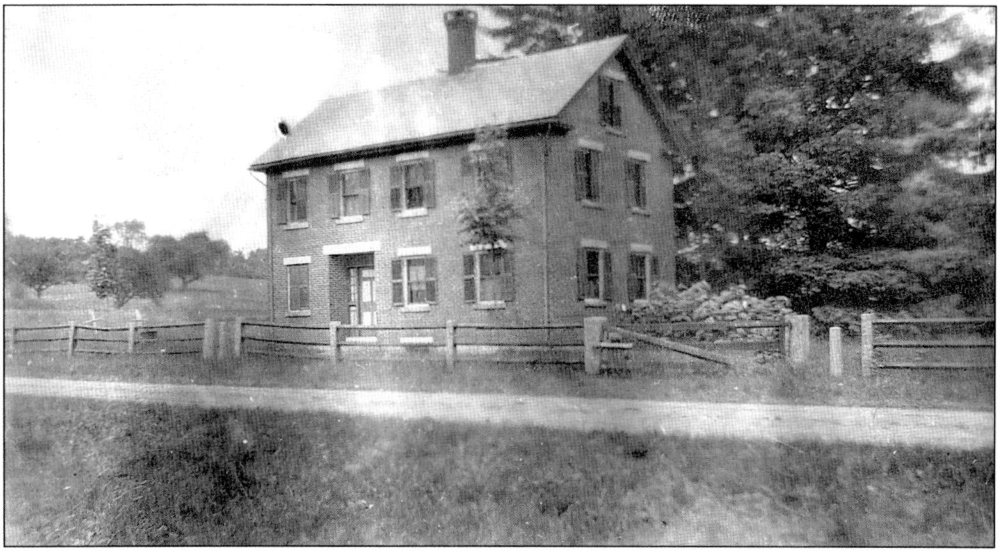

This is the ministry shop in the Harvard Shaker village that was built by Augustus Grosvenor in 1843. Grosvenor was the probably the first Harvard Shaker to cover new building exteriors with brick.

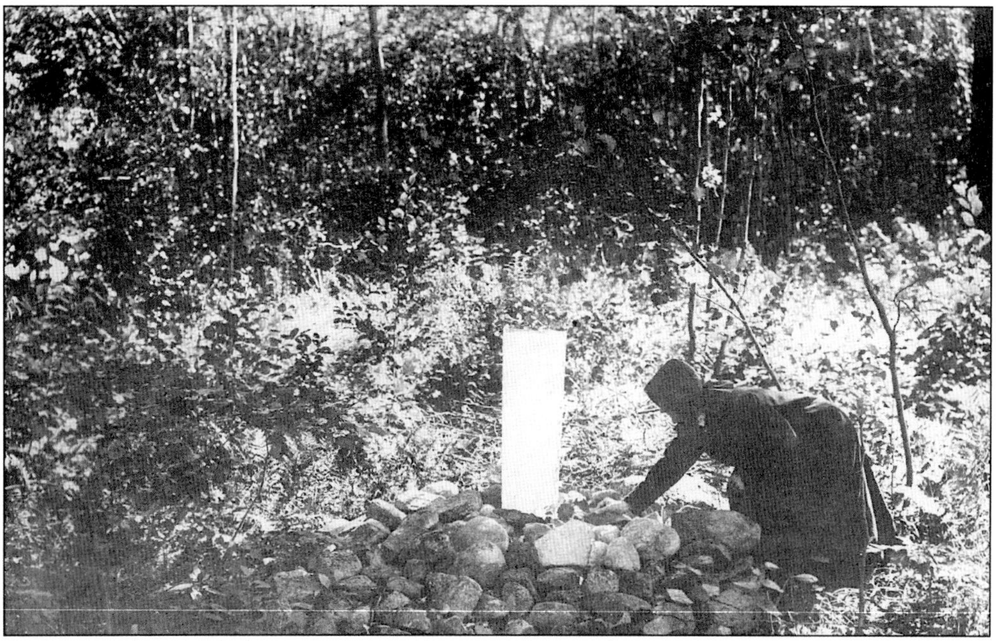

This image shows a Shaker woman near the spot where Father James Whittaker was whipped by disgruntled residents of Harvard in 1783. Early Shaker behavior was considered indecent, and townspeople suspected Shakers of being British sympathizers. A town meeting in 1781 voted to prosecute them.

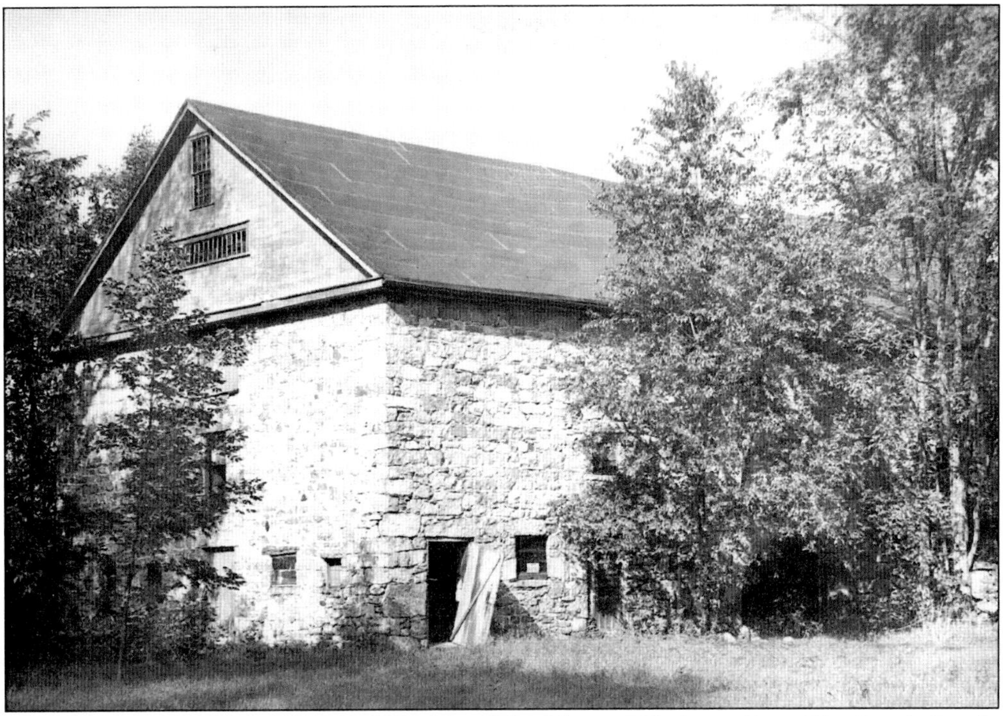

This is the stone barn in the South Family of the Harvard Shaker village. The South Family closed in 1895, and this image was taken c. 1905 after the property had fallen into neglect.

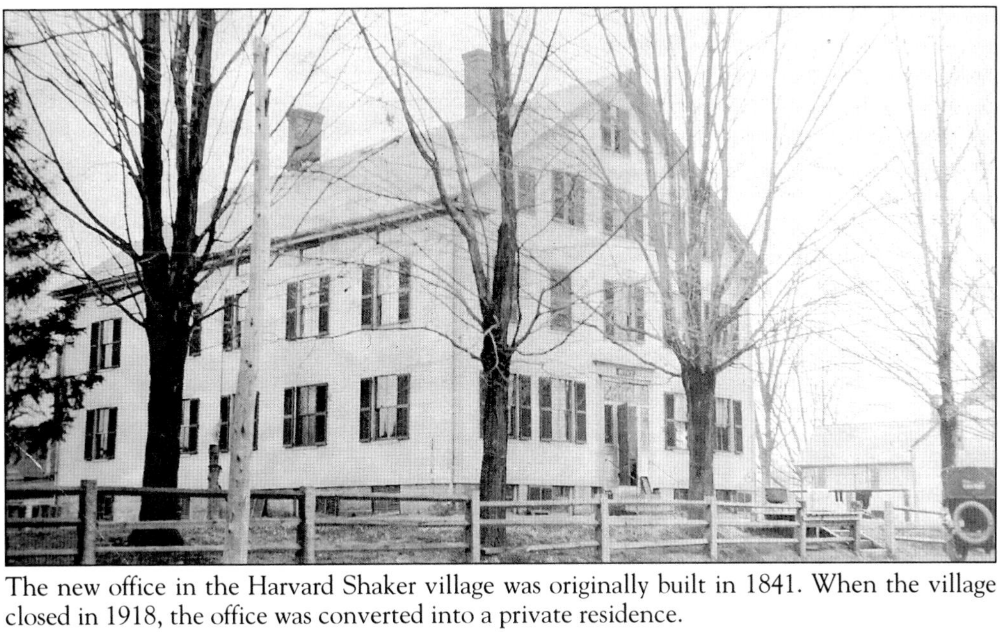

The new office in the Harvard Shaker village was originally built in 1841. When the village closed in 1918, the office was converted into a private residence.

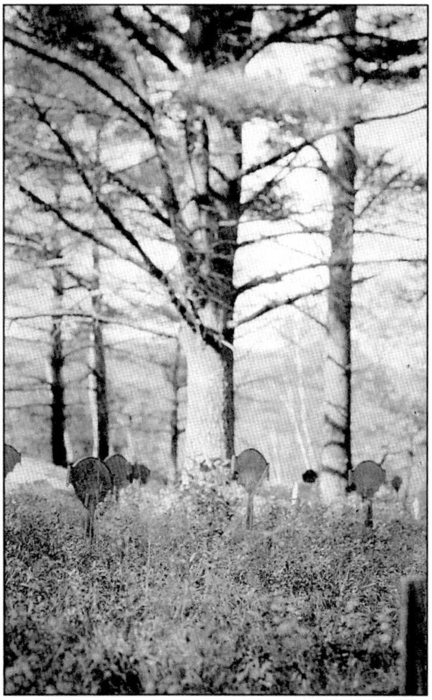

Some 330 Shakers are buried in the Harvard Shaker cemetery, and many have unique cast-iron lollipop grave markers.

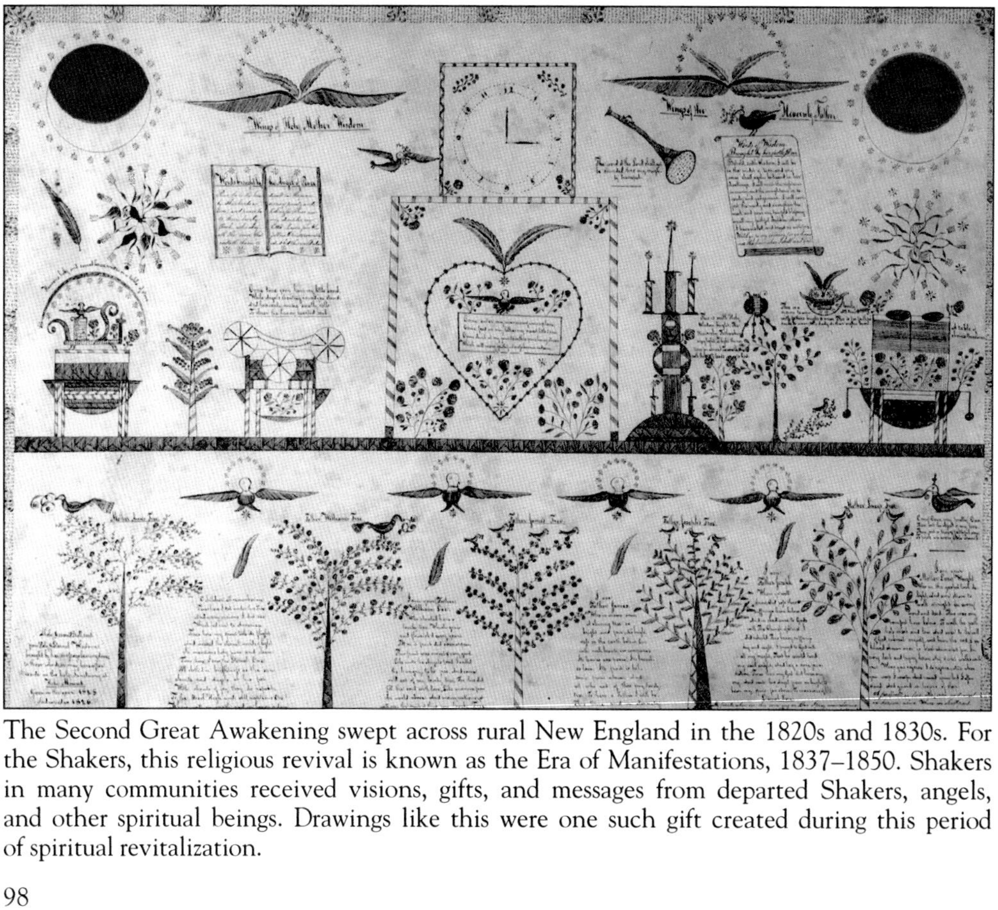

The Second Great Awakening swept across rural New England in the 1820s and 1830s. For the Shakers, this religious revival is known as the Era of Manifestations, 1837–1850. Shakers in many communities received visions, gifts, and messages from departed Shakers, angels, and other spiritual beings. Drawings like this were one such gift created during this period of spiritual revitalization.

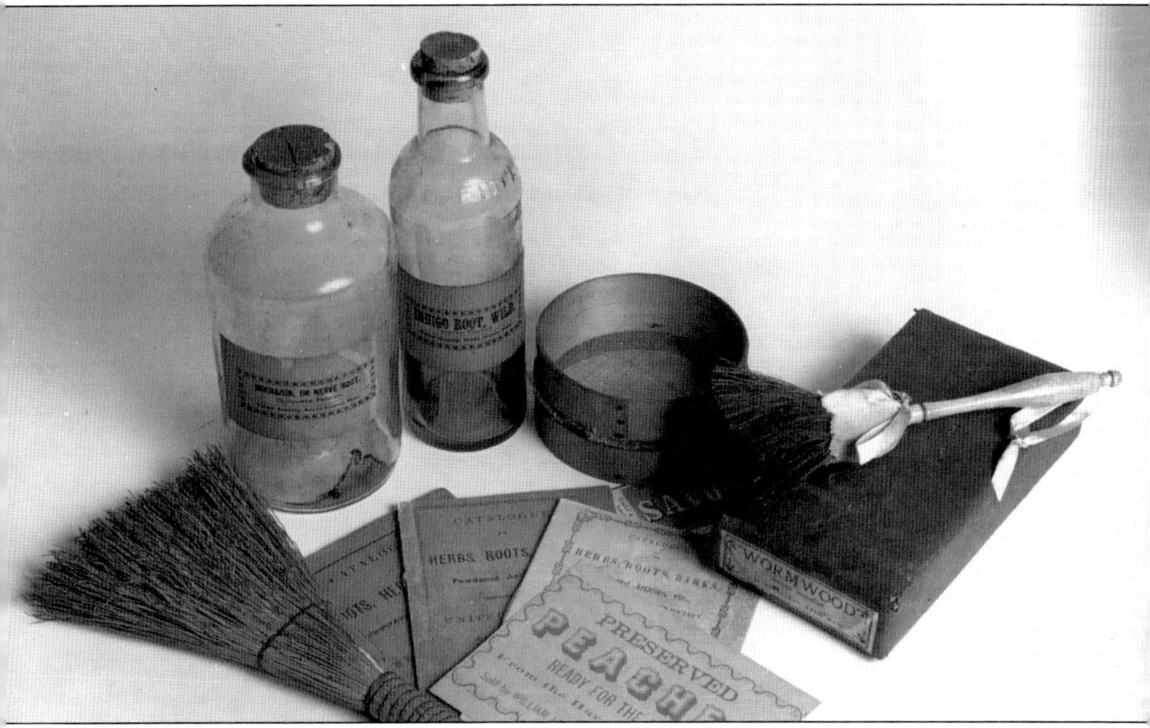

Shakers produced a variety of goods for sale. Of their many marketing innovations, the Shakers were one of the first groups to use color in labels and advertising. Shaker villages sought to provide for their basic needs of food, shelter, and clothing. They also developed commercial enterprises to generate the capital necessary to buy goods and services from "the world." Early industries formed around the skills of early converts and trades learned from Shakers in other communities. The success of any of these industries required the strength of individual Shakers to provide the energy and ingenuity that enabled success. It also relied on the more anonymous community members whose many labors provided the raw materials, labor, and community support.

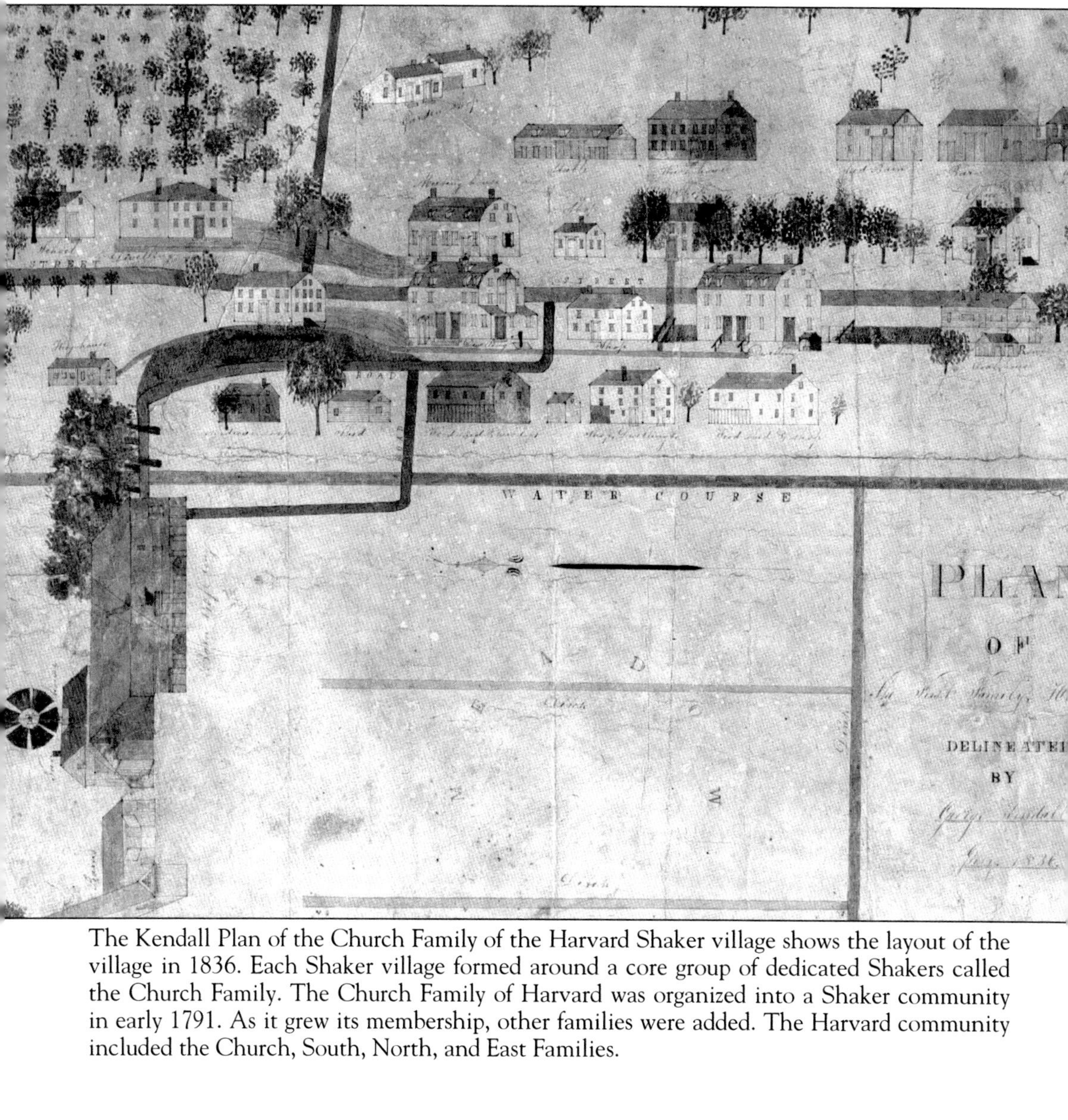

The Kendall Plan of the Church Family of the Harvard Shaker village shows the layout of the village in 1836. Each Shaker village formed around a core group of dedicated Shakers called the Church Family. The Church Family of Harvard was organized into a Shaker community in early 1791. As it grew its membership, other families were added. The Harvard community included the Church, South, North, and East Families.

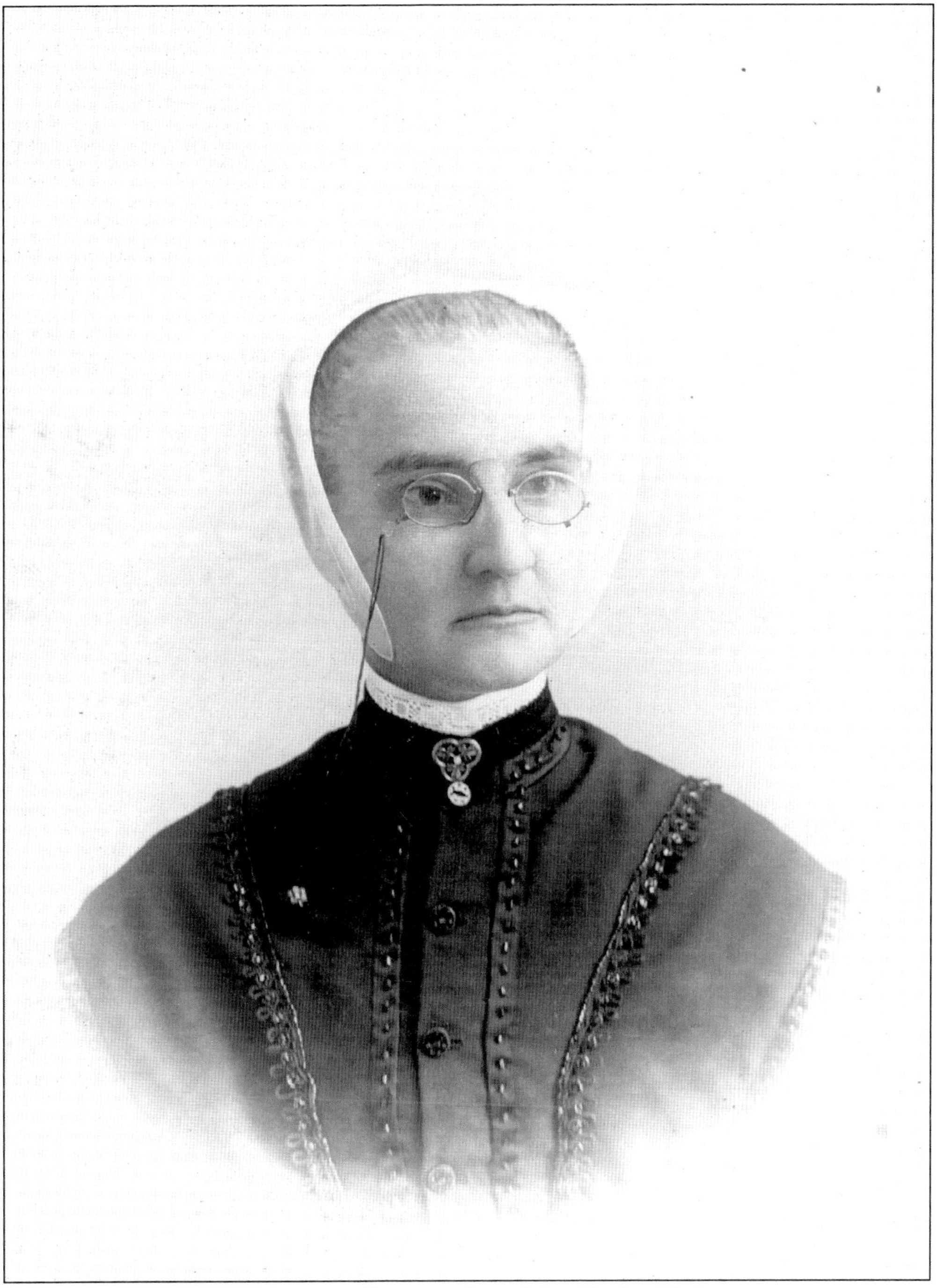

Eldress Josephine Jilson was originally a member of the Shirley Shaker community, joining at the age of three in 1855. When it closed in 1909, she moved to Harvard with Laura Beal and Anne Bell Tuttle. Jilson was very interested in preserving the Shaker legacy. She set up a modest museum of Shaker relics in a small building, eventually installing a display in the Square House. Many of the most cherished items were given by Eldress Josephine to Clara Endicott Sears for her Shaker Museum at Fruitlands.

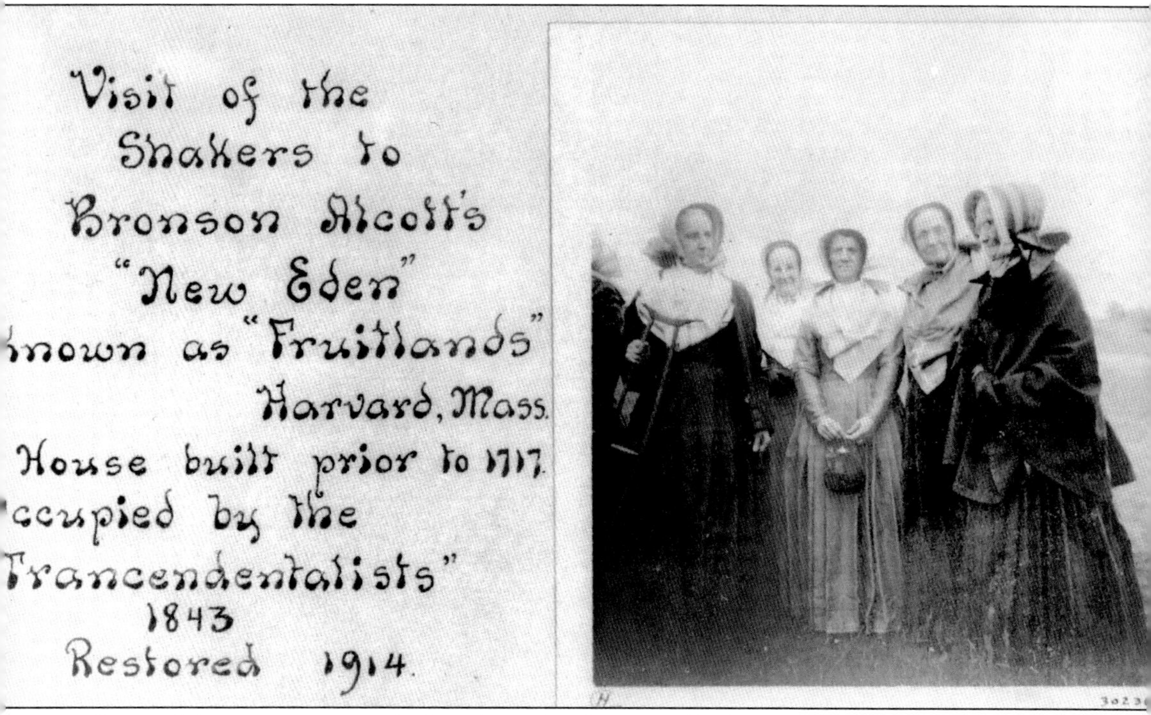

Harvard Shaker sisters visit the Fruitlands farmhouse in 1914.

Three

The Fruitlands Experiment

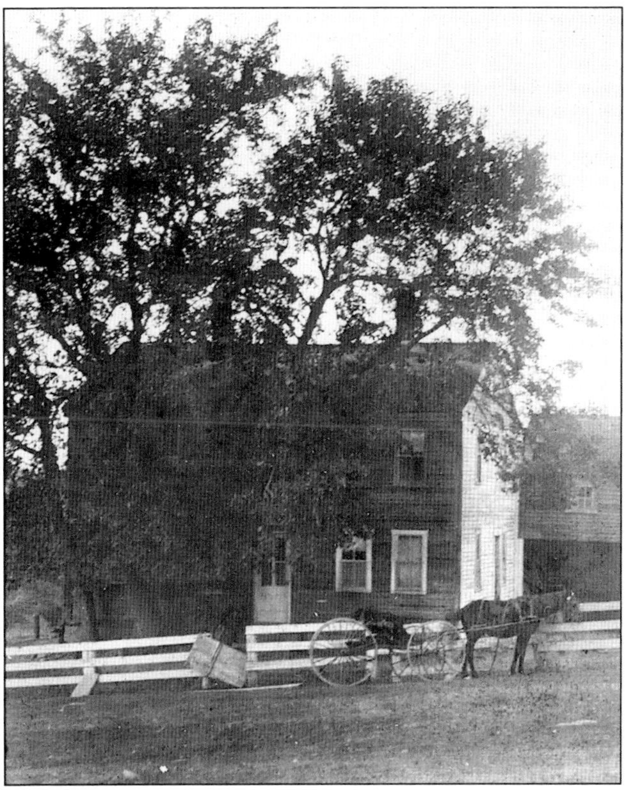

The Fruitlands farmhouse, seen here in 1900, was the site of the Fruitlands experiment, a transcendentalist commune that sought to live off the "fruits of the land." Unfortunately, the lack of practical farming experience and poor planning caused the early demise of this experiment in early 1844.

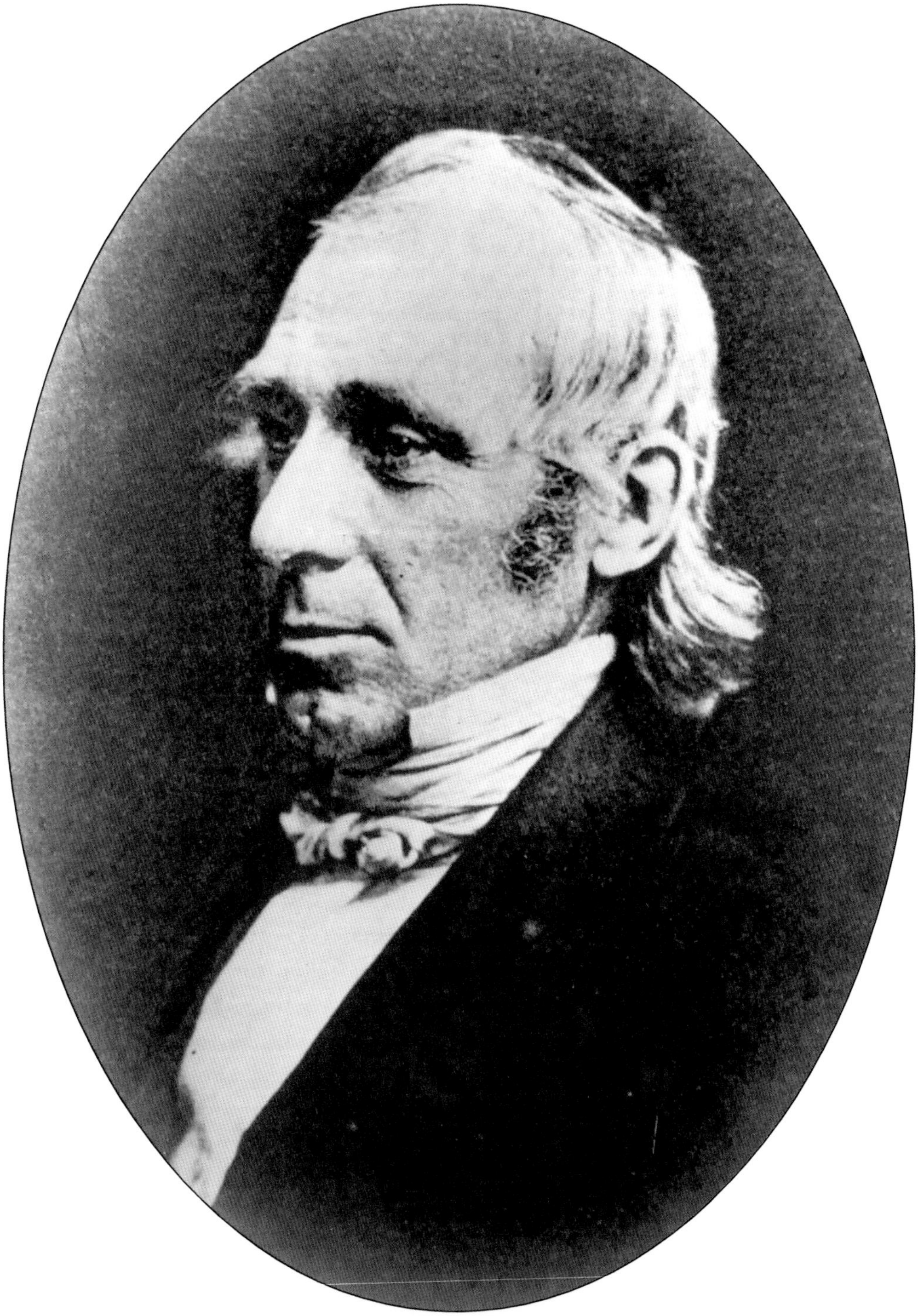

A. Bronson Alcott was an important educational reformer, abolitionist, and transcendental philosopher in 19th-century Massachusetts. He and partner Charles Lane began the ill-fated Fruitlands experiment in June 1843 to test some of the more idealistic aims of their branch of transcendentalism. When the experiment failed in January 1844, Alcott's dream died with it.

Charles Lane was an English journalist and educational and spiritual reformer. He came to America and helped Bronson Alcott create the transcendentalist experiment in communal living called Fruitlands. Lane has been criticized as a tyrant whose divisive influence contributed to the failure of the experiment.

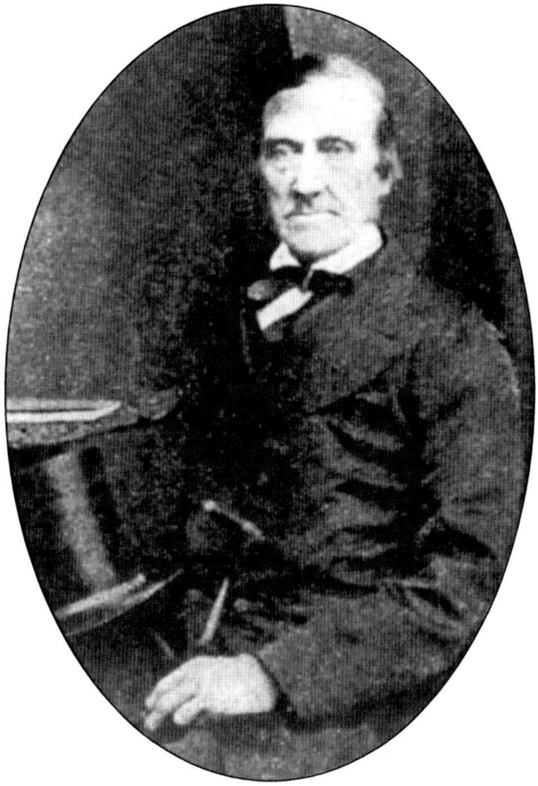

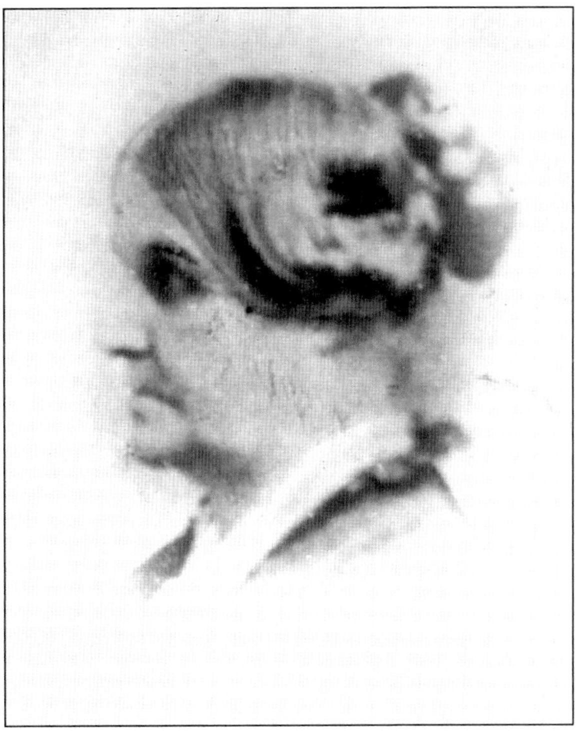

After Abigail May Alcott married Bronson Alcott, her brother Samuel May helped fund the Fruitlands experiment as well as the purchase of Orchard House in Concord. Mrs. Alcott fought hard to maintain their family during and after the tumultuous Fruitlands experiment.

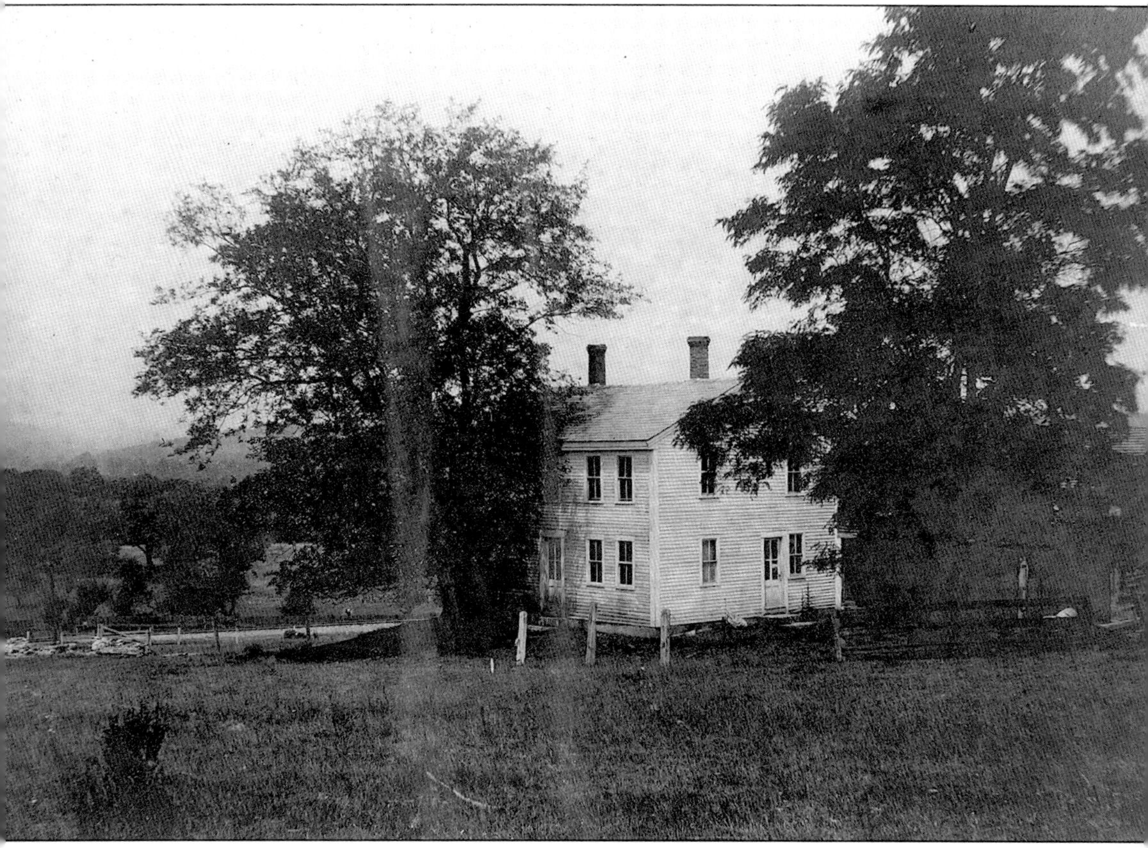

Prior to its restoration as a museum in 1914, the Fruitlands farmhouse originally had two chimneys, as seen here. The original structure on the site dates from c. 1700. The original farm was approximately 140 acres laid out during the second division of Lancaster.

Louisa May Alcott, author of *Little Women*, spent some time as a girl in the Fruitlands farmhouse as part of her father Bronson's transcendentalist commune called Fruitlands. Ironically, the Fruitlands experiment and Bronson Alcott are probably best known today due to the literary works of his daughter Louisa May Alcott.

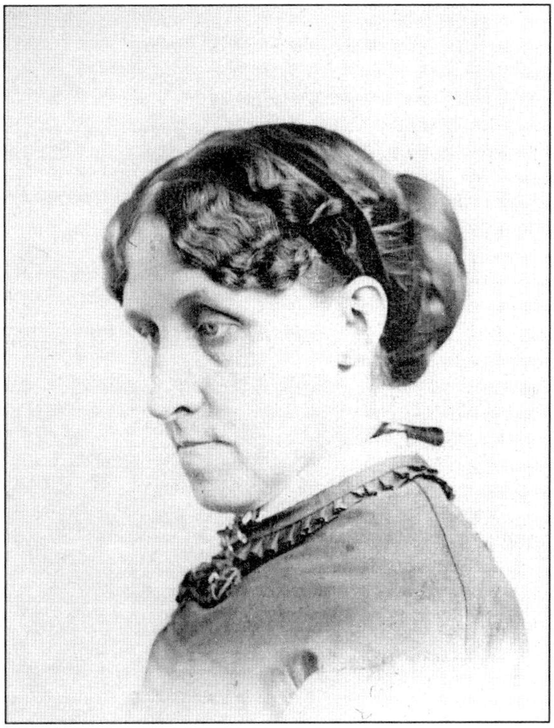

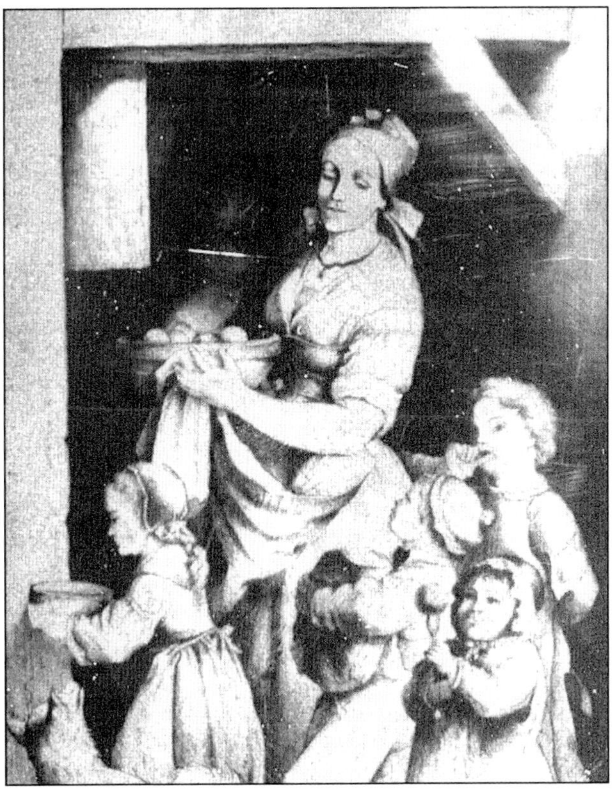

May Alcott was the younger sister of Louisa whose successful literary career enabled May to attend art schools in America and Europe. This drawing was done by May Alcott *c.* 1860.

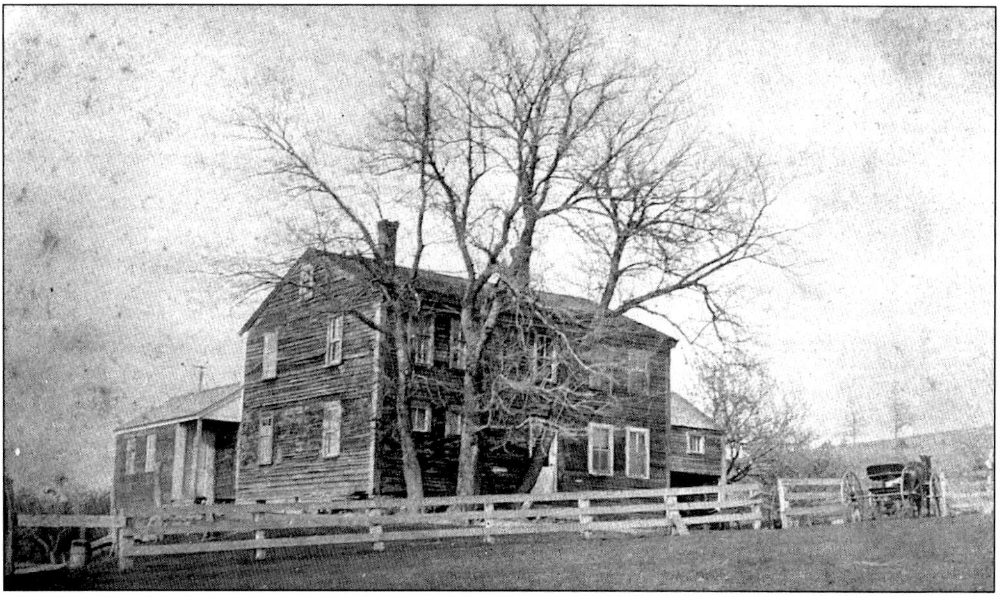

The following people participated in the Fruitlands experiment for some time between June 1843 and January 1844: A. Bronson Alcott, Abigail Alcott, May Alcott, Louisa May Alcott, Abby Alcott, Charles Lane, William Lane, H.C. Wright, Sam Bower, Isaac Hecker, Christopher Greene, Samuel Larned, Abraham Everett, Anna Page, Joseph Palmer, and Abraham Wood.

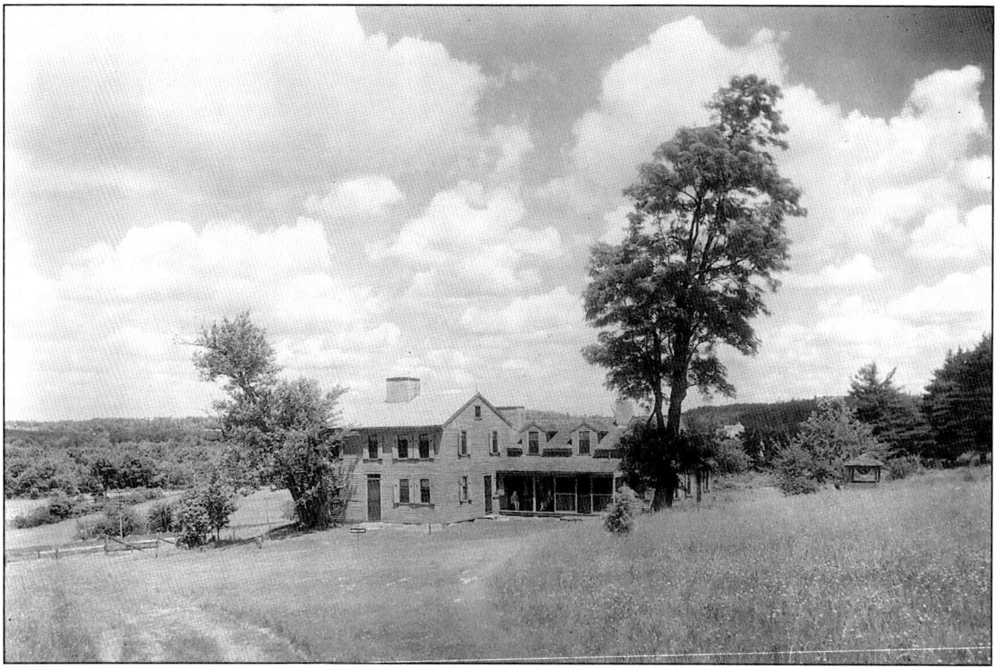

The Fruitlands experiment did not allow use of stimulants such as coffee and tea, and no meat or animal products or labor were used, including wool, honey, wax, or manure. They also refused planting roots, tubers, and vegetables that grew into the ground. In theory, the women spent the day working in the farmhouse while the men worked in the fields. They discussed philosophy at night.

Louisa May Alcott is shown here later in life. She published her first book, *Flower Fables*, at the age of 22 in 1854. This led to a successful career writing children's literature. She published more than 30 books and stories before her death in 1888.

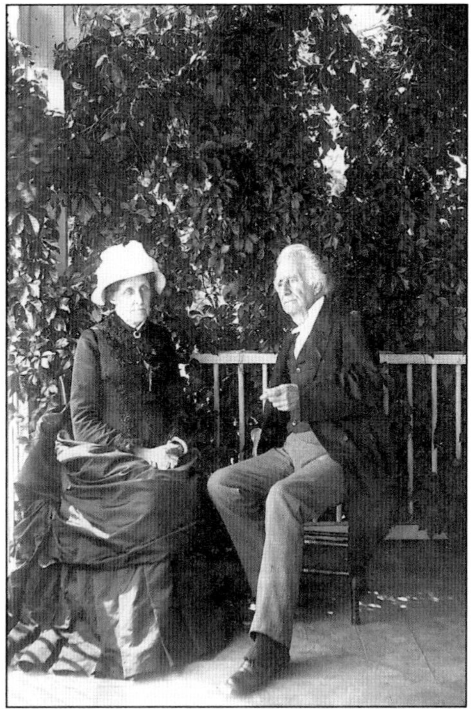

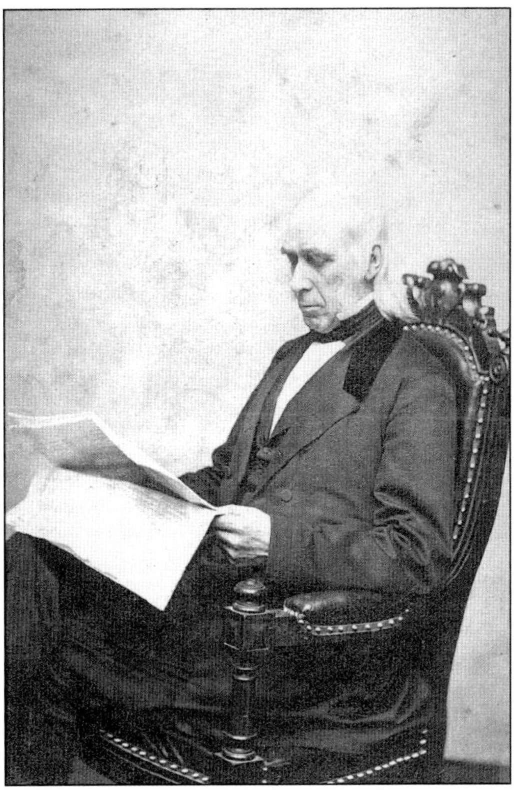

Bronson Alcott is seen here in later life. Born in Wolcott, Connecticut, Alcott married Abigail May, sister of Samuel May. He and his family moved to Concord, Massachusetts, and were surrounded by their friends, who included Thoreau and Emerson. Alcott believed childhood education must be moral, intellectual, spiritual, and physical.

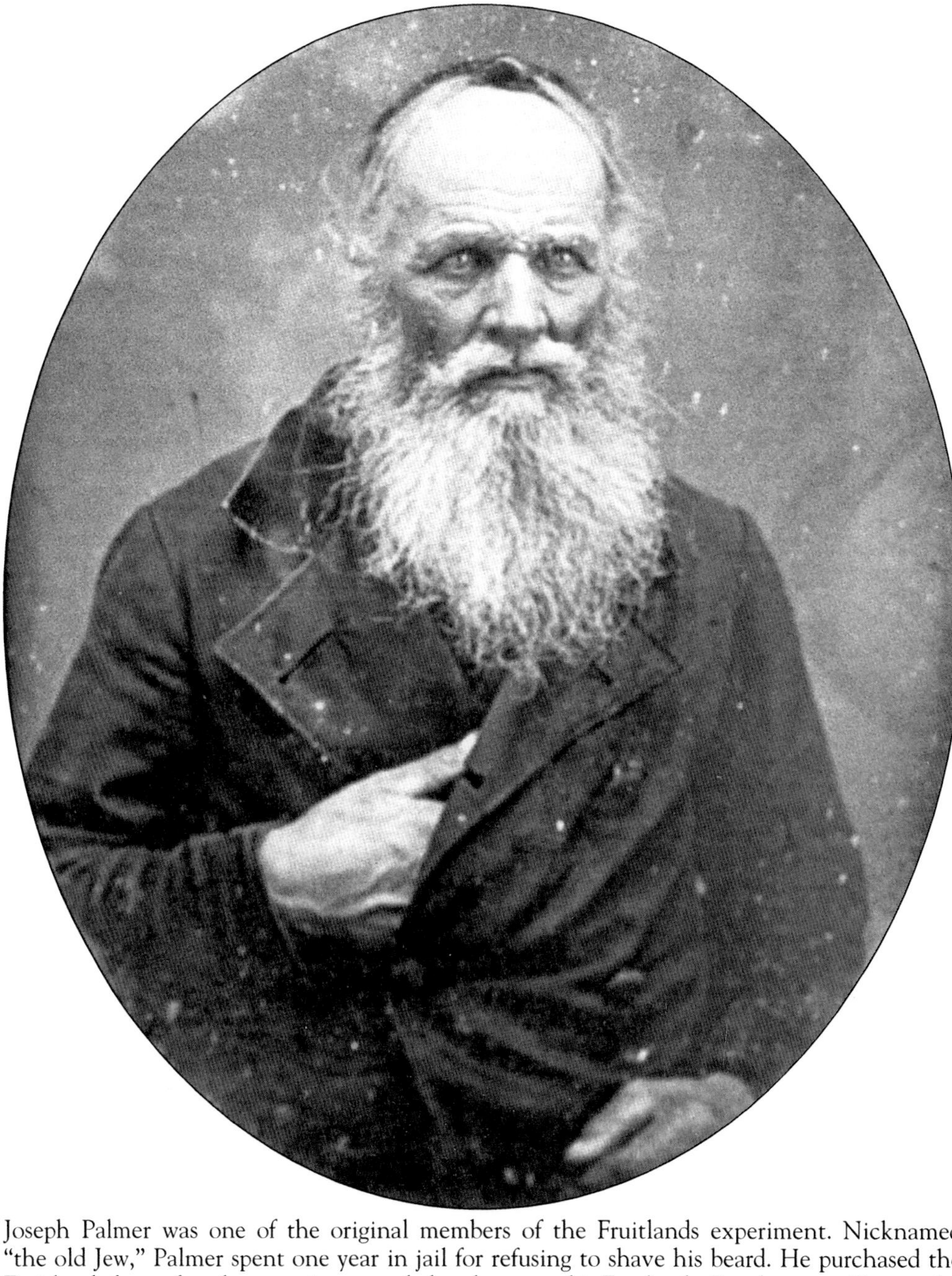

Joseph Palmer was one of the original members of the Fruitlands experiment. Nicknamed "the old Jew," Palmer spent one year in jail for refusing to shave his beard. He purchased the Fruitlands farm after the experiment ended and renamed it Freelands. For the next 40 years, he farmed the land and provided food and shelter to the destitute. He actively resisted all forms of oppression and was involved in prison reform, abolition, and defending the rights of the homeless and poor.

Four

FRUITLANDS MUSEUMS

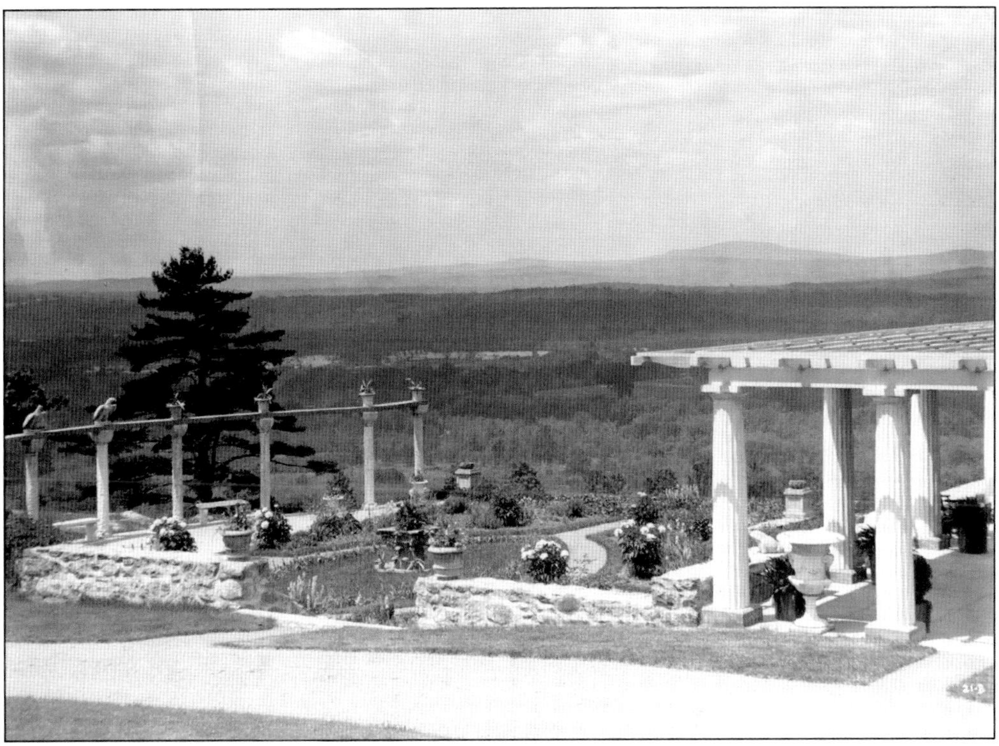

This view shows the Pergolas, the Byzantine temple imported from Turkey by Clara Endicott Sears for her garden on Prospect Hill Road. Sears founded Fruitlands Museums in 1914. Mount Wachusett is visible in the background. The view from Prospect Hill Road is as appealing to people today as it was to Miss Sears when she moved to the area in 1910.

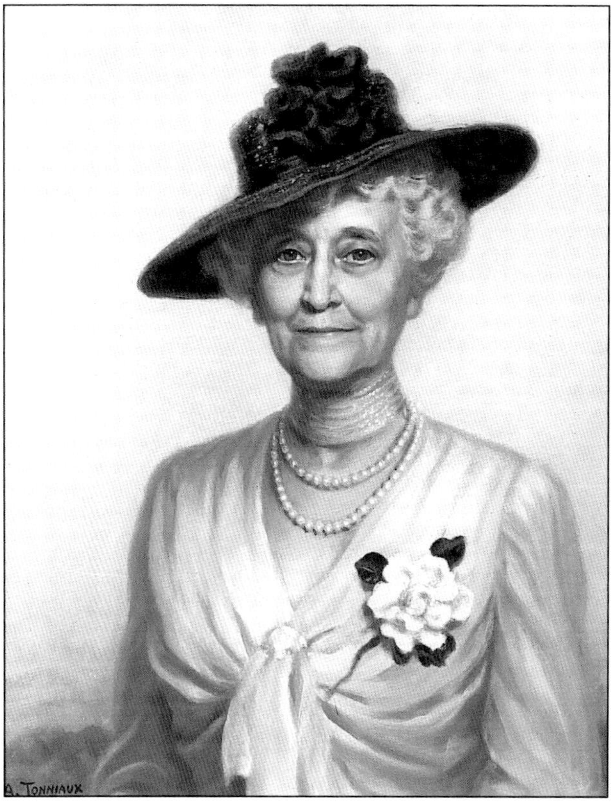

Clara Endicott Sears was a wealthy Boston Brahmin who in 1910 purchased a farm in Harvard as a summer estate. When she discovered her farm contained the original farmhouse of the Fruitlands experiment, she began to create Fruitlands Museums. She ultimately built four museums: Fruitlands (1914), the Shaker Museum (1922), the Indian Museum (1928), and the Picture Gallery (1940).

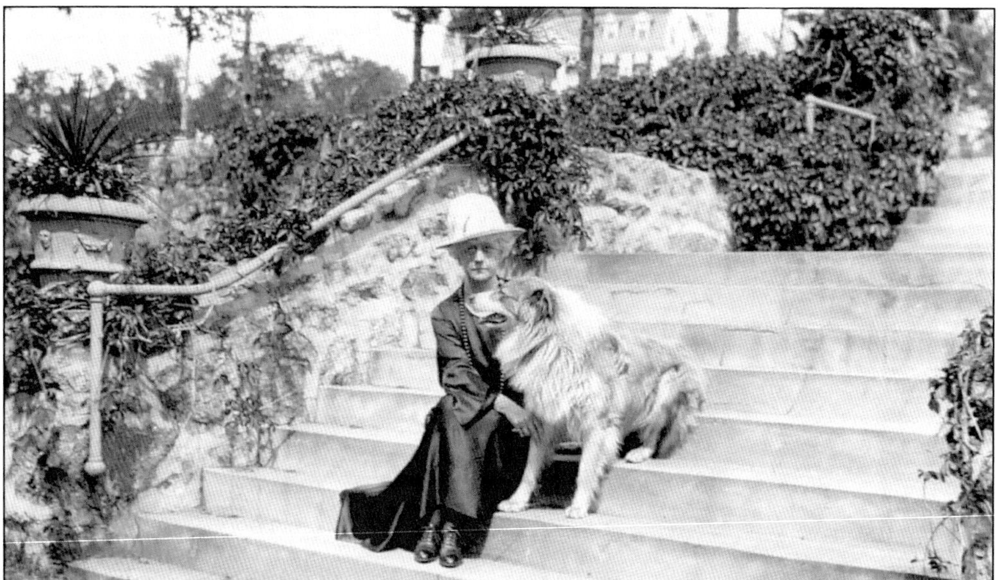

Miss Sears was born in 1863 and lived to be 97. She thought of herself primarily as an author and wrote historical books about each of her four museums, as well as romantic novels and poetry. During World War I, she published the popular song "Unfurling the Flag."

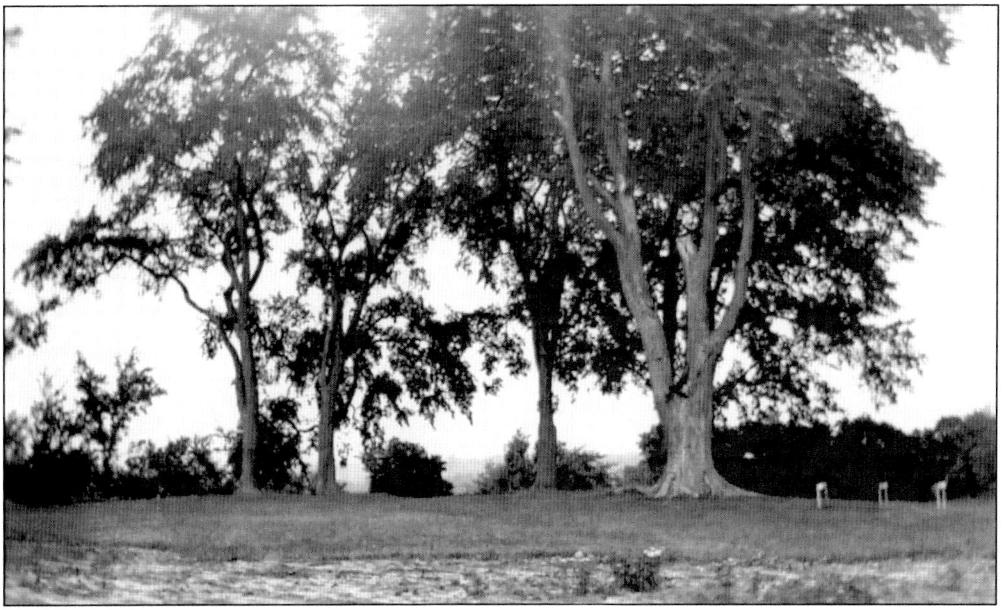

This is a picture of the site of Miss Sears's summer home called the Pergolas prior to its construction in 1910.

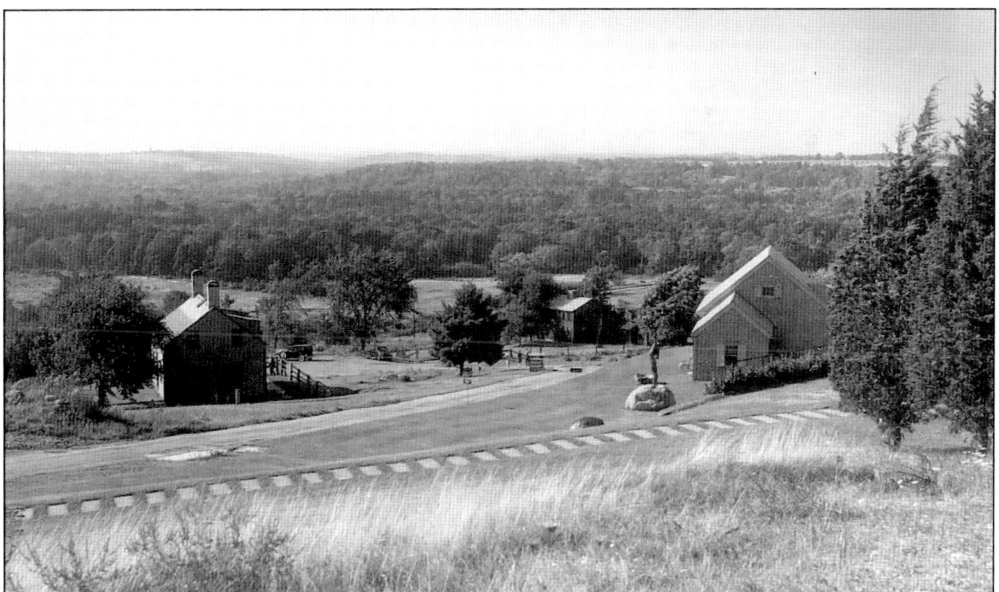

The Fruitlands Museums contains 210 acres overlooking the Nashua River Valley. The four museum buildings each educate visitors about an important aspect of 19th-century social history.

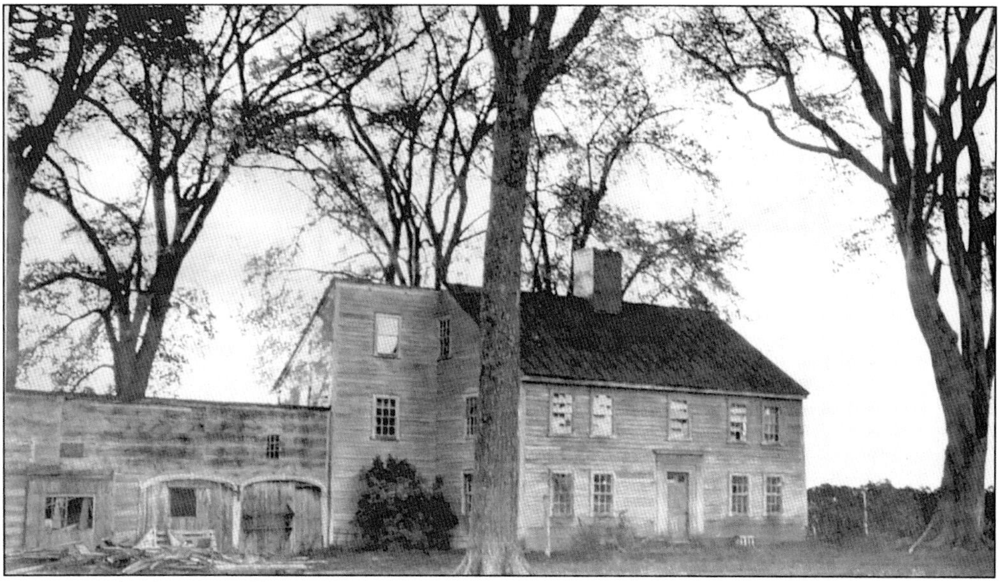

Miss Sears built some of her collections by visiting old farms and families in the local area and inquiring after the things in their attics.

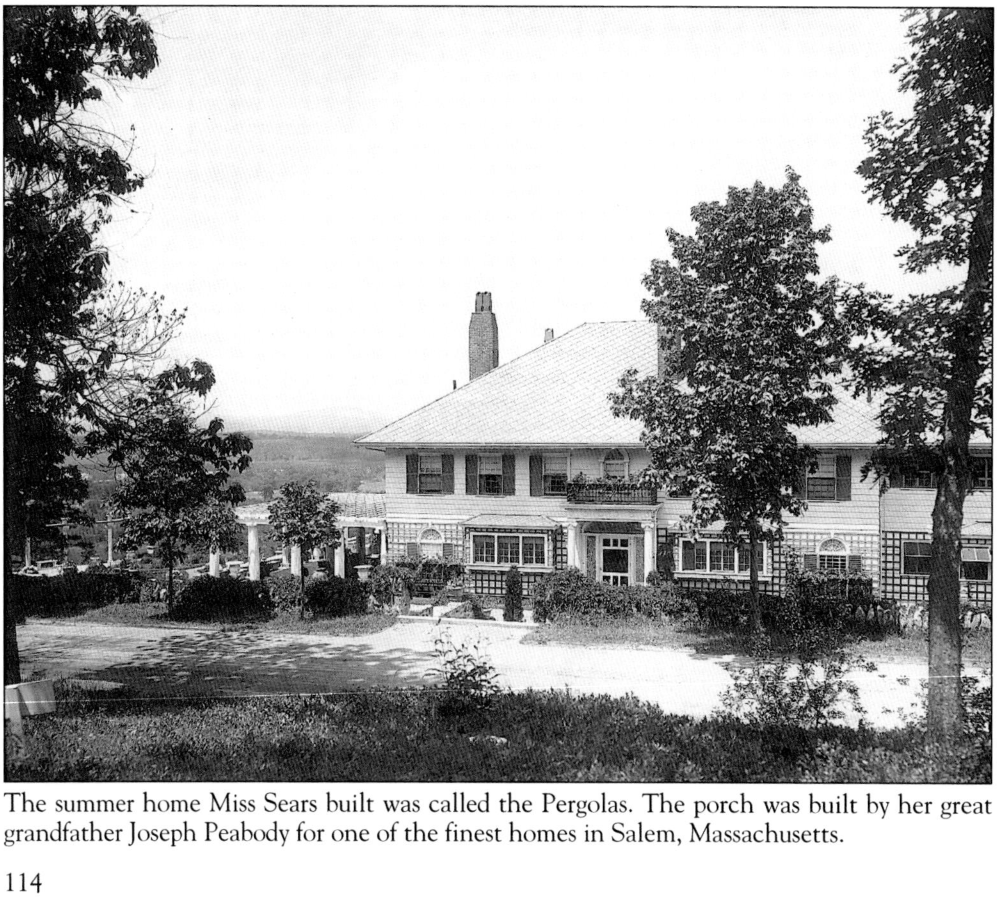

The summer home Miss Sears built was called the Pergolas. The porch was built by her great grandfather Joseph Peabody for one of the finest homes in Salem, Massachusetts.

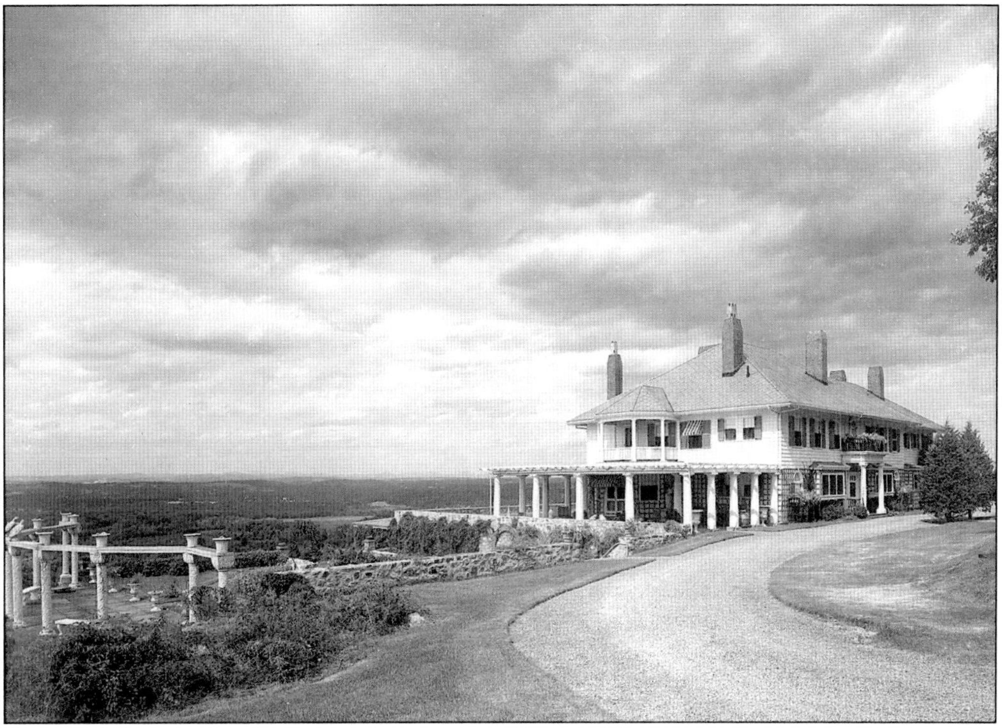

The Pergolas was a large, lavish summer home with an unparalleled view to the west and north. Miss Sears spend the summer here in Harvard and returned to Beacon Street in the fall.

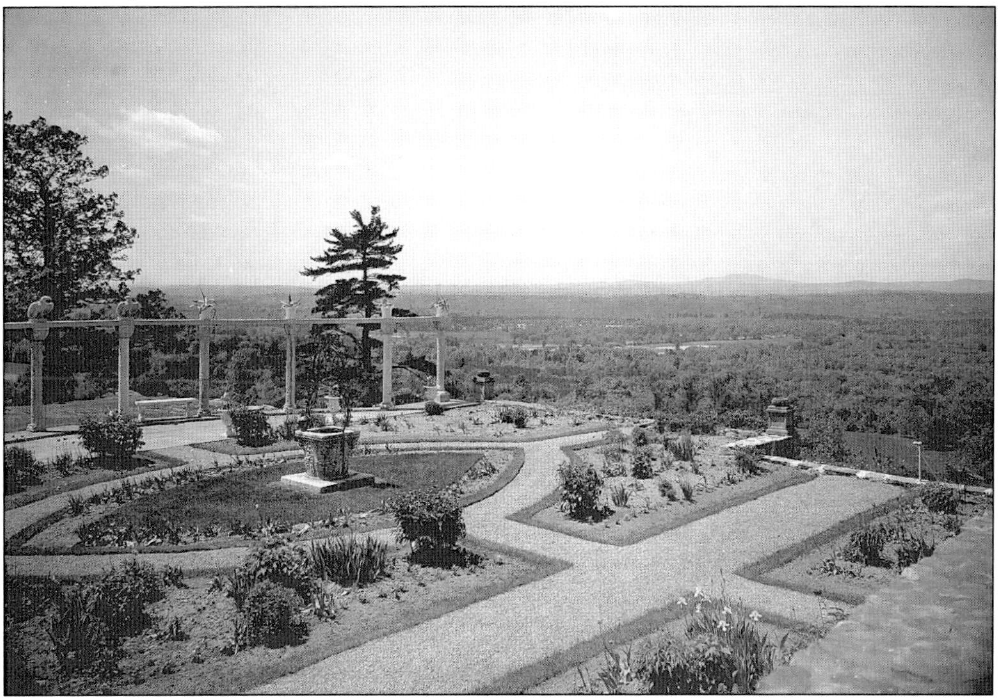

The stone columns in the sunken garden were imported from Venice. They are all intricately carved and many centuries old. They originally came from western Turkey.

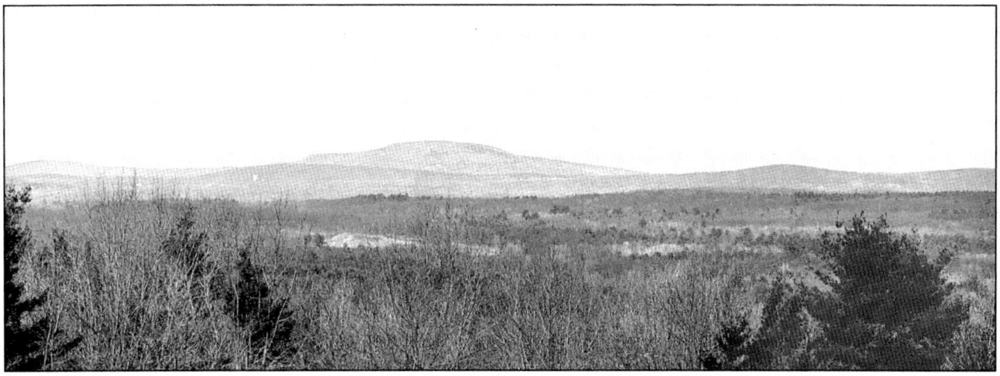

Mount Wachusett (2,000 feet) is the highest peak in Massachusetts east of the Connecticut River. It has the classic shape of a New England mountain that was once scoured by glacial ice.

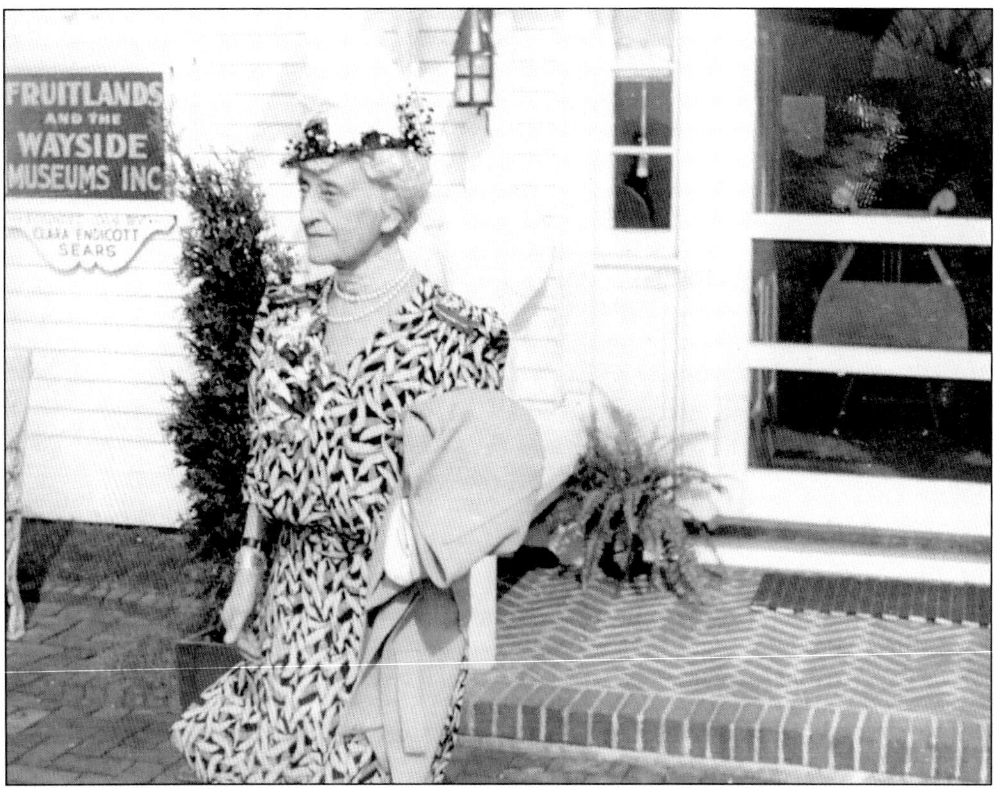

Miss Sears added a restaurant in 1935 called the Tea Room to her museum complex.

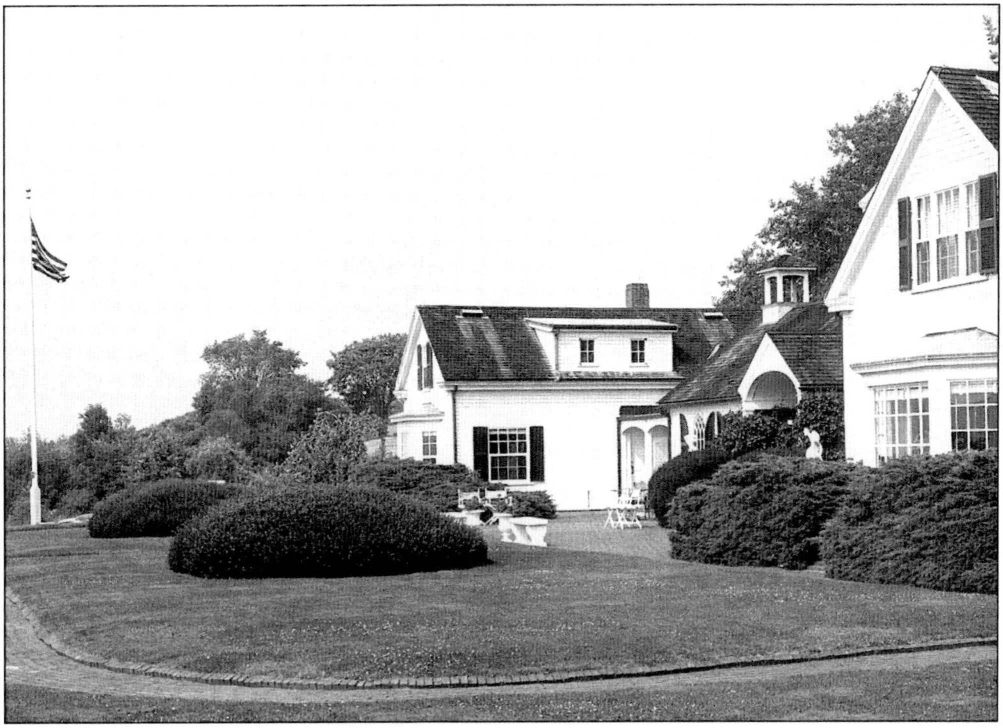

In order to create the Tea Room, Miss Sears had two cottages and a barn moved to the site and assembled together. She called this building Prospect House.

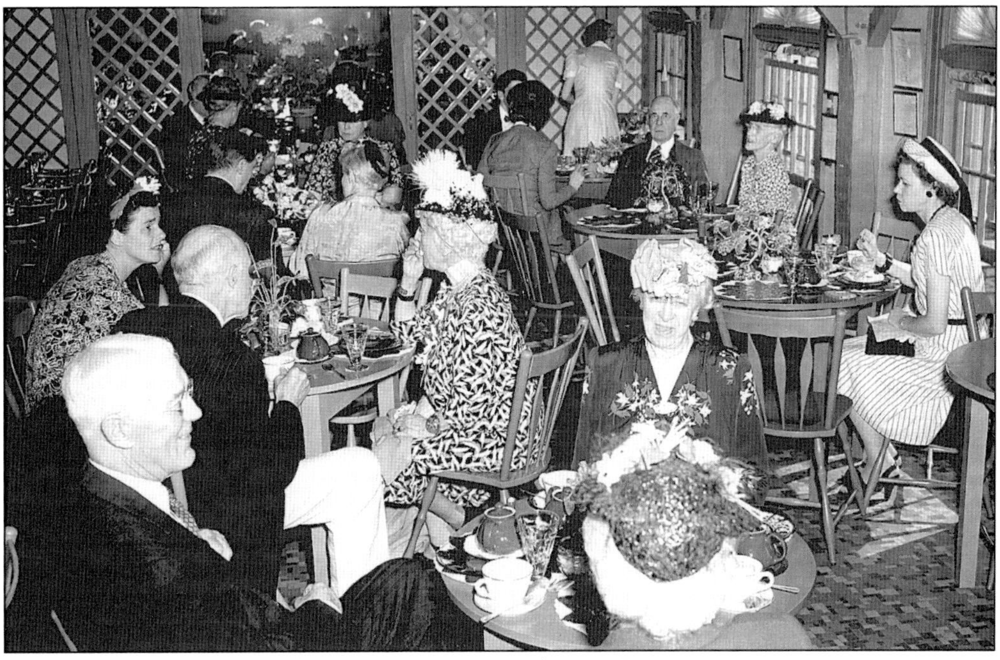

This is a photograph of a gallery opening event in the Tea Room in 1949.

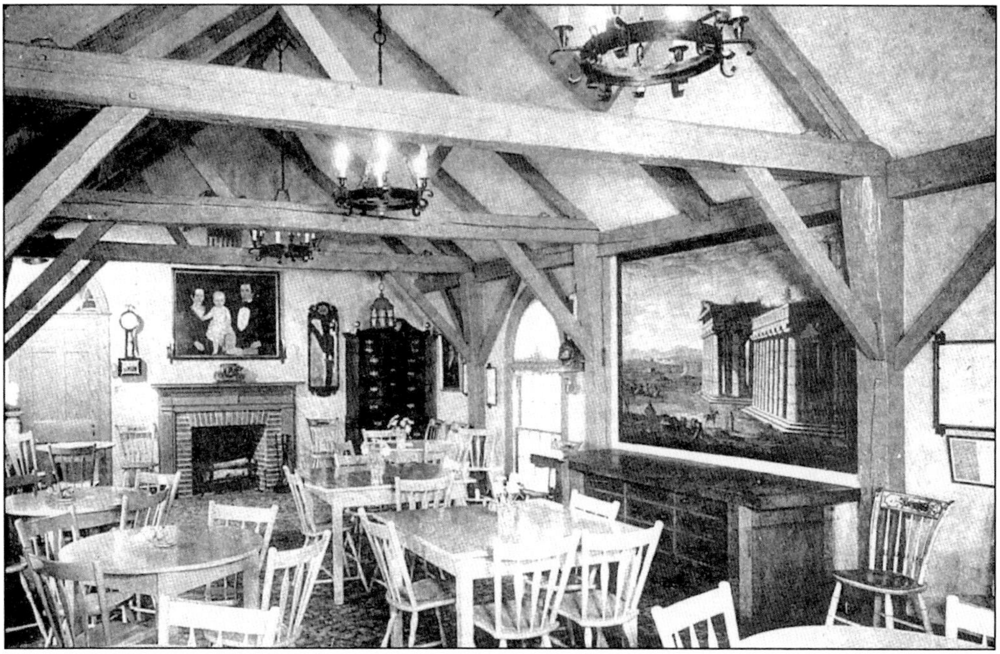

Shown is an interior view of the Tea Room *c.* 1940.

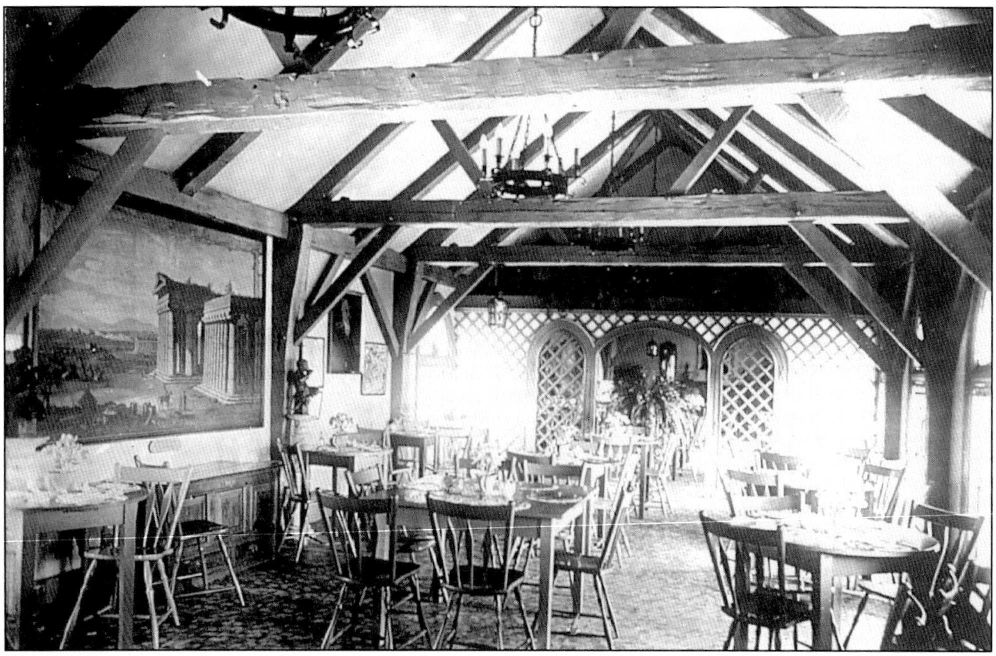

This photograph offers another view of the Tea Room *c.* 1940.

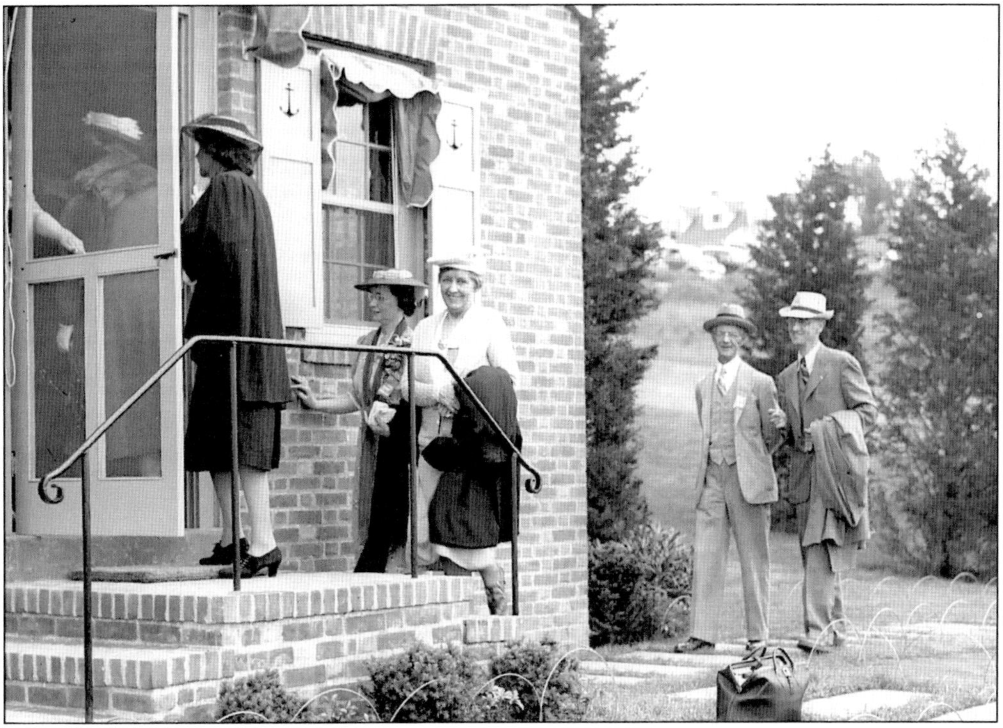

Mr. and Mrs. Carlton Hayes and others of the Boston Authors Club are shown entering the Picture Gallery for an exhibit opening *c.* 1940.

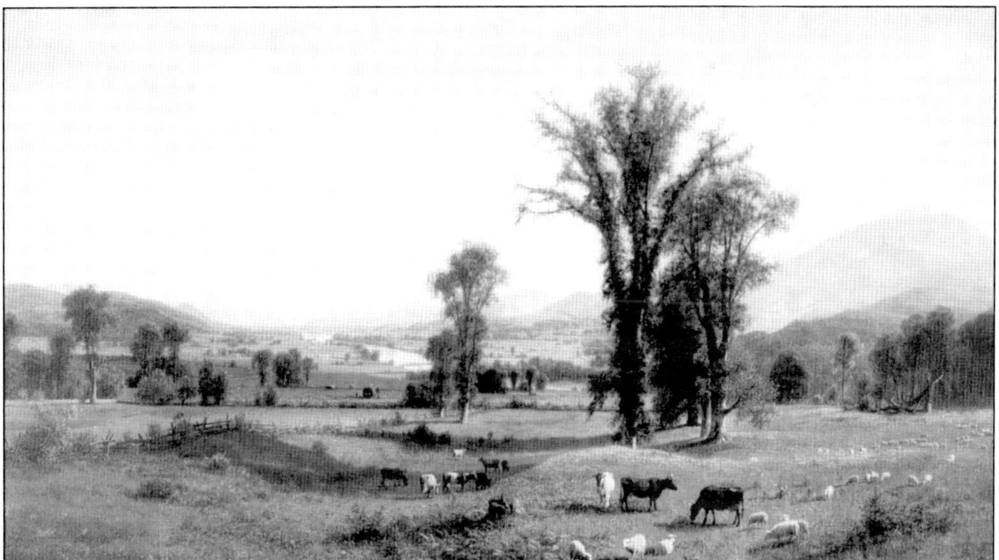

This painting by Albert Bierstadt is entitled *The View of Mount Ascutney from Claremont, New Hampshire.* Bierstadt is one of the most accomplished and well-known artists of the Hudson River school.

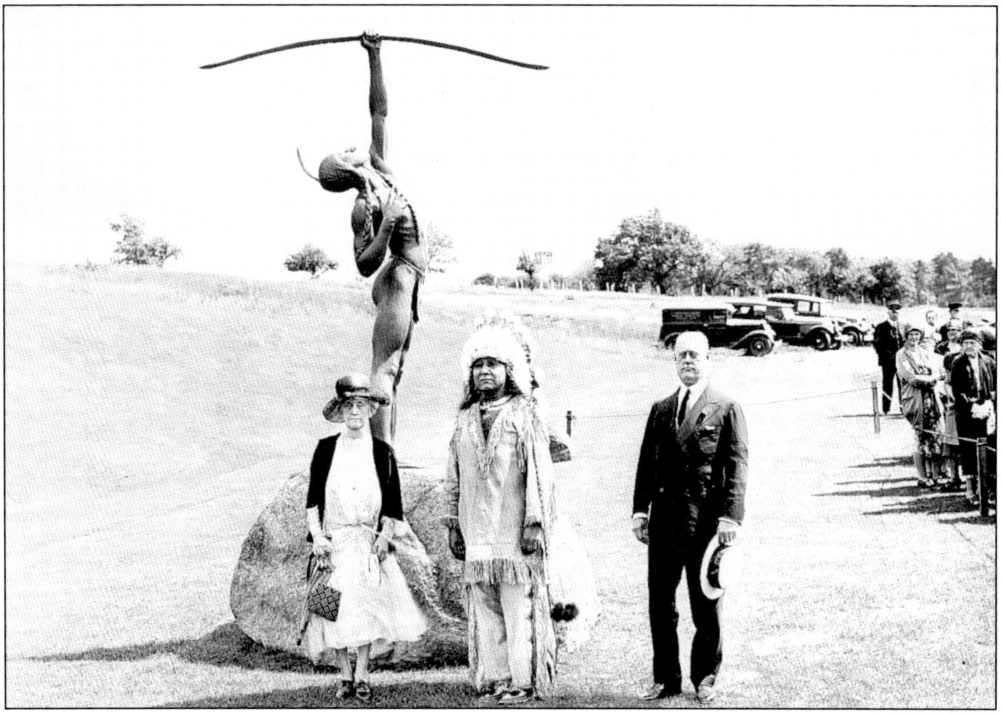

Seen in 1931 are Clara Endicott Sears, Charging Bear, and sculptor Philip Sears during the unveiling ceremony for *Pumunangwet,* or "He Who Shoots the Stars."

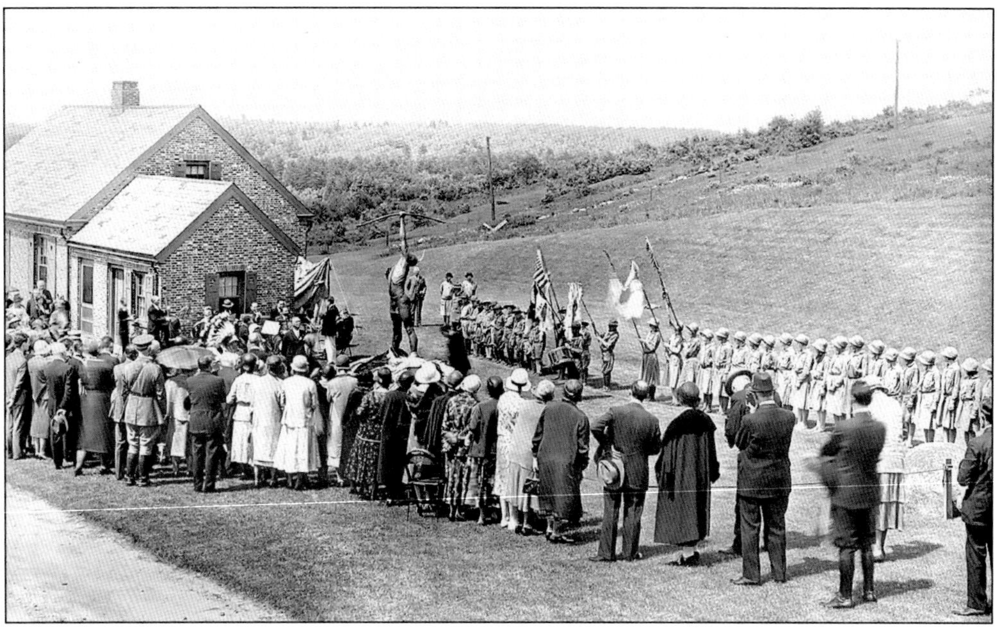

This is the unveiling ceremony for *Pumunangwet* in 1931.

In 1929, Miss Sears commissioned this heroic-sized statue, entitled *Pumunangwet*, for the exterior of the Indian Museum. She felt that New England lacked fitting memorials to its Native American past.

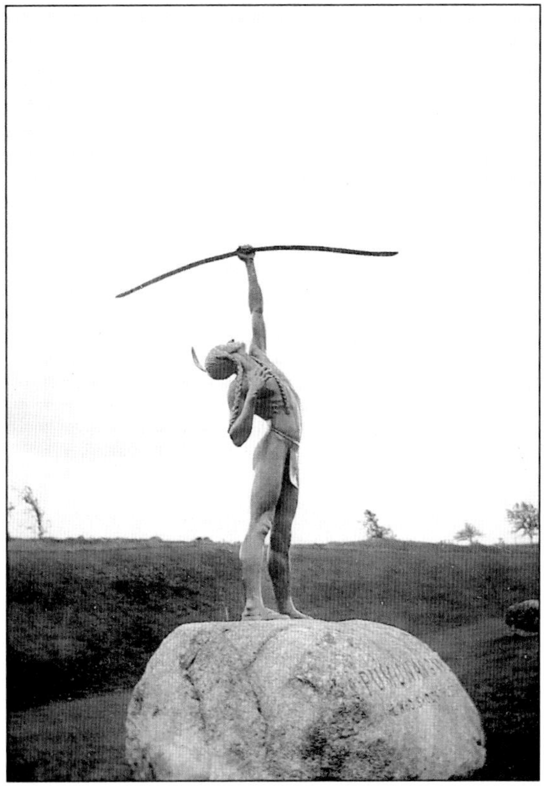

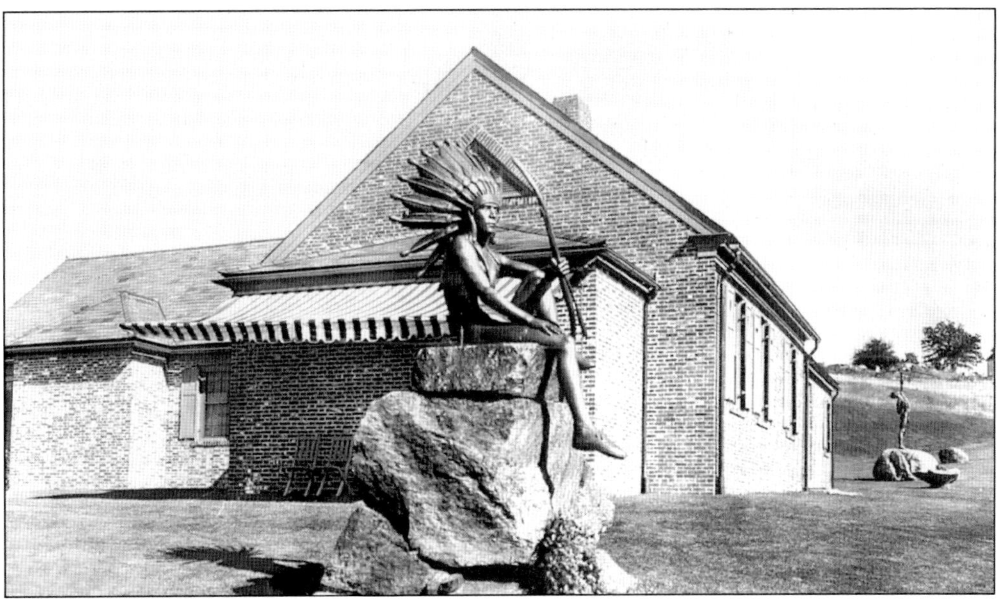

As a counterpoint to the active stance of *Pumunangwet*, Miss Sears also commissioned *Wo Peen the Dreamer* for the other side of the Indian Museum. *Wo Peen the Dreamer* was modeled after a Pueblo artist of the same name, wearing Plains regalia. Sculptor Philip Sears was Miss Sears's cousin.

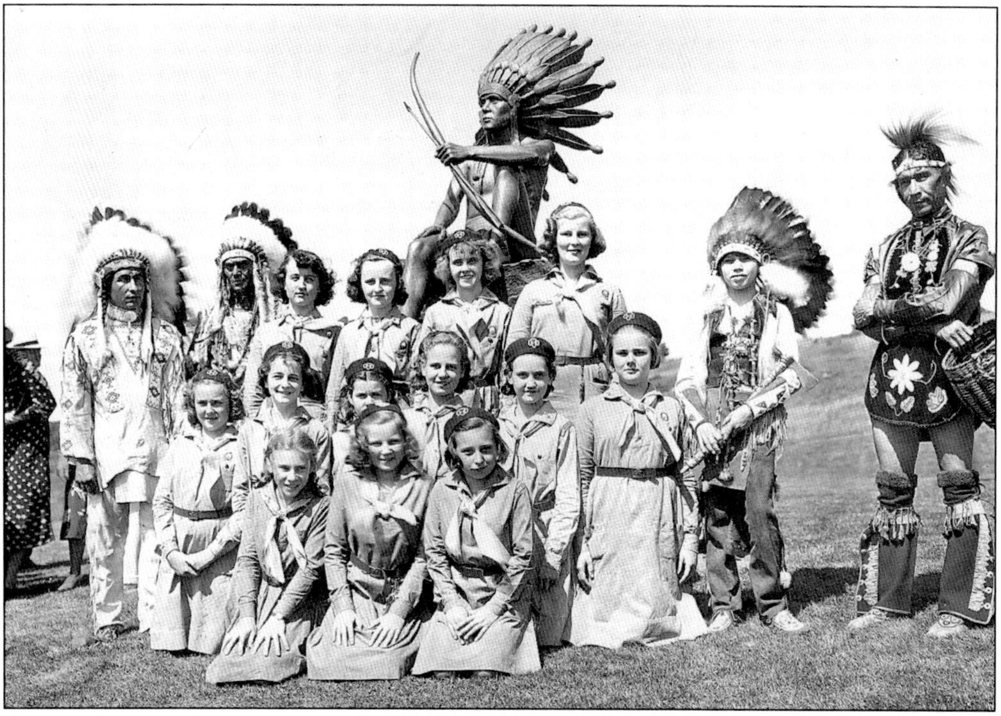

This is the unveiling ceremony for *Wo Peen the Dreamer*. The man on the right is Harold Tantaquiddeon, a Mohegan from Connecticut, wearing traditional Eastern Woodlands regalia.

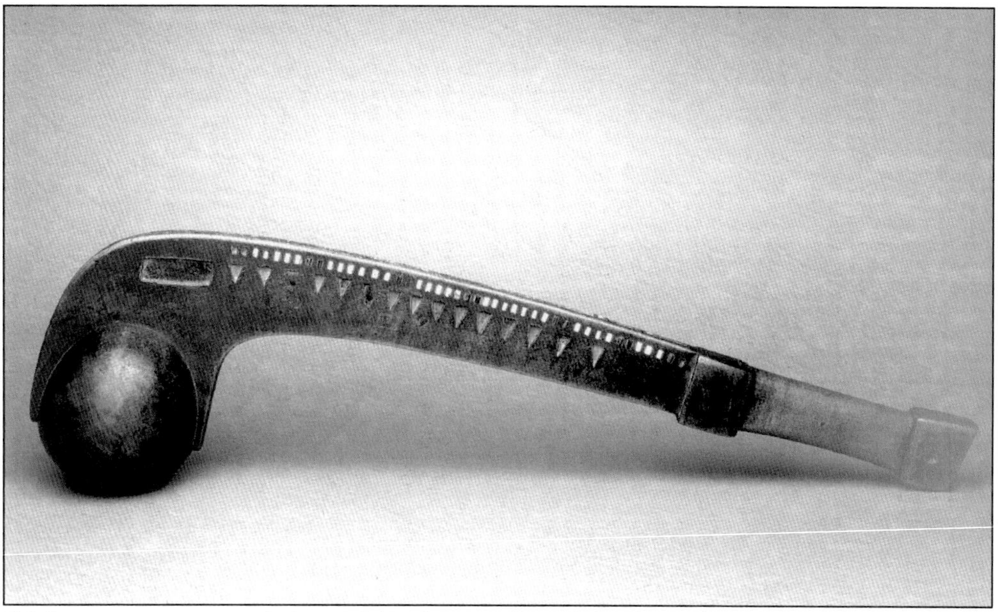

Of the many exceptional objects Miss Sears collected for the Indian Museum, King Philip's war club is one of the most famous. It is an authentic 17th-century ball club probably from southern New England.

Another interesting local item in the Indian Museum is this 1690 deed from the Native Americans to the English colonists for an area of land in Natick, Massachusetts. It is called the James the Printer deed after a famous Native signatory.

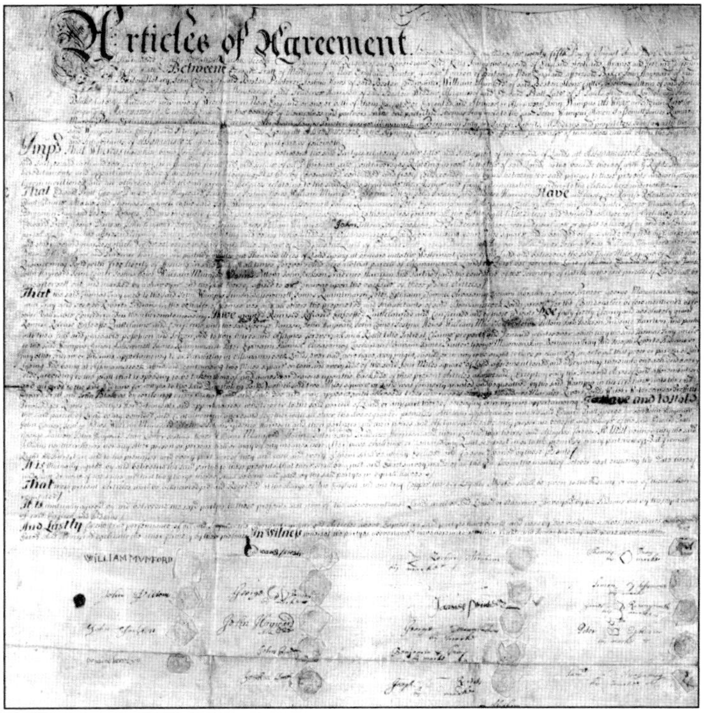

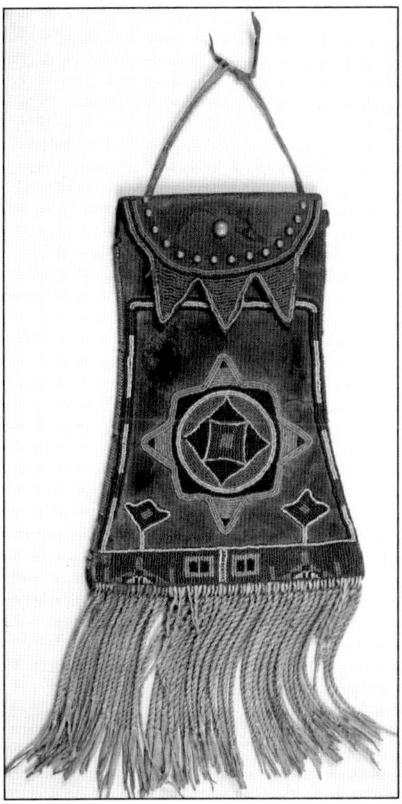

This Kiowa dispatch bag is one of the finest examples that survives. Bags like this were used for carrying a mirror and face paints, among other items.

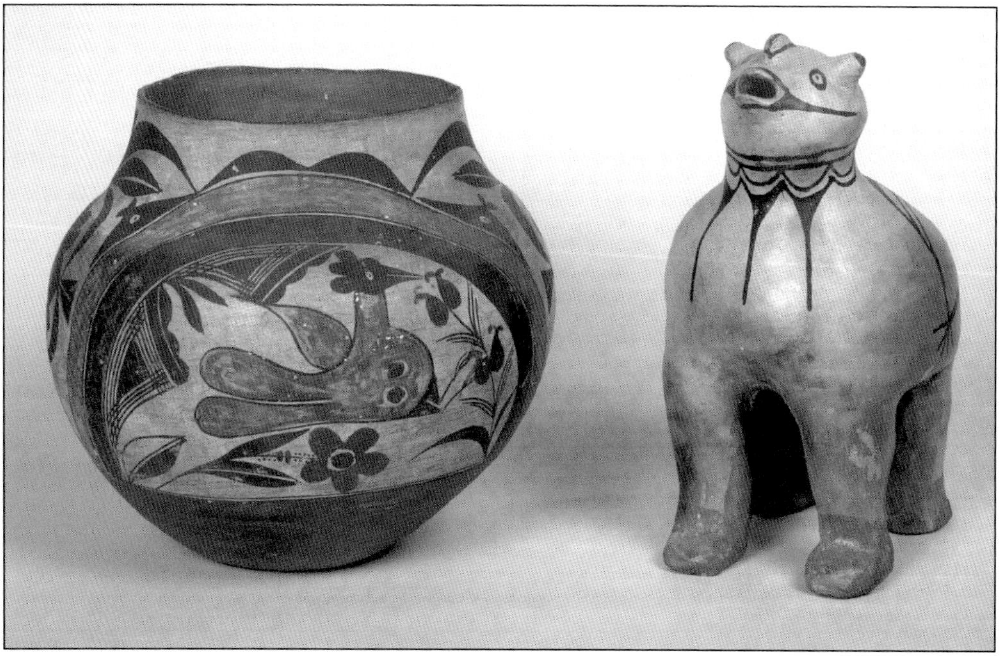

These southwestern ceramics were both made c. 1920. The object on the left is from the Acoma pueblo, and the figure was made by the Cochiti.

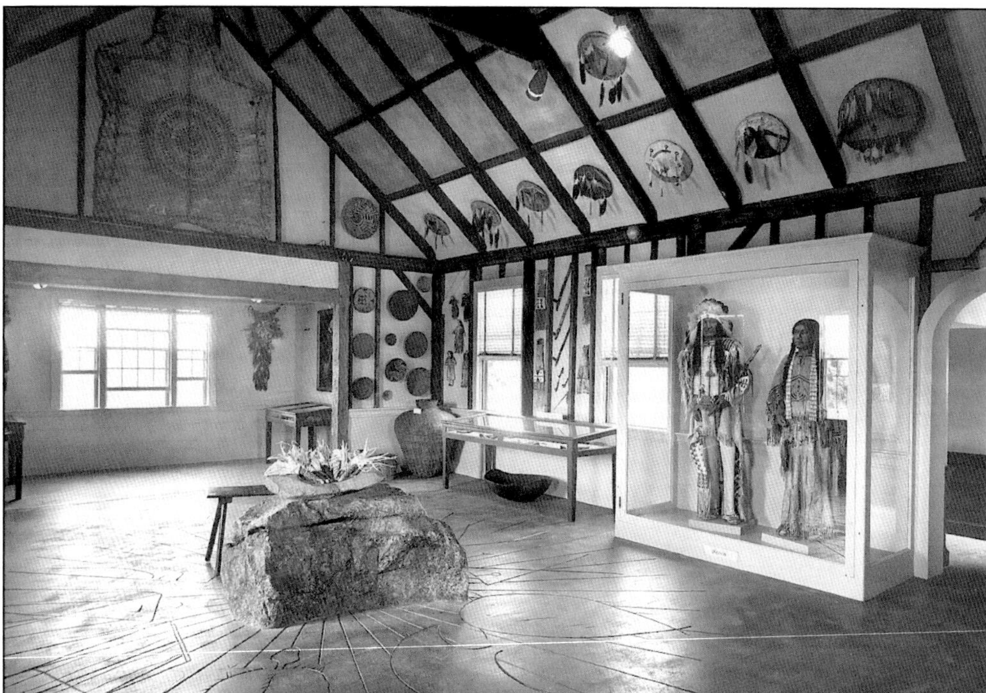

The interior of the Indian Museum is shown as it was created by Miss Sears in 1928. The rock in the center of the floor symbolizes the enduring power of the Great Spirit. Miss Sears collected Native American materials that often included stories to enrich the visitor experience.

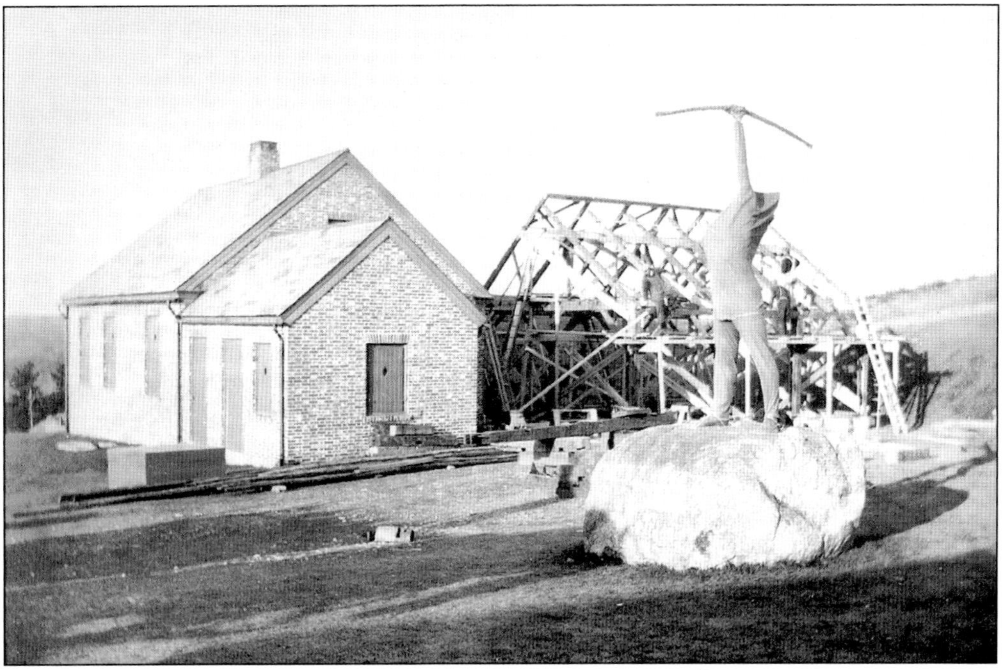

The Indian Museum was expanded in the 1930s to create more gallery space.

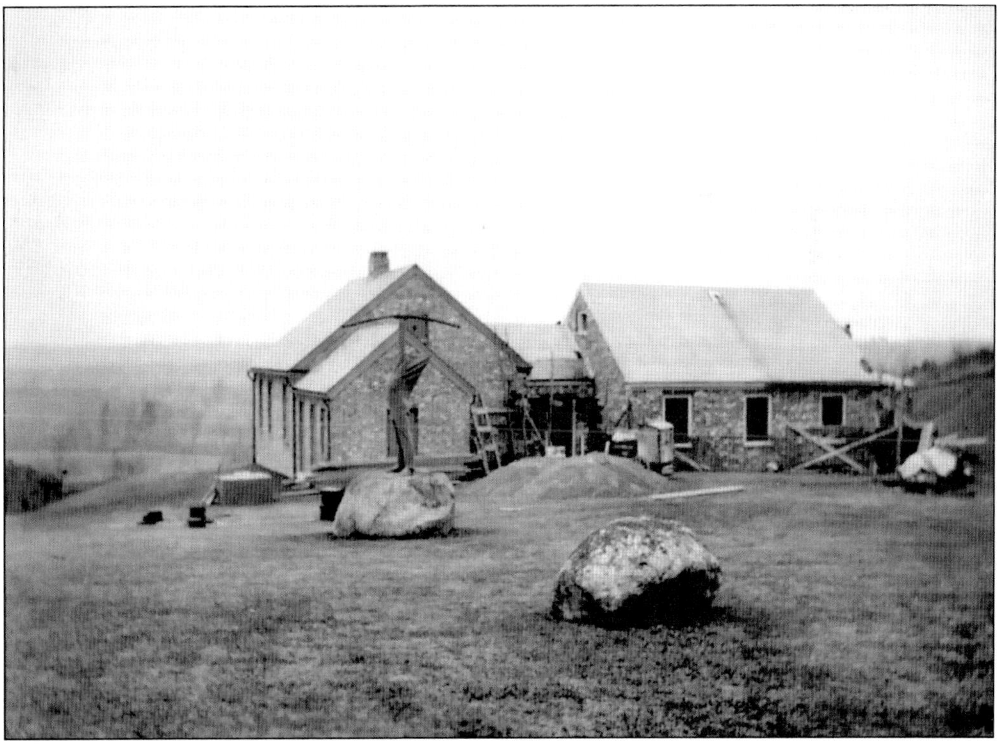

The museum's frame timbers were taken from an old building in Harvard, and the bricks were from another building in a nearby town.

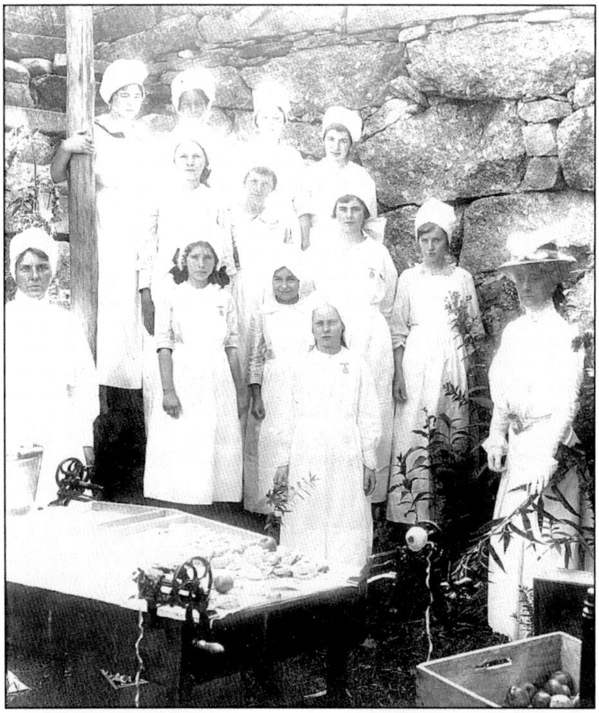

Miss Sears was very patriotic. During World War I, she organized and ran a food-canning and drying operation to prepare and ship food to the troops.

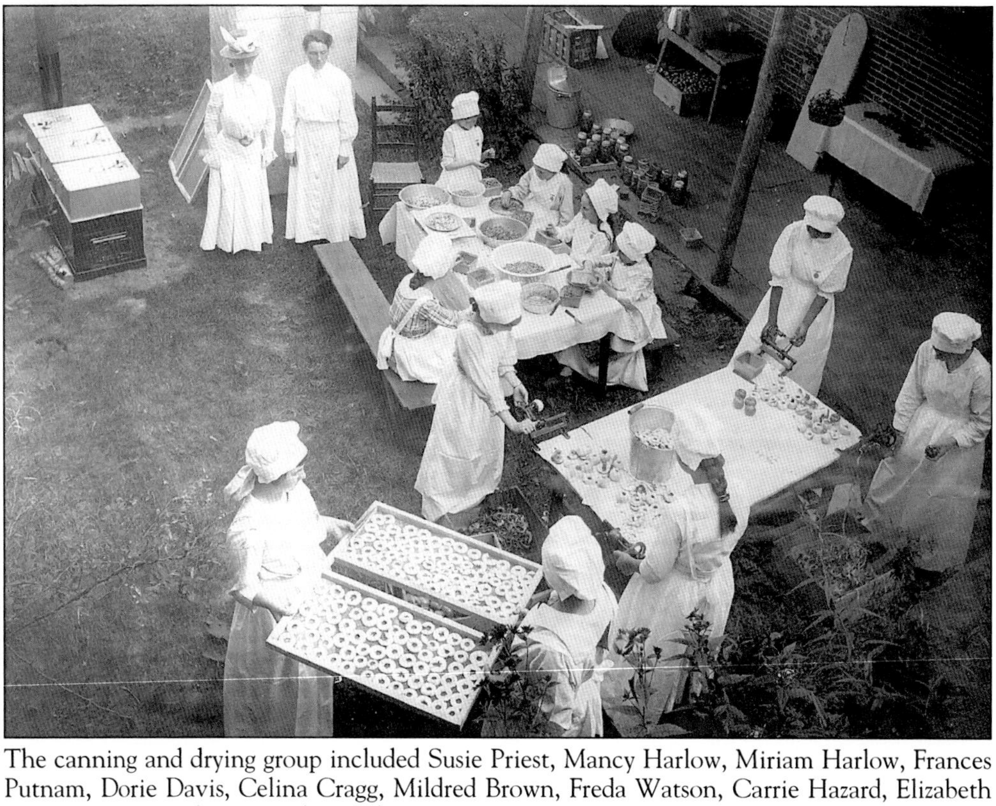

The canning and drying group included Susie Priest, Mancy Harlow, Miriam Harlow, Frances Putnam, Dorie Davis, Celina Cragg, Mildred Brown, Freda Watson, Carrie Hazard, Elizabeth Avery, Marjorie Cleaves, and Dorothy Stone.

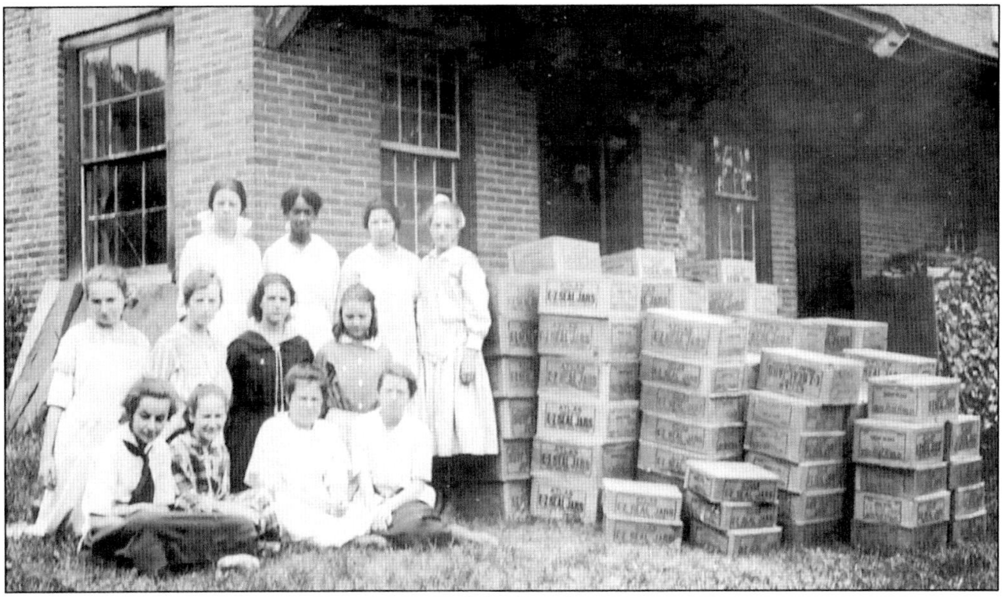

The canning group shipped over two tons of food to the troops in Europe.

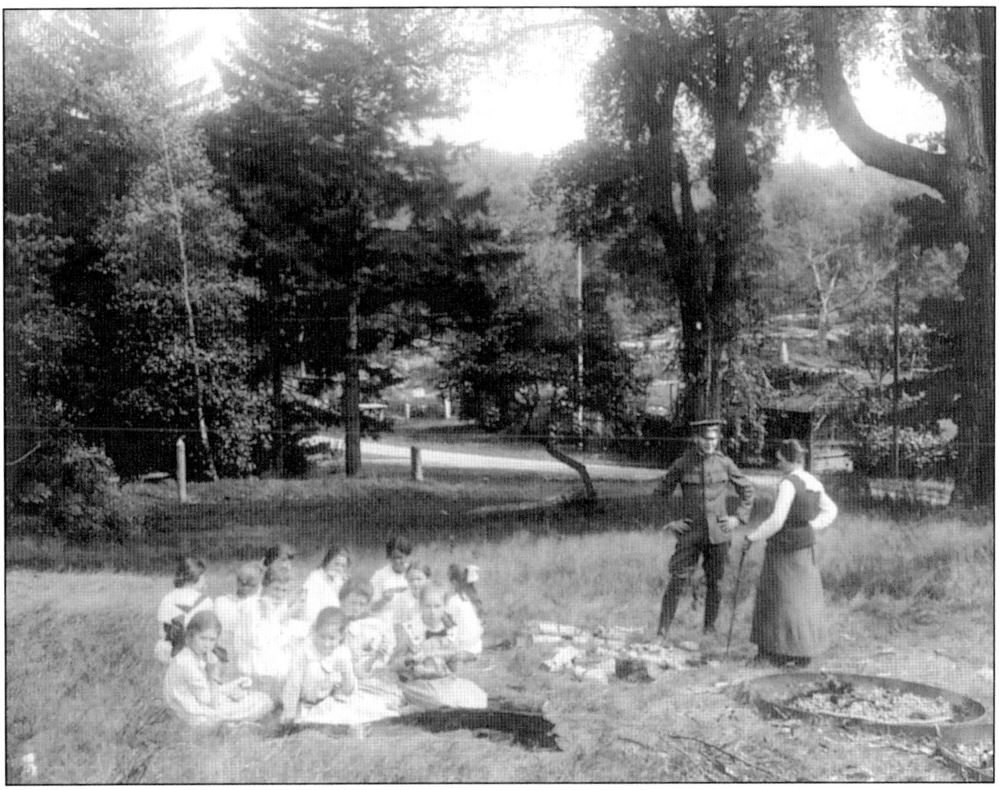

Nearby army officials oversaw the food preparations for the canning group.

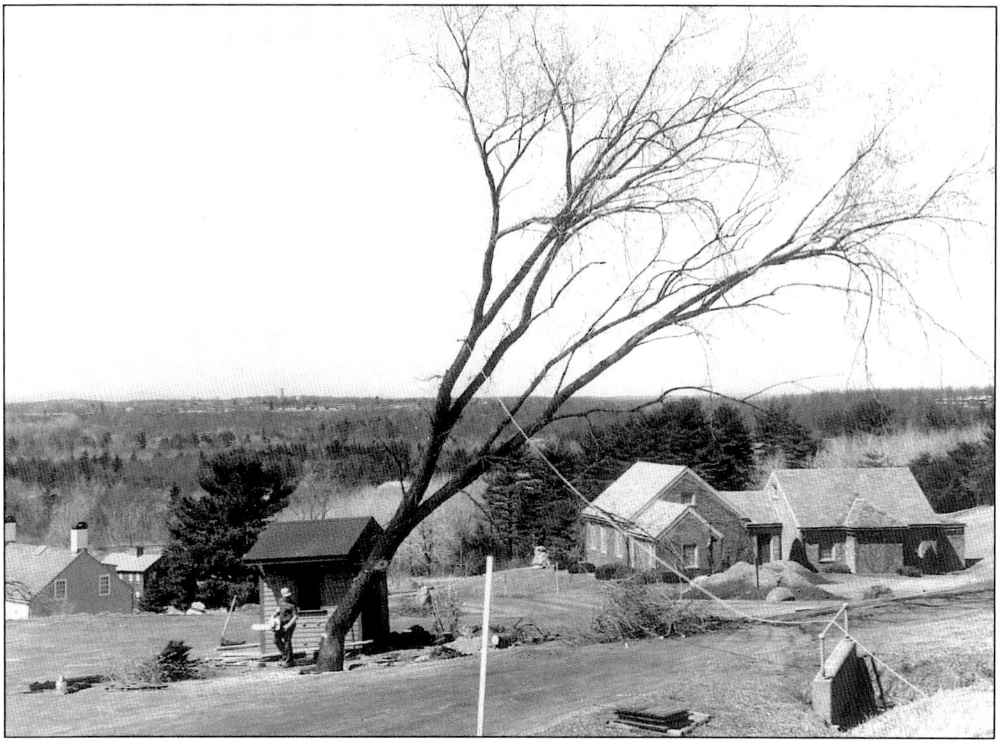

While Miss Sears created and operated the museums, for many years she also had a dairy farm on the property.

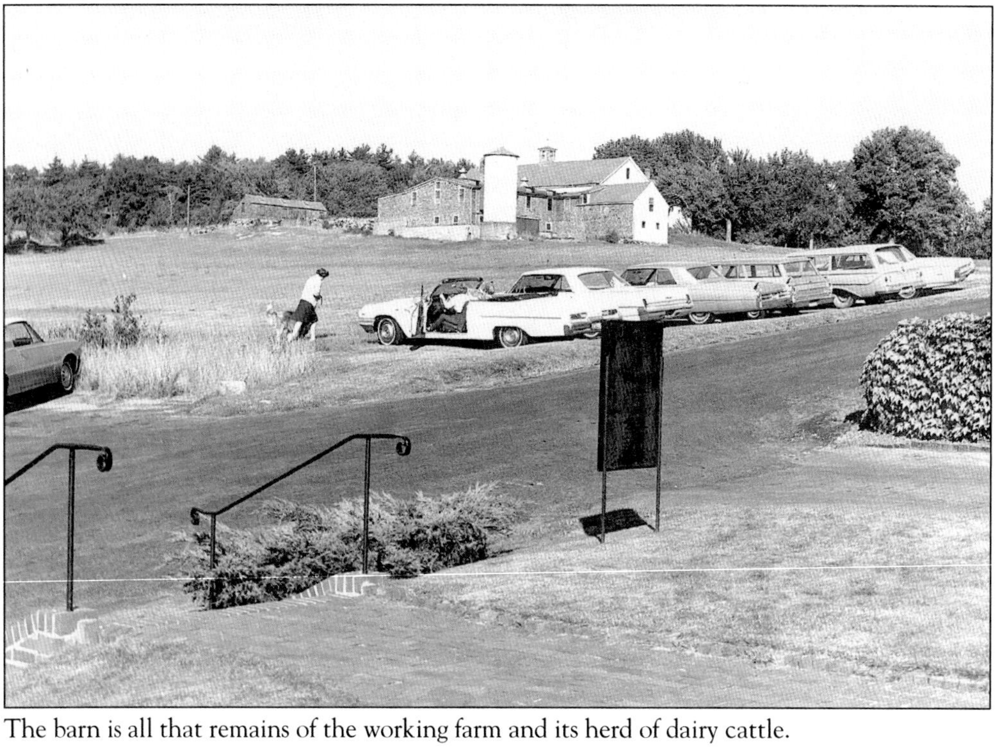

The barn is all that remains of the working farm and its herd of dairy cattle.